# THE
# LONG ROAD
# TO HOPE

*a day of small beginnings*

Jennie Dangers

# DEDICATION

To my dear grandparents, Jack and Jeanne, the first "Dangers of Africa" to blaze a trail in that remote continent we now call home.

# TABLE OF CONTENTS

*My object is that their children may see with what difficulties their fathers had to wrestle in accomplishing the first beginnings; and how God ultimately brought them through, notwithstanding all their weakness and infirmities; also that some use may be made of them later, by others, in similar important projects.*

-William Bradford, History of Plymouth Plantation[1]

*We have heard with our ears, O God; our fathers have told us what You did in their days, in days long ago. With Your hand You drove out the nations and planted our fathers....*
*It was not by their sword that they won the land, nor did their arm bring them victory; it was Your right hand, Your arm, and the light of Your face, for you loved them.*

Psalm 44:1-3, NIV

---

[1]William Bradford, The Plymouth Settlement; Mantle Ministries, San Antonio, Texas, 1988. P. 48.

# PREFACE

## *It Takes a Mad Man*

**It takes a mad man not to acknowledge the Almighty God
for all He has done in Kasana.**
*– The Honorable Sayida Bbumba,
our district's Member of Parliament and good friend to Kasana,
speaking at the Annual General Meeting at Kasana in 2005*

As Moses Kisakye and Joel Ruyondo, two of the Kasana boys who have been part of Kasana most of their lives, began to set up the sound system in the church for our annual staff "Envisioning Week," I was struck by how time flies and how things have changed! Who would have thought, years ago, as thirty people – the entire Kasana family (staff, children, and village church members)—gathered outside under the Mugavu tree near the first mud building on site, that one day the staff alone at Kasana would be more than eighty people!

How things have changed!

Today, New Hope Uganda is responsible for over five hundred children. Its Kasana Children's Centre is the home of over one hundred twenty children and nearly eighty staff members. Essuubi Eppya Vocational Primary School gives free education, vocational training, discipleship, love, food, and medical care to approximately three hundred children. New Hope Academy now has eighty-five secondary students, and the New Hope Vocational Institute graduates at least twenty students each year. The New Hope Institute of Childcare and Family now trains and sends over thirty committed servants of the Lord each year into the "harvest field" to work with orphaned and destitute children across the world. The number of people who have come through Kasana in teams or as short-term missionaries and visitors reaches well into the thousands, each individual contributing their own part to the "Kasana Story."

Todaty an aerial view would show the perfect shape of the original plans. A circular road that encompasses the primary school, the girls' tailoring school, and the church; off of this road seven "spokes" (roads) lead to seven circular family villages, each with five round buildings that are the homes for the children and a living and dining area, and one rectangular building for the family parents. Along these "spokes" is staff housing. Throughout the site there are also the clinic, barn, administration block, guesthouse, and eight buildings that make up the Institute of Childcare and Family. Across the main road, on a separate site, are now the secondary school, more staff housing, Hope House, and the Launch House.[2] On both sites are acres and acres of gardens that grow the daily food at Kasana. Three kilometers up the road is yet another site, the New Hope Vocational Institute, where young men are trained daily in auto mechanics, carpentry, and masonry. Two out of three sites are powered by generators to provide needed electricity when the "UMEME" Electricity Board supply fails. There are *computers* (who would have thought!), and what's more, there is Internet access! Some say the changes are good; others miss the "good old days."

Kasana is a beehive of activity. People are constantly going in and out, working, walking, moving: children playing football...students being called in for classes...staff gathering for fellowship...families working in the gardens...guitar lessons being held under a tree outside...oxen plowing fields. The lives of over five hundred people are intertwined twenty-four hours a day, seven days a week.

---

[2]A Home where our older girls, who have completed school, live for one year to be prepared for independence.

Then there are the construction, childcare, education, and administration departments. There is the accounts section, and the "store." There are early adulthood and follow-up, childcare extension, and family leaders. There's Hope House, the Enterprise Farm, and the Kasana Community Church. There are children who live on site and day students that either walk to school or ride the bikes provided for them due to the distance from New Hope to their homes in the village. There are the university students, the vocational students, the A-level students, the Investment Year students, and those doing apprenticeships that leave during the school terms and return home for their holidays.

There is the prison ministry, the outreach teams, choirs, and the village caretakers. There is the National Reconciliation Movement, the new site starting in Kumi, and the relationships forming with other ministries across the country and the world who are in similar work. There is the New Hope Institute of Childcare and Family. There is the guesthouse and teams, and there are visiting speakers and family friends. There are staff members from tribes that formerly hated each other, tribes whose languages are very similar and those that could not be more different. There are Americans, British and Scottish, Rwandese, Congolese, Sudanese, and Kenyans. People from Holland, Canada, New Zealand, Germany, India, and Israel have also served here.

This is Kasana today – 2006.

But while the appearance of the land, the number of buildings, the makeup of the staff, and the number of children have changed drastically, the vision remains the same. It is still the vision of bringing glory to our Father in heaven by bringing the "fatherhood of God to the fatherless," of putting the lonely in families, of bringing His love and healing to the broken.

Yes, there are always struggles. There are always frustrations, setbacks, and confusions. But the One who calls us has been and will continue to be faithful to guide and direct each step of the way.

Kasana Staff, January, 2005

# INTRODUCTION

## *Had It Not Been for the Lord*

The contents of the old box were covered in cobwebs and dust. "I don't know what you'll find in it," my dad told me, "but maybe it will be of some help." For the next several hours I was engrossed in letters, lists, and documents that communicated so much of the story that I want to share with you through this book. It all started from a vision, an idea, a sense of urgency to reach the "unreached" with the love of the Father. There was nothing else to show, no experience or finances, nothing more to build on – just a vision. And yet, the Lord's hand took that idea and conviction and has fashioned it into a ministry that has touched hundreds of lives.

As I read through the letters and other manuscripts that were haphazardly collected in the dusty old box, my emotions went from one extreme to the other. Here were the stories of successes, of failures and disappointments, of broken trust, of heartbreaks and lessons learned. At times I wanted to stop reading immediately. The pain of reliving all the difficulties that the ministry, the children, and our family had gone through was too great. Then the next letter would bring encouragement and a reminder that the Lord *was* on our side and would remain faithful to us, even when we failed to be faithful to Him.

As I rummaged through the stack of papers, I especially enjoyed looking at my dad's old notebooks. They are filled with lists, designs of new buildings and furniture, children's names, prayer requests, my mom's notes to my dad, sermon notes, and especially new ideas. These notebooks and the messages they contained are what really tell the Kasana story – the day-to-day decisions, heartbreaks and joys, the questions, steps of faith, failures and successes, and always new ideas and ways of solving problems. "How can we do things in a more godly way? How can we reach the kids and change their lives? How can we improve? What should our next step be?"

As I laid down the last paper and thought about all I had read, I was flooded with questions, emotions, hurts, and joys. But one thing was so evident it must not go unmentioned: the Lord's never-failing love and unchanging faithfulness toward us, His weak and fallible servants. The words of David best express what I want to communicate, and they have become a theme and encouragement to all of us at Kasana:

> If the LORD had not been on our side –
> let Israel say –
> if the LORD had not been on our side
> when men attacked us,
> when their anger flared against us,
> they would have swallowed us alive;
> the flood would have engulfed us,
> the torrent would have swept over us,
> the raging waters
> would have swept us away.
> Praise be to the LORD,
> who has not let us be torn by their teeth.
> We have escaped like a bird
> out of the fowler's snare;
> the snare has been broken,
> and we have escaped.
> Our help is in the name of the LORD,
> the Maker of heaven and earth.[3]

---

[3]Psalm 124, NIV

Before you read the history of Kasana, I would like to introduce you to the key people in this book. My name is Jennie Dangers, and as I began to write this story, I was working at the Kasana Children's Center as a tutor/teacher for my sister Joyanne and as a "miscellaneous" staff member, filling in where there was a need. When I signed up to work here that year, I had no idea what that commitment would lead to. I had only been here a couple of weeks when New Hope's Ugandan and North American directors asked me to write a book on the history of New Hope. I was asked mainly because I had the time. But I was also asked because I had the extreme blessing of being a part of New Hope since its beginning, actually since the time it was just an idea in someone's mind – a dream, a vision. You see, my father is Jay Dangers, New Hope Uganda's founder and director.

My father was born to missionary parents, Jack and Jeanne Dangers, and grew up in the heart of Africa, the Belgian Congo (later known as Zaire and then the Democratic Republic of Congo). It was there that he first began to feel called to a life of service in Africa. Many of his beliefs, convictions, and philosophies were born in Africa under the influence of his godly parents and the Zairois and missionaries with whom he lived.

My father is usually a fairly quiet man and very serious, though those who know him know that he loves to laugh. He is a man of conviction and purpose who believes that the Word of God must determine and define every aspect of his life and ministry. Consequently, my dad believes with his whole heart that "religion that God our Father accepts as pure and faultless is...to look after orphans and widows in their distress."[4] My father's heart is constantly burdened by the plight of the fatherless. Indeed, one of the few things I ever remember reducing my father to tears were issues involving his own family or the plight of an orphan or abandoned child.

---

[4]James 1:27, NIV

But, unlike many missionaries who are impassioned by a love for the Lord and a desire to see His kingdom advanced on the earth, my father's first commitment and love are to his own family. He continuously sought to never allow the ministry to come between him and his family; he always promised us that if this were to happen, he would return to the States and make things right.

Because of his love for us and his commitment to making our family as godly as he could, my father always encouraged and enabled us to become part of the ministry. It was never *his* ministry; it was *ours*. He did not want the Lord to remain only his and my mother's God, but he wanted us children to know Him as our God as well. My father wanted to share with us the experience of fighting battles with the Lord's strength and seeing His victory. Consequently, we worked together, talked together, prayed and cried together over failures, and rejoiced together over successes. Discussions around the table almost always included the children or staff and focused on how we could improve things or what our concerns were.

It is an indescribable blessing to know that this story is not just something Josiah, Jamie, Joyanne, Jeremiah, Julia, and I only know about from a distance. My parents allowed us to be part of it. And though it was often painful, I would not change our experiences for the world.

My mother, Vicki, was born to Calvin and Dorothy Young, and she grew up mainly in Southern California. When my mother was nine years old, her aunt led her to the Lord, and from that point on she knew that she would one day be a missionary. She and my father were married in 1977 and, just over a year later, moved to the jungles of Zaire. From the beginning my mom's perseverance in the face of overwhelming odds and difficulties was amazing. Just twenty-one years old and seven months pregnant, she left a life filled with every comfort and luxury she could want to follow my dad into the unknown. But she was committed to following him in whatever the Lord called him to do.

Her first home in Congo was a mud-brick house with a thatched roof and a pit latrine. Later, their accommodations were downgraded to a one-room corn storage shack. There was little or sometimes no money. There was no plumbing or electricity, and to reach the closest place to purchase food required a two-day drive over horrible roads. In addition to all of this, she also had the responsibility for a newborn – me![5]

In regards to the living conditions and availability of supplies, our times in Uganda were not nearly as difficult as those my parents faced in Congo. However, the struggles and heartaches have continued and have often been far too much for my mother to handle in her own strength. Yet, with the Lord's strength, she has persevered and remained faithful. Her gift of hospitality and her ability to make feasts appear from a small kitchen with limited resources and no grocery store conveniently up the street have amazed and blessed hundreds. Her heart, too, is burdened for the lost children. And, like my father, her primary focus has always been her family and those the Lord brings into our home. Six more children were added to the biological six children in our home. Sennyonjo Robert, Bizimungu Charles, Esther Birabwa, Paul Kusuubira, Wasswa Michael, and Richard Kato each joined the family at different times and in different ways, and though they've all grown up and moved on, each one will ever remain part of the Dangers family.

Jonnes Bakimi, my Ugandan father, has served with New Hope since the beginning. The work he has done for the fatherless and the importance of his friendship and support to my father and the rest of my family can never begin to be measured. He gave up the offer of a lucrative position with Pepsi Cola in Kampala and came to the bush to join my parents and an organization that could only be seen with the eyes of faith. His willingness to move to the Luweero Triangle also took much humility and reliance on the Lord.

---

[5] I was born in February 1979 at the Tandala Mission Hospital.

According to tribal customs, one of the last places a man from his tribe would choose to live would be this area. Yet he humbled himself and was willing to learn the language and serve the people of a tribe his own people would have shunned.

Raised an orphan himself, due to living yet absent parents, Jonnes' heart understands the pain of rejection and loss, and the Lord has used him in amazing ways to touch the hearts of the Kasana kids.

Jonnes' wonderful wife, Gertrude, joined the Kasana family in 1988 when she married "Uncle" Jonnes. She too gave up a prestigious position in Kampala as a lecturer of home economics in the nation's leading technical college and came to work at her husband's side. Their first home at Kasana was a broken-down brick building with a roof that leaked like a sieve. Despite much ridicule from friends and relatives in the city, who failed to comprehend what it was that possessed her to come to Kasana, she has remained an integral part of the Kasana family.

Often it is the sacrifices of the foreign missionaries that are praised and recognized. However, the men and women who have given their lives to serve the Lord in their own nation sacrifice just as much or more than the foreign missionaries. The daily struggles and inconveniences Auntie Gertrude faces – the constant interruptions and pressing needs of staff, villagers, and children; the hundreds of visitors and countless people living in their homes; the cramped living quarters and primitive facilities; and the continuous reminder each time she goes into the city of what she could have had – are just some of the sacrifices she has made for the children at Kasana and for the kingdom.

Their own children, Joshua, Joanna, Jordana, Joseph, and Jonathan, are also an important part of the Kasana family. Two of their nieces, Judith and Eva, have also been part of their family for more than ten years now, and their home has become home to countless others – Joy, Esther Mbabazi, Ruth Batamuliza, Sam Mugabi, Atuhiire Evelyn, Angelight Kirungi, Noellina Katabazi, Godfrey Ngabirano, and so many more!

<hr>

While I have enjoyed the opportunity of researching, remembering, and writing down these memories and the stories of the Lord's faithfulness to us, I know that I am not nearly competent or worthy to do justice to such a story. The story of New Hope is one that would take an expert to properly explain. It truly is a tapestry with each strand being the life of a child, a staff member, a friend, or a supporter; a lesson, failure, disappointment, success, heartbreak, or joy. As the years progressed the vision was brought to life, day by day, one brick at a time, one child at a time, one story at a time.

The purpose of this narrative is not to boast of our successes or tell of a great vision my parents had. Indeed, if that is the result of this book, then I have utterly failed in the task I was given. The purpose of this narrative is to bring glory and honor to the One who is the Author and Finisher of it all – the Lord Jesus Christ. It was He who gave my father the first conviction to begin working with children. It was He who gave my mother and father the strength to take a leap of faith and move to Uganda. It was He who brought Uncle Jonnes and Auntie Gertrude and every other staff and board member, each child, each team and visitor, each supporter, each encourager, sponsor, and friend that make up the tapestry of Kasana's story. It is He who calls Himself the Father of the fatherless, the Defender of widows. He did not need to use us, weak and fallible vessels that we are, but for some reason He chose to. He allowed us to take part in the indescribable blessing of carrying His Father's heart to those who only know rejection and pain. But it was the Lord who initiated it all, enabled it all, and holds it all together. Indeed, our prayer is that of the psalmist:

> *Not to us, O LORD, not to us but to your name be the glory, because of your love and faithfulness.*[6]

---

[6] Psalm 115:1, NIV

The Dangers' family, December 2004.
Left- right: Back row: Jamie, Josiah, Jay, Jennie
Front row: Autum (Josiah's wife), Jeremiah, Vicki, Julia, Joyanne

Most of the Bakimis, July 2005
Left to right: Front row: Joseph with Joy on his shoulders, Jonny, Jordanna,
Evalyn, Joanna, Fatuma,
Back row: Joshua, Gertrude, Jonnes, Angel

# Section 1

*The Early Days*

# Chapter 1
## A Jeep, a Brick Machine, a Wife, and Three Kids

∽◦∾

There are a few things important enough to lodge themselves permanently in the memories of very young children, such as the birth of a younger sibling, the death of a parent, or a drastic change in environment because of a family move. Our first trip to Uganda is one of those memories for me. Never will I forget the emotions, the fears, the sights, and the smells that began after Josiah, Jamie, and I were told that we would be moving to Uganda.

Because I was born into the Dangers' family, talk of Africa had never been unusual. My grandparents had begun our family's involvement in that remote continent, and after them my uncle, aunt, and parents had followed. Though I couldn't remember my time in Africa, my life had begun there, and I knew that if my father had his way I would one day spend much of my life in the place he dearly loved as home.

Yet, until I was seven, Africa remained a distant and imaginary place. It was a place that Grandpa and Grandma frequently showed us pictures of and reminisced about, a place with rough roads and snakes, a place where women braided their hair in amazing ways and carried things on their heads, a place where the people spoke in a language that most of the adults in my family could speak. We children enjoyed listening to the language but failed to understand it. Africa was a place of strange foods, of hunting and swimming, of wonderful drum beats (which my father would frequently demonstrate to us), and where, during an outdoor bath, one could hear lions roaring in the distance. To my seven-year-old imagination Africa was an exciting place, but still so distant. That is, until my parents said, "We're moving to Uganda!"

Suddenly, all that had been fantasy was about to become part of my life. All that I was comfortable with was to be replaced with unfamiliar things. As my parents prepared us for the drastic change in our lives, my romanticized view of Africa was replaced with more realistic facts. The part of Africa to which we were headed was different from the Congo I had heard so much about. It was a place where wars and strife had devastated the people and the land. I understood that we would be taking care of children who had no mothers and fathers. There would be soldiers everywhere, and we would be learning a new language (one even my parents didn't know). We would first live in the city, and my mom, Jamie, and I would have to wear dresses every day. Of all the changes I knew we would face, wearing skirts every day was one I remember thinking much about. It was like a new identity or role I would begin to play, and it made the trip all the more exciting.

Our flight was scheduled to leave early in the morning on September 11, 1986, from Los Angeles, California. For several days before, we packed and prepared. While my mom and her mother organized, kept us three little ones out of trouble, and purchased all we would need but could not buy in Africa, my dad began the arduous task of fitting our belongings into bags and boxes that would pass international travel codes. Known for his "missionary kid" packing skills, my dad began to pass on the tricks of the trade to the three of us prospective MKs.

"Did you know," he would ask, "that there is air in clothes? You have to squeeze all the air out by rolling several items together as tightly as you can. Once you have squeezed all the air out and the clothes are compacted as firmly as possible, you then tie the roll with twine. This way we can make the most of every centimeter of space."

We did our best to listen and help, although I'm sure our presence was often more of a hindrance than a blessing. Still, we aided the packing process by sitting on the rolls of clothes, towels, and sheets to hold them in place until he tied them securely together. Somehow, Dad managed to make all of our things disappear into the bags that were piled up in my grandma's living room.

Finally the long-awaited morning came. After a tearful parting with my mom's parents, we boarded the plane. Though we children felt excitement, there was also a measure of apprehension. Our overall understanding of what our future held was very limited, yet we all knew that this airplane was taking us away from all we had ever known to a new life, new adventures, new experiences, and challenges.

After several hours of flying, I awoke to the pilot announcing our arrival at the airport. Confused as to where we were, I immediately assumed that we had landed in Africa. After all, we had been flying for so long, and my mom, Jamie, and I were all wearing dresses. At the baggage claim we were met by friends of my parents who welcomed us warmly and led us to their car.

*Strange*, I thought, *everyone here is speaking English. Maybe we will find some Africans soon.*

As we drove through town, I began scanning the crowds of people we passed, confident that I would catch a glimpse of some orphans very soon. I was sure I would recognize one when I saw him. In my imagination and day-dreams of Uganda, I had assumed that all orphans must look the same and must be easily identified. Maybe they wore a sort of uniform, or maybe they had name tags or something. In any case, I knew we would all be able to find them quickly and begin to help them right away. By the end of the drive, I had not found a single one of my self-created orphan stereotypes, but I had discovered that Africa wasn't at all how I had expected it.

"But then," I reasoned, "I hadn't really known what to expect before we left America."

Then, I tuned in to the adults' conversation. Bewildered, I realized that this, in fact, was not Africa, but Washington, DC! Knowing that they might be gone for several years, my parents had planned a stop in DC to visit college friends before they left the country.

I had spent what seemed like ages trying desperately to make what I saw out of the car window fit what I had envisioned Africa to be like. Then, when I had utterly failed, I resolved that I had been wrong and needed to change my expectations entirely. Now, I was forced to change my thinking drastically once again. We were not in Africa at all! In fact, we had not even left the continent!

*Well, I guess it is okay to wear dresses every day in Washington DC, too,* I thought after I had finally been able to wrap my mind around the reality of the situation. *People will probably know we are missionaries, though!*

As our plane made its first jolting contact with the pavement, after an hour of circling the airport due to stormy weather, we breathed a sigh of relief. We were in Africa! Finally.

Because Uganda had been the scene of a five-year civil war, it was nearly impossible to obtain needed supplies or a reliable vehicle there. Aware of the situation, my parents had chosen to land in Nairobi, Kenya, and spend several days there before completing our journey to Uganda. Doug Judson, a veteran missionary whom we had met in the United States just months before, was there to meet us at the airport and to help us make all the necessary preparations to move to Uganda.

During our stay in Kenya, Josiah, Jamie, and I spent much time exploring the grounds of the missionary guesthouse where we were staying and visiting with the other company. Although Nairobi was quite developed, the combination of British and African influence in the culture, architecture, and language was new to us. Skeleton keys to lock our rooms, afternoon "tea" when the guesthouse bell rang, and new British-English and Kenyan-English words such as "water closet," "trousers," "rubbish," and "to converse" were some of the new and exciting discoveries we made each day.

Doug was able to help my parents purchase a 1971 Suzuki jeep. Its two bucket seats in the front did not make it very conducive to functioning as a family car; still, it would have to suffice as that and also as our only ministry[7] vehicle for the next year and a half. In addition to the jeep, Doug and my dad had also obtained a trailer that would be secured to the back of the jeep, and a brick machine – our first official ministry purchase. We three children, thankful that we didn't have to wear seat belts anymore, quickly found our niches in the jeep: Josiah and I perched happily on the two wheel wells in the back, and two-year-old Jamie was placed on a pillow between my parents, her legs straddling the emergency brake. During the long trip, Josiah, Jamie, and I would sit and sleep on top of the pillows, suitcases, and sacks of flour and sugar that completely hid our formerly claimed territories.

Eleven days after our arrival in Nairobi, we said good-bye to Doug and began our two-day drive to Kampala. The Suzuki and trailer were laden with all of our worldly possessions: clothes and school books, as many food supplies as we could squeeze into the car, and a brick machine. Needless to say, we were quite a sight, as the jeep's 831cc engine struggled to climb the hills out of the Rift Valley at 25 kilometers per hour.

Our arrival at the border town of Busia introduced my mom and me to one of the many sensations forever burned into our memories – a sick, nervous feeling that occurred whenever we knew we were at the mercy of government officials and soldiers with machine guns. Upon our arrival at the border, my dad was led into a room while we were instructed to remain in the car and wait. And we did wait – for what seemed an eternity. Finally, he emerged carrying our passports and new documents, followed by an armed soldier. Unsatisfied with our explanation of what was in the vehicle, the man with the machine gun searched our car and interrogated us about each item he found.

---

[7] For my Ugandan friends who are reading this book, the word *ministry* here and throughout the book does not refer to a government department, but to a Christian ministry.

As soon as we crossed the border from Kenya into Uganda the atmosphere seemed to change, and my mom and I felt an uneasiness in our stomachs. The roads were terrible, and every hour or so we were stopped by armed men who carelessly rested their machine guns in the window of the jeep as they questioned us. Sometimes they searched the car. Attempting to intimidate us (and succeeding at least with my mother and me!), they asked to see our passports, drilled us as to why we had come to their country, and walked back and forth slowly and deliberately, glaring into the car. Throughout each episode we children sat quietly and tensely, praying that they would let us go. A huge sense of relief swept over us each time a soldier would mumble, "Proceed."

We finally arrived in Kampala late at night. Exhausted, dirty, and still uncertain about the safety of our new environment, we pulled into the Anglican guesthouse. However, we were so late, the manager had assumed we were no longer coming and had given away our room. Thankfully there was room in the inn down the road, a Catholic guesthouse managed by nuns. Well, there *was* room, but we could only have a minute portion of it.

For some reason we still do not understand, although we were the only visitors in the large guesthouse, the five of us were given only one small room with two small camp cots for furniture. Unwilling to make a bed on the floor with the cockroaches, whose quiet evening it seemed we had disturbed, we all squeezed into the cots for our first night in Uganda. My mother and I slept in one cot, and my dad, Jamie, and Josiah tried to sleep in the other.

Under most circumstances, though there are "tears in the night, there is rejoicing in the morning." However, the next morning we awoke to find that my dad was terribly sick, the bathrooms were closed for cleaning all day every day, and the closest pit latrine was a 50-meter walk down a steep hill. Too sick to drive into town and look for a place to live, my dad lay on a cot for several days enduring severe pain. The rest of us became well acquainted with the cockroaches, visited with the nuns, and waited and prayed for Dad to recover – *quickly.*

Our stay at the guesthouse introduced us to Ugandan food for the first time. While we thoroughly enjoyed the breakfasts of sweet milky tea, buttered bread, and scrambled eggs with milk in them, our first encounters with Ugandan food[8] and sauce, I'm afraid to say, was not the most pleasant experience. On the second night of our stay, a friendly nun ushered us into the dining room and seated us among the other nuns for the evening meal. Trained to eat everything we were served, Josiah and I took one bite of the matooke (cooked bananas) and the boiled eggplant sauce and stared at each other. It was one of the most disgusting things we had ever tasted. The consistency was almost impossible to handle. How on earth were we going to finish our meal without embarrassing our mother or hurting the nuns' feelings? Our prayers for Dad's speedy recovery intensified.

It was not only minor discomforts that made our first days in Uganda a stretching experience for our family. During the daytime, the view we had of Kampala from the guesthouse was very peaceful and beautiful. At night, however, the stillness was replaced with the sounds of war very near and very real. Yet again, we were introduced to a new emotion that would become familiar to us over the next year and a half – the feeling of terror and nausea that came over us when the first gunshot broke the night's silence and screaming was heard nearby.

As he lay in the cot on our second night, still very sick and weak, and listened to the gunfire and shouting all around us, my dad's thoughts were far from unreasonable. *What have I done?* he wondered. *Where have I brought my family? O Lord, what have I done?*

---

[8] In Uganda, bread and other light edibles such as eggs, fruit, and sauces are not food. In order for a Ugandan to regard any form of nourishment worthy of the title food, the substance must be something starchy that has been boiled, steamed, or "mingled," and then served hot with a sauce ("soup") poured next to it on the plate.

Our 1971 Suzuki Jeep.

# Chapter 2
## *Adjusting*

After several days at the Rubaga Catholic Guesthouse, we received news from a Ugandan friend that a house had opened up for us in Nateete on the outskirts of Kampala. With great excitement, we packed our things into the jeep again and set out for the final leg of what had seemed like a never-ending journey. Josiah, Jamie, and I overflowed with thankfulness for our release from "captivity." We ran back and forth from the trailer to the house carrying whatever our small bodies could lift and our parents would entrust to us. What had seemed like far too much to fit into the tiny jeep and trailer now disappeared in the house. After our last trip from the car, we realized how empty our new accommodations were. Without a single piece of furniture, the house echoed, as if to remind us of how much work it would take to make our new house a home.

Our new residence was far more agreeable than what we had anticipated – at least on the surface. With three bedrooms, two bathrooms,[9] electricity, and a phone, we felt so blessed. A phone! We could hardly believe it when we saw it. And we did actually receive one call once! But we could hardly hear the person's voice. Then the phone cut off and was never resurrected during our fifteen-month stay in Nateete. My dad's trips to the local telephone company proved fruitless and only ate away his valuable time. He was usually given answers such

---

[9] Please forgive my American English, all my Ugandan and European readers! To us, a bathroom is the room that contains a toilet, shower, and sink.

as, "The road is being worked on, and we can't fix the telephone cables until the road is fixed," or "Yes, the work on *that* road is finished, but now they are working on another one, so when that one is finished...," or "The rain has flooded the system, and no phones are working." And so the telephone sat a lifeless reminder of what we *almost* had.

As we began to unpack and organize as best we could, given the lack of furniture and storage options, we realized that we were not the only tenants in the house. In fact, our housemates outnumbered us by the thousands. Hiding in the kitchen cupboards were cockroaches bigger than any my siblings and I had ever seen. My mom shuddered when she saw them, remembering her ongoing battle with the very same pests in Congo.

"Well," my mother said with determination (and has said numerous times since in other homes we've lived in), "someone has got to go, and it's not going to be me!"

Armed with one of our life's new necessities, an insecticide appropriately known as "Doom," my mom and dad went to work exterminating hundreds of the crawling, winged creatures. Judging by the amount used that afternoon, had Doom been harmful to humans I doubt any of us would have survived. As my parents sprayed, the cockroaches swarmed up the walls by the hundreds, frantically making their way onto the ceiling and then dropping to the floor, intoxicated by the powerful chemical.

Satisfied with their efforts, my parents closed all of the windows and doors to the kitchen and let the Doom carry out its work overnight. In the morning we knew we would have to face the distasteful task of sweeping up piles and piles of roaches. Sure enough, the next morning Josiah and I were given the job of carrying one dustpan full of dead cockroaches after another and dropping them down the pit latrine in the back yard. Though it was a disgusting job, at least we had won the battle and could take dominion as originally intended. We did not realize that there was still one more major battle to be fought.

Only minutes after we dumped the last pan full of insects down the latrine, Josiah and I noticed something rustling in the grass all around us. "Daddy!" we yelled, running toward the house. "Hurry! *Please!*" Swarming out of the pit latrine holes came what seemed to be an army of cockroaches that made the first ones seem like mere youths. The Doom that had successfully exterminated the smaller household roaches had aggravated the grandfather roaches that inhabited the pit latrine, and they began fleeing for their lives.

Like many young American girls, I had an intense and extremely unreasonable fear of all crawling creatures. It had taken every ounce of courage I had ever had, and much prodding from my parents, just to carry the pans of dead cockroaches. Now I was surrounded by living roaches the size of small mice. My dad quickly handed each of us a long stick and said, "OK, you know what to do!" My first strikes were weak and timid, but within minutes I had abandoned my cowardice. I knew that if I lost this battle, I would never win again. With a vengeance, for the next several hours Josiah and I mercilessly beat to death every cockroach we could find.

Once we had rid our home of as many undesirables as we could, we began to settle in. Our books lay in straight lines against the wall on the living room floor, and our versatile dining room "table," two large trunks pushed together, provided a place for us to set our food while we sat on the floor and ate. Those trunks also held all of our clothes.

Due to the destruction war had brought to Kampala's businesses and economy, there was virtually no place in the entire city to purchase furniture. Eventually, though, my dad was able to procure six matchstick-like used chairs and a dining room table from a small used furniture shop. As the weeks progressed, we were able to purchase a bed here, a couch or shelf there, and so on until we were quite sufficiently established.

Electricity was another intermittent benefit in our house. Though it did appear fairly frequently, it was completely unreliable, often coming on during the day and turning off as soon as the sun began to sink below the horizon. Sometimes when the lights would go out in the evening they would not turn on again until the middle of the night, delivering a rude awakening to anyone who forgot to turn off the light switch. Other times the electricity would not return for a week or ten days.

Not only was the power sporadic, but the *amount* of power available was also unreliable. Just because electricity was flowing through the wires did not guarantee that it would be in a usable form. We became well acquainted with "candle power," a frequent electrical malfunction that provided enough power to barely activate a light bulb, yet far too weak to operate any appliance. Candle power light dribbled out of the bulb and hung suspended around it like a halo. It never quite reached beyond the bulb to illuminate anything else in the room. In contrast, at other times the power source would be far greater than necessary, causing a power surge that "fried" whatever appliance was plugged in at the time.

One night, around midnight, Jamie called my parents to come to her room. She was sick and needed help quickly. My mom, awakened from a deep sleep, jumped out of bed and switched on the light. Suddenly there was a flash of light, a loud pop, and then it was pitch dark again. Still confused and a bit groggy, she was not sure what had happened, but she knew Jamie needed her. As she took her first groping step toward the door, her bare foot felt something cold and sharp. The light bulb had exploded, and the floor was covered with tiny slivers of glass – and there was no light to reveal where they were.

---

Though we had come to Uganda to start a children's center for orphans, it often seemed that my dad would never be able to give that his full attention. During the majority of our first year in Kampala, my parents' primary activity was finding ways to survive. Things as fundamental as purchasing groceries, gas (petrol), or obtaining Ugandan currency without losing nine-tenths of the original value in the transfer were incredibly tedious.

When we first arrived in Uganda, there was no way to buy flour or sugar and many other staple supplies. Eventually, a sugar ration monitored by the

Local Council members was established. Every two months, each family was authorized two kilos of sugar. The amount was quite generous, and even a sweet-loving family such as mine would have been quite relatively satisfied had the ration been regular. However, after standing in line for several hours, frequently my father was told, "Sorry. The sugar is finished."

Had my mom only been feeding our small family, the limited resources Uganda could offer most likely would have been quite relatively adequate. However, from the beginning my mother was not only wife, mom, secretary, and teacher, she was also "hotel manager." Almost every week we hosted visitors from all over the world – other missionaries, Ugandans, short-term mission teams, pastors who came to Uganda for conferences. Two kilos of sugar were never enough.

In addition to the scarcity of supplies in Kampala, the cost of what was available was far more than we could afford. According to the official exchange rate, one U.S. dollar could purchase 1,400 shillings. However, it was not the official rate, but the black market rate shopkeepers used to determine their prices. The "under-the-table" rate was one U.S. dollar to 15,000 Ugandan shillings. Based on this black market rate, a bar of soap sold for 14,000 shs, almost ten dollars according to the official rate. Our limited missionary funds would never stretch to cover such prices. While we had to purchase all of our fresh foods locally (my dad would have to carry a briefcase full of bills just to do a weeks' worth of grocery shopping), we had to find a more efficient way to find our more substantial supplies.

At least twice a year we would climb into the jeep, retrace our initial journey in Africa, and return to Kenya for several days of "grocery shopping." Here we purchased everything we might need for the next six months – soap, toilet paper, Safari Land milk powder, Blue Band (margarine) and Kimbo (shortening), sugar, flour, and, of course, more Doom.

One of my parents' "favorite" pastimes was obtaining fuel. During our first few years in Uganda, there was never any certainty that petrol would be available from one day to the next. Indeed, trips to Kasana, where land was being cleared for the children's center, and shopping trips to Kenya were often postponed or canceled because of fuel shortages.

During these shortages petrol stations in Kampala that actually *had* petrol were permitted to sell only 20 liters per customer per day. With this amount, my dad could make one round trip to Kasana and back to Kampala.

Reminiscing over those patience-trying times, my dad recalled, "After one trip to Kasana, we would go and find a petrol 'queue' to join. Being overly optimistic, we would drive past some queues, certain we could find a shorter one. This was seldom the case, however, and we were usually forced to join an even longer line. We knew that if we returned to the first station, we would run the risk of it being even longer, and we would also lose that much more petrol. Often, our search for a line would begin at 4:00 a.m. Once we had found one, we would try to sleep, but to no avail. Henry (named changed for privacy) and Jonnes, our Ugandan staff members, and I would take turns waiting. Hours would turn into days. And still no petrol. Then, after a day or two, we would hear that there was gas at another station. We would quickly start the engine, hoping to reach the source before the crowds. But upon our arrival, we would either be told that it was a false alarm, or the line would already be far longer than the previous one. Our only option was to wait, or go look for the next line!"

In a letter to my grandparents dated April 1987, my mom described one of the many fuel crises:

> The fuel shortage has lasted for the last six weeks. The lines outside the stations are at least a quarter of a mile and often three or four cars deep. Many even stay overnight. There are supposedly 100 fuel tankers waiting at the Kenya/Uganda border, but Kenya's upset with Uganda for something, so they're not letting the trucks across.

Earlier in the year, she had written,

> No one is getting gas at all in Kampala, and in

Luweero town, the station was only given 3,000 liters last time. They weren't selling to the public, but when we drove into the station, the owner's son, a pastor, said he knew Jay, and his father filled our tank! God is good!

In the daytime, Kampala remained relatively peaceful. And so long as one cooperated with the soldiers at the checkpoints and took no pictures of public buildings, there was usually little to fear (having one's camera visible in many public places could result in its confiscation or the owner's arrest). However, as the sun began to set, the peacefulness that comes with daylight was always displaced with a feeling of fear and restlessness. Out of the stillness around us, gunshots frequently rang out. The war *was* over, but it was hard for us to believe at times! Almost every week we would hear stories from both expatriates and Ugandans of armed robberies they experienced by thieves either breaking into their homes and stealing everything they could, or hijacking their car and leaving them stranded on the roadside. Many times these robberies brought no physical harm to the people, but frequently the thieves were very violent and had no regard for the condition of their victims. Anyone who escaped alive and untouched considered himself very blessed indeed. As we heard such stories, we were thankful that our dilapidated '71 jeep was not even a slight temptation to anyone seeking quick wealth!

Though the machine gun fire we heard was not a nightly occurrence, its frequency caused each night to be ruled by a sense of insecurity. Though it had not reached our home previously, there was no guarantee that it might not be at our door next. Time and again we inquired about the gunfire, asking who was firing and who was being fired on. The only answer we ever received was that the police were chasing thieves away. While there could easily have been truth in such an answer, the screaming that accompanied the blasts and the frequency of the gunfire caused us to wonder if this was really the case.[10]

As the nights progressed we became as accustomed as possible to these sounds of war. Still, the terror remained. At the sound of nearby gunfire, our family would immediately fall to the floor, my parents quickly pulling us children to themselves for comfort and protection. As quickly as we could, we crawled away from a window or door that led outside, usually to a room that was protected by a thick wall and as far as possible from the direction of the bullets. As we crawled toward a place of safety, my dad would turn off the lights in the house, and we would remain silently still until my dad was certain it was safe again.

Once, as we lay still in the dark, we watched tracer bullets fly over our roof. On several other occasions the continuous gunfire was just next door or in the surrounding neighborhood. With our hands clasped over our ears, we children pressed our faces into our parents' sides as they held us tightly. Trembling with fear, we prayed for our safety and that of our neighbors, whose terrified cries tore at our hearts.

As my dad's work on the children's center began to increase, he frequently had to travel to Kasana for one or two nights at a time. On nights that he was gone we felt a particular vulnerability and prayed even more fervently for our safety. When he had to leave for a week of surveying the new land, my parents decided that it was not wise for us to be in the house alone without my dad for such a long time. Feeling the same way about leaving his own family, a missionary friend who had volunteered to help with the surveying brought his wife, Debbie, and their two boys to stay with us for the week. Comforted by the strength that comes with numbers, we tried to ignore the feelings of anxiety that began to settle in our stomachs as the sun set. Then we heard the haunting sounds of explosions in the distance.

---

[10]Through to us these were sounds of war, to our Ugandan friends it was nothing in comparison to the terror that had reigned in the former regimes, and was actually proof that peace had come!

Although they did not voice their fears to us children, I know my mother and Debbie were silently wondering what their best response should be. Would it come closer? Should they continue with the evening plans or begin to take safety precautions? As the distance between our house and the explosions lessened, my mom and Debbie called us all together to sit low and wait for the gunfire to cease. As we waited, the bullets did not die away. Instead they began to come more frequently and seemed to get ever closer. Knowing that our safety was now being threatened, the adults decided there was only one place safer than where we sat.

"Children," they spoke calmly but firmly, "quickly, crawl into the hall. Stay low. Don't worry. We'll all be fine. Jesus is with us. Just go quickly."

Crouching down, we crawled quickly into the hall, and Debbie and my mom securely locked all the doors of all the rooms that led to the hallway. We lay there quietly huddled together in the dark as the bullets came in showers. We hoped that the distance between us and the outside of the building was sufficient to shield us from the night's peril.

Another situation that remains one of my most vivid childhood memories occurred late one night. Earlier in the day I had asked my dad to hammer a nail into my wall so that I could hang a calendar on it. He had agreed to do so, but told me that I would have to wait until the next day when he had more time. After supper, Bible stories, and prayer, we all headed to bed. Not long after I heard pounding in my room. Confused at being awakened from a deep sleep, I assumed my dad had decided to hammer the nail in for me at that moment. I rolled over to go back to sleep again.

Suddenly my dad was next to me, kneeling by the bed. "Jennie," he whispered, "come quickly." He wrapped his arm around me and quickly pulled me off the bed and onto the floor next to him. "The gunfire is next door. We've got to hide under the window."

I was instantly awake. The noise I had heard had not been my dad hammering on the wall but machine gun fire next door. The automatic weapons were being fired on the side of the house where my room and my parents' room were located. My dad and I crawled along the floor in the dark into my parents' room. My mom sat crouched under the window. Suddenly, I realized there were only three of us in the room.

"What about Jamie and Josiah?" Fear gripped my heart. "We can't leave them in their room! We've got to get them."

"It's OK," my dad assured me. "They are on the other side of the house. They're actually safer where they are than where we are here."

I couldn't go back to sleep alone in my own room that night. After the commotion had died down next door, my dad decided it was safe enough for us to return to our beds. We prayed together, and then he escorted me back to bed. But this time I joined Jamie in her bed. Oblivious to all that had just occurred, Jamie rolled over and made room for me without even opening her eyes. Her childlike peacefulness despite the night's terror gave me comfort, and the rhythmic sound of her breathing gradually lulled me back to sleep.

First day of homeschooling.

New friends...outside our house in Nateete.

# Chapter 3
## *First Wait*

᷈᷍

Uganda's capital today, a city of cyber cafés and cell phones, paved roads and fashions, street lights, shopping centers and traffic jams, can hardly be called the same city as the one we moved to in 1986. Outside the protective borders of our compound's evergreen hedge, life in Kampala continued with daily difficulties and crises, scarcity and confusion, fear and danger. Still reeling from the devastating effects of the war, the nation's economic, political, and social structures were forced to begin the uphill struggle of reclaiming all that had been lost.

Throughout the city signs of the recent war were clearly visible: bombed-out buildings, deserted shops, cardboard or rusted iron sheets instead of glass in windows, an army barracks with bullet holes in every wall. Our home too had its own battle wounds. There were several bullet holes on the outside walls. What was once Kampala's finest hotel, a beautiful twenty-story building – the International Hotel – had been completely gutted and destroyed. Anyone who chose to could walk freely in and out of the structure. The only remaining evidence of the hotel's former glory was a grand piano, riddled with bullet holes, that stood in the main hall. Not far from the International Hotel stood a skyscraper abandoned during the middle stages of construction because of the war. For several years it stood there with scaffolding gradually crumbling away. A large crane, still carrying a heavy load, was suspended in midair and hovered near the top of the building as a silent and constant reminder of all that had occurred to cease its work.

There were more potholes than tarmac in many places on the roads, and large trucks frequently were stranded, blocking traffic for everyone else. When the rains came, the potholes filled with water, and one could never be certain how deep a hole was. One must either risk sitting for hours in the middle of the road, unable to move, or find an alternate route to ensure a safe passage. And in the middle of many roads stood a pile of rocks covered with branches, signaling a mandatory military checkpoint. Usually there would be several armed soldiers resting in the shade by the road, waiting to interrogate the drivers and search the vehicles that passed.

Perhaps one of the most shocking and saddening sights that we witnessed frequently in Kampala were the many young soldiers, boys as young as nine, who carried full-sized machine guns. In an attempt to protect the thousands of orphans that flocked to him during the war, Museveni had resorted to his only option – training these young boys to defend themselves and take on roles that even many men struggled to carry. The boys' hardened faces, still unable to hide their tender ages, revealed the horrors they had witnessed and the physical and emotional traumas they had experienced.[11] These "kadogos," as they were called, frequently "manned" the roadblocks. With a sense of authority and fearlessness, as if to prove themselves and their capability, they carried out their responsibilities with roughness and severity.

————————— ༒ —————————

In Uganda today, even thieves and pickpockets carry cell phones. Almost *everyone* is "connected." When the sound of a phone ringing is heard in a public area, almost everyone reaches down to check if it is their phone. How things have changed!

When we first arrived in Uganda, only the privileged had telephones in their homes or offices. And even these seldom worked. Usually it was not even worth asking for someone's phone number. There was almost no

---

[11]Once the nation became more stabilized, Museveni's government established schools and homes whose purpose was to restore some of the boys' lost childhood and to provide education and training for them to become regular members of society.

chance in the world that both your telephone and his would be working at the same time.

International calls were another near-impossibility my parents continued to attempt. Whenever they needed to send an urgent message back to the States, my mom and dad would drive into town to the office that we shared with several other people above an Agip petrol station.

"We'd call the international operator and tell her what number we were calling," my dad recalled. "Then we'd hang up and wait for her to reach our 'party' and call us back. It could be hours, or it could be days, or it may never happen."

Receiving letters and packages was another opportunity to wait. I remember receiving a letter from our grandmother – six months after she sent it. Then there was the time that we received a package from a supporting church. It was filled with Christmas gifts for Jamie, Josiah, the baby-on-the-way (who turned out to be Joyanne), and me. But we received it several months after Joyanne's first birthday!

One huge disappointment I clearly remember was when we received a package from our Aunt Dottie. We were so excited to open it and were even more thrilled when we saw what was inside – a box of chocolate *See's Candy* – a family favorite. Anything sweet was such a luxury we could hardly wait to take a bite. As soon as the entire family was together we let my mom take the first piece. It was almost impossible to hold back the tears when every piece we touched disintegrated into a heap of stale chocolate dust. The package had taken so long to reach us that the chocolate was completely inedible. (And we *did* try to eat the dust – it was disgusting!)

---

We had come to Uganda to set up a children's center for orphans, but my parents often wondered if they would ever be able to actually begin what they had come to do. The war's devastation had not only affected the general appearance of the nation and its communication systems, but the political and bureaucratic structures were also thoroughly disorganized. After the overthrow of the former government, new political appointments had to be made and new laws and policies passed. However, by September 1986, just eight months after the war officially ended, that arduous task seemed to have only just begun.

When we arrived, the nation was caught between the jurisdiction of old policies and the creation of new ones. But what should happen in the meantime as this lengthy turnover followed its course? The old offices were now being manned by men and women who did not yet know their new jobs. And if they did happen to be familiar with the former policy regarding a specific situation, there was no way to be certain whether or not the regulation was still valid, if it was one that would be kept or if a new one had been created to take its place. Until this was determined, the job of people like my dad was to wait.

Day after day my father visited one government office after another in a determined effort to register WorldCare, the organization we had come under. But for months he would receive an answer that would bring him back the next day: "First wait, sir. We do not have that paper as yet. Please come back tomorrow." Or, "First wait, sir. The man who needs to sign the paper is not around. But he's coming. You wait."

In a country where men and women are struggling to survive and where every sense of stability and structure has been destroyed, the concept of efficiency has low priority. Often, the reason for a paper not being processed was merely that the man who changes the date on the stamp had not arrived yet. "First wait."

We later discovered that there was another cause for these months of delay. Due to insufficient wages, it was not at all uncommon for government employees to carry out private business during office hours or to hold a second full-time job – somewhere else in the country! Carefully arranging papers on their desk and placing their coats in an obvious place to give the impression that they were nearby but had just stepped out of the office momentarily, they would instruct their secretaries to concoct necessary explanations for their absences. "He is in a meeting," or even, "He has gone to bury his relative in the village; he will be back next week." The list was never-ending. Sometimes their desks would remain vacant for only a day, sometimes a week, but often it was longer. Other times, the government official was simply waiting for "chai" (a small bribe to buy some tea).

The words of Gad Gasatura, a Ugandan friend who had been in exile in America during the time of Idi Amin, always provided comic relief during extremely frustrating and upsetting times and perfectly summarized the situation in which we found ourselves. "In America," he would say, "people say, 'Wait a second.' In England, they'll say, 'Wait a minute.' But here in Uganda, we say, 'Just wait!'"

"Just wait." How true were those words! Take opening a bank account as an example. While most would assume this to be a fairly simple and straightforward task, anyone who has lived in a nation that is reestablishing itself will know that such a presumption is preposterous. In order to keep WorldCare's funds in U.S. currency rather than the rapidly devaluing shillings, my dad's first step in securing a bank account for the organization was to obtain a letter from a high-ranking commissioner in the Ministry of Finance to allow him to begin the process. But this first step soon proved to be nearly impossible. As many as three times a day my dad would climb the stairs to the official's office. Day after day, week after week he was told, "He's not around. Please come tomorrow," or, "He's in a meeting, first wait." A likely story! Finally, my dad gave up.

"I didn't want to make a career out of getting a bank account," he explained. "I knew I'd have to access our money another way."

The situations where we were forced to "first wait" were never-ending. We couldn't buy food because we didn't have Ugandan money. So we tried for months to get Ugandan money in both a legal and cost-effective manner. When that failed, we decided we would have to return to Kenya. At least there we could exchange money fairly easily and could purchase needed groceries. But then, there was no petrol. So we waited. By the time there finally *was* petrol, our Kenyan license plate had expired.

Looking ahead, my dad had begun the process of exchanging the Kenyan plates on the jeep for valid Ugandan plates not long after we entered Uganda. But the story of the license plates was similar to the story of the bank. Month after month, he was only issued a provisional license to accompany his now expired Kenyan plates. "First wait, sir. We do not have the papers necessary to issue a permanent license," they would explain. That was well and good if we were just driving in Uganda. But a provisional Ugandan license would not get us across the checkpoint at the Ugandan-Kenyan border. Kenya would not allow a vehicle with expired plates into the country, and we still needed to buy groceries...

# Chapter 4
## *Puzzle Pieces*
❦

*The theme of "first wait," though a frustration, was not a new theme in my parents' life by this point. Before I go on with the Uganda side of this story, it is essential to take a few steps back to gain a clearer understanding of the events leading up to Uganda – the waiting and the "no" answer whenever my parents asked "Lord, is it time to return to Africa?" But God was at work during the years of stateside waiting. There are so many pieces to the puzzle of our lives, and thankfully, He sees the whole picture and lays down each piece in its assigned place at the proper time – His time! Often it means waiting for us, but it always means He's working!*

*Much of the ideas and philosophies upon which the work in Uganda was built started with the puzzle piece of my father growing up in Congo. However, there were several more pieces that must be put into place during our years of waiting. While it seemed to my parents that our six years in California were years of waiting, of treading water until they were finally given the go-ahead to swim, they can now look back at the invaluable lessons they learned during this time and the precious relationships that were started then that we still enjoy today, and give thanks that His ways are not our ways, nor are His thoughts our thoughts!*

❦

"I was just fifteen months old when my parents first moved to Congo," my dad began his story. We were sitting in my living room in Kasana, and I was thoroughly enjoying having my parents all to myself as they reminisced about their past!

"My parents wanted to go where the greatest need was," he continued, "and didn't want to be where other missionaries already were established

51

and were at least partially meeting the needs of the Congolese around them."

With a heart for the lost, my grandparents sacrificed their careers, comforts, and safety and moved to the Congo. They frequently sought to live outside the established mission stations and relate as closely as they could with the Congolese.

"I think there was a bit of independence in them," my dad confided, "a pioneering spirit that certainly influenced me. During my high school years at the Ubangi Academy,[12] I began formulating a lot of ideas regarding missions and methods to reach the locals. Sometimes these ideas and the way I chose to voice them got me into trouble, but I believe my time in Congo was a very crucial part of my life and has had an impact on the ministry we've had here in Uganda.

"By my senior year of high school, I was convinced that I was going to be a missionary and always assumed it would be in Congo. I never had any interest in going anywhere else."

With this in mind, my dad chose to attend John Brown University in Arkansas where he studied building construction and design.

"That's where I met your mother," he smiled and continued. "From the age of nine she had felt called to be a missionary, and particularly to Africa. When we got married there was no question in either of our minds that we were headed to Congo. In December 1978, after nearly one and a half years of marriage, we left California for Congo. Vicki was seven months pregnant, but she had decided it would be easier for her to get used to living in Africa *without* a baby first, rather than getting used both to having a newborn and living in Africa at the same time. So, since you were on the way already, that's what we did!"

My parents planned to be "tent makers," or self-supported missionaries, instead of the conventional missionaries that must raise support through a

---

[12]Ubangi Academy is a boarding school in Congo for missionary children.

mission agency and churches. However, dealing with contractors that failed to pay my dad for his work, losing every coin they owned when the currency changed, and living in an impoverished community, caused the first year on the mission field to be far from easy for my parents. "We had a really rough time making ends meet," my dad continued. "We were also a bit of an enigma to some of the other missionaries around. While they were very kind and generous to us, many couldn't quite figure out what to make of us. No one else in that area had ever done anything like what we were doing."

"Looking back," my mom interjected, "with the experience we now have as long-term missionaries, I can see exactly why they didn't know what to make of us! We went out there completely on our own. Your dad was going to work and earn money, so we didn't have supporters to whom we were accountable. We didn't have a governing authority over us at all. We weren't sent from a church or a mission, and I think, from the missionaries' perspectives, we looked like free agents who didn't have to be accountable to anybody."

"My parents, who were still in Congo when we lived there, were also viewed as a bit different," Dad continued. "I think this was because they lived where there weren't other missionaries. Though they were never in any way against socializing with other missionaries, they didn't seek the company of the other missionaries that much. They spent more time with Africans. That whole outlook on missions certainly also influenced me and set a precedent for how your mom and I chose to work in Congo. But while there are many things I would do again, we did make a number of mistakes during our time in Congo!"

After fifteen months in Africa, my parents decided it was time for us to return to the States for a while. Emotionally burned out and nearly penniless, they planned to return to the U.S. for a year and, when things had come together again, return to Congo. However, after a year in the U.S. the door back to Congo was still firmly closed. Confident, though, that one day the

Lord would give them their heart's desire to return to Africa, my parents settled down in Southern California to work...and wait.

During this time, my dad worked for a construction company in Ventura, and though his heart was in Africa, the Lord used this time to introduce my father to Lin Franklin, one of the owners of the company for which my dad worked and a man who, along with his wife, Judy, would be extremely pivotal in the New Hope story in the years to come. It was another piece of the puzzle our heavenly Father carefully laid into place without our knowledge.

In 1982 Adoniya, a Ugandan man, came to Christ's Church in Ventura where my family had been attending. He told about the thousands of men and women – educated, Christian, or from the "wrong" tribe – who had died at the hands of Idi Amin and his men and of the huge number of orphans the regime had created.

Uganda. It had never even been a thought before. But maybe, just maybe, the Lord had closed the doors in Congo only to open them in a needy yet unexpected place.

"After hearing of these atrocities," my dad continued, "I began formulating an idea of starting an orphanage. It would be a center where the children would be cared for and would also spend time each day working. Their work would be geared toward learning trades and being trained in self-sufficiency."

Still rough around the edges and with countless unknown details to work out, the vision of what would one day be New Hope Uganda was born. My parents continued to mull over this new idea, to pray about it and seek the Lord's will. Dad soon put his ideas down on paper and began to share them with friends, family, and churches. The responses he received were unanimously enthusiastic, and my parents were convinced that in no time the funds would come together, and we[13] would be heading to Uganda as soon as possible.

---

[13] My brother, Josiah, was born in Camarillo, California, in 1981, and at this point, our sister Jamie was on the way!

However, while there was much verbal encouragement, my parents were unable to raise a single dollar to make this new vision possible. No, the Lord still had three more significant puzzle pieces He must lay down during the next two years before He said, "Go!"

<hr>

My mom met Christina Kirk through a women's Bible study they both attended. At the time, my parents were looking for a Christian school in which I could be enrolled for my first year of academics. Christina's husband just happened to be the principal of a newly founded Christian school; would my parents like to come and visit? Little did we know that from that "chance" meeting in a large community Bible study the Lord would lead us to a couple whose influence would have an immeasurable effect on our family, the work in Uganda, and countless lives throughout the world!

As I began my first year of school at the Master's School in Camarillo, California, my parents were introduced to the concept of a truly Christian education.

"I always thought I'd received a Christian education," my dad recalled. "Yes, the curriculum was the same as that in a public school, but my teachers were Christians, and we prayed before each class and had chapel once a week, so I assumed that made my education a Christian one. What we were hearing at the Master's School was something new."

Ron and Christina Kirk taught that the fear of the Lord is the beginning of *all* knowledge – of knowledge about math, science, literature – everything! He is the author of all things, and in Him all things hold together! He created the world with laws and patterns, with one nonnegotiable standard of truth – Jesus Christ.

"Indeed," they said, "the fool has said in His heart, 'There is no God.' It is all too often that Christians base their educational principles, psychology, philosophies, and belief patterns upon the *wisdom* of men and women who have said there is no God."

However, the Kirks, and many others with them, believed that every aspect of their curriculum (one that was extremely rigorous and surpassed that of most schools around), and their methods of child discipline and discipleship must all be reasoned biblically. For two years, my parents were immersed in the exciting and freeing biblical principles – the Principle Approach – that the Kirks and others taught.

Ron and Christina spoke "kingdom language." They not only talked of how the knowledge of the glory of the Lord must permeate every aspect of the classroom but also of how the Word of God was the answer to every question on how to raise children in the home and how to have a healthy marriage. Though my parents sought to be good parents, they were frustrated with what they saw in our family. They had listened to the teaching of Christian psychologists on family issues and sought to implement their methods to the best of their abilities. However, so much of what they were hearing was a complicated and confusing mix of biblical and humanistic approaches to discipline and child-raising, and my mom's frustration and discouragement grew. In fact, Josiah and I were such a struggle for my parents that when my mom found out she was pregnant with Jamie, child number three, she burst into tears!

"I can't even control the two I have!" she cried. "How on earth will I handle a third child?" But with the Bible as their reference and guide, I remember Mom and Dad repenting to Josiah and me of how they had failed to be godly parents and how they were, from then on, going to instill biblical principles as the new and only foundations of our family. What our family experienced was almost immediate change. There was a new consistency in our family – a consistency in discipline – that provided clarity for Josiah and me to understand where our boundaries were, enabling us to be truly free. Under the counsel of the Kirks and with the Scriptures as our new *practical* guideline for every aspect of our lives, our family was revolutionized.

"Our time in Southern California and as part of the Master's School was a very major turning point in our lives," my dad said, "and since that time, it has become an ongoing hobby of ours to study these biblical concepts and to find ways of implementing them practically into all we do. Our time being discipled by the Kirks greatly helped mold what Kasana is today."

❧❧

# 1985

*There was a big chart on the wall above our dining room table – sort of a makeshift calendar. To each of the twenty-one days on the chart, my mom had attached a piece of plastic wrap with a ribbon tied around it filled with six chocolate malt balls – two for Jamie, two for Josiah, and two for me. Every day when I returned home from kindergarten, Josiah, Jamie, and I would rush to the chart, taking turns pulling off the bag from the box and dividing the malt balls. Then came the most exciting part – taking the big black marker and putting a giant "X" through the box. We were one day closer to the last box on the calendar – the day when my dad would return to us in the huge airplane that first took him away.*

He had traveled to Uganda with a team of nine other men to do a feasibility study on the situation we had heard so much about and how the new vision might possibly be carried out. Maybe it was to be Uganda where the Lord wanted us after all – at least for a while until we could return to Congo. Among others, the team consisted of Dr. Tim Donahue, our family doctor and friend, Jeff Johnson and Glen Cravig, pastors of Calvary Chapel Downey, and William Morgan, a landscape architect. The Lord would use each of these men throughout the years in unique ways to bless and grow the vision that had been born.

Upon arriving in Uganda my father was shocked to see the difference it had undergone since he had visited as a child and what was before him. During the mid-sixties Kampala had been modernized with excellent roads, skyscrapers, and everything a recently decolonized nation could boast. Now, the capital was in shambles, and each night they could hear shooting and people screaming in the valley below Namirembe Hill, the "Hill of Peace."

Making various helpful connections with government officials, several members of the team were soon free to travel under government protection to different parts of the country to carry out medical missions. Dad and a few others stayed in Kampala, praying that the Lord would guide them to see the plans He had for them. Where did the Lord want us? With whom did He want us to partner? Little did we know the Lord had arranged to use someone to both refine us and help us.

"It was during this time in Kampala that I met Henry[14] through a mutual friend," my dad recalled. Henry – tall, friendly, and charming – offered to show my dad around. The two traveled to several different pieces of land with the hopes that one of them might be the future home of the center. Henry also began to give my dad a clearer understanding of the political situation.

"When I came to Uganda while Obote was in power in the sixties," Dad explained, "Uganda was so amazingly developed, I assumed Obote must be a good man. I knew Amin was not good, so I assumed that it was wonderful that Obote was back in power and that this rebel group fighting him was the one causing all the trouble."

All talk about the government and the current regime and current rebel movement was done quietly. As they stood looking out across Kampala on one of its seven hills, Henry's mood became somber. Pointing to the north he said, "That is where my people are dying." In hushed tones he spoke to my father of how Museveni's rebel movement was fighting to overthrow Obote's government and how Obote's men were slaughtering thousands of innocent people from Henry's tribe.

"It was the first time I'd heard anything negative about the government," Dad recalled. "It became hard to know whom to believe now. We couldn't travel to Henry's home area to see if his allegations were true, as it was the hot spot of the guerrilla warfare. I just had to begin piecing together bits of information I could gather here and there."

---

[14]Name changed for privacy.

However, while Dad was still unsure as to where the problem really was politically, there was no question of the need of thousands of orphaned children. As the African proverb says, "When the elephants fight, it's the grass that suffers." Regardless of the innocence or guilt of these different political "elephants," children – the "grass"—were most definitely suffering.

Henry and my dad were able to find a large piece of land in Lugazi, just outside of Kampala, that would work perfectly for a children's center. It was 530 acres and was being sold for $70,000. Unaware that this was "highway robbery" according to the Ugandan economy, my dad was amazed to find such cheap land according to American standards.

Three weeks after their departure, the team of ten returned home with countless stories of hair-raising experiences of the Lord's protection and of the great need they witnessed throughout the nation of Uganda. Mom and Dad were even more convinced that this was the time and the place. We knew what piece of land we wanted and were convinced that the money would come in no time. Oh, but God's ways are not our ways, and once again, the answer was no! As my parents continued to share their burning vision they were again met with positive responses from those who listened. However, a total of $137 was all that we had to show for dad's fund-raising efforts. For a family of five, cross-Atlantic tickets alone would require significantly more than this! Not a cent came in for the piece of land.

In January 1986 my dad received a call from Henry. The war was over. Obote had been overthrown by his own men and had fled the country. In his place, Lutwa was named president for a short time. Then, on January 26 Museveni's forces had surrounded Kampala and overthrown Lutwa. The country was finally at peace. Henry's phone call also brought word that if we would come and start the center in his home area of Luweero, his grandfather, Daudi Mukubira, would donate whatever land we needed. His grandfather owned twelve square miles of land.

Suddenly it became clear why the Lord had caused nothing to come in for the Lugazi land! Excited with the new possibility, my parents continued to tell others of their plans. But *still* nothing came in to make the vision a reality. Maybe this wasn't the time and place. Maybe God had something else in store.

In addition to their discouragement from the lack of funding and the closed doors everywhere they turned, my parents had also begun to be concerned about the timing of our departure to Africa. Our home church was struggling, and my parents were tired and discouraged from the struggles that come from church politics. They certainly didn't feel equipped and overflowing with a burning message to share with those who've never heard. Finally, in March 1986, my parents, thoroughly confused as to why the Lord had seemed to make things so clear but still kept all doors closed, spent time seeking the Lord in prayer.

"It was then that we realized that we were waiting for the Lord to pave the road for us before we were willing to step out in faith," my dad recalled. "We wanted all the money ahead of time, or at least to have it clearly promised. We wanted our uncertainties answered, and *then* we would step out 'in faith.'"

But the Lord seldom calls us into the "known" or well-planned situations. He was not calling them to go when it made sense or when they felt ready. He was not calling them to the known, but to the adventure of the unknown, where only He was certain of the next step, where their faith could be in no one or nothing else but in Him.

From that point on, things began to move fast. My parents put our house up for sale, Dad gave his notice at work, and we set a departure date. Very quickly, our house sold, and suddenly people began to take their talk seriously. Money began to come in for our monthly support, and prayer support was quickly promised. Soon also, we met Bill[15] who was in the process of beginning a new organization, WorldCare, and wanted us to be its pioneering family. Bill came with outstanding references from the leaders of several

---

[15]Named changed for privacy.

large and respected organizations, and although my parents had never heard of him before, they knew he must be what he said he was! My parents agreed to join Bill, and soon everything fell into place.

Before we knew it, we children were sorting through our belongings and "helping" our parents prepare for our huge yard sale. I'll never forget sitting on our couches out in the yard and wondering which neighbor would take them home that night. Once our furniture was all sold, we moved in with my Grandma Dorothy until our departure date. We children were excited! An adventure had begun!

The Lord used each of the puzzle pieces from my parents' past and from the previous "waiting" years to better prepare us for the work He wanted to begin in Uganda. Because of our connection with the Franklins at Dad's work, years later New Hope Uganda Ministries, Incorporated was started as a sister ministry to the work in Uganda. Because of our connection with and training under the Kirks, the ministry at Kasana now is family-focused and based on biblical Christian education and biblical child-raising. Because of William Morgan's time spent in Uganda with Dad in 1985, he added his own mark to the ministry by designing the original plans of the "Children's Farm Home." Convinced even more that it must be family-based and not dormitory style, Dad shared his ideas with William Morgan, and he drew up the blueprints for the Farm Home – family homes surrounded by family land for farming, instead of in a typical "orphanage" setting.

The plans were originally designed for the land in Lugazi, but when we later received sixty-six acres from the Mukubira family, the plans William Morgan had designed fit our new land precisely, just on a smaller scale – another affirmation of the Lord's hand on the new work! Because of Dad's childhood experiences in Congo, the design of the new Farm Home would also include staff housing for both foreigners and Ugandans side by side. Our future connections with Calvary Chapels in California would come through that initial trip to Uganda with Pastors Glen and Jeff. And the list went on and on. The Lord had carefully laid each puzzle piece, and it was now time.

Spiritually, however, Dad and Mom were dry and struggling. For several years their church had not been providing the nourishment my parents needed. But that piece of the puzzle, too, was just about to be put into place – almost as soon as we entered Uganda.

Mom and Dad, 1977.

The family vehicle, Congo, 1979

Mom and Dad with me, Congo 1979.

# Chapter 5
## *Refreshment*

❧❦

When one steps out in faith and walks according to God's will, even though there may be difficulties, the Lord's blessings far outweigh the frustrations. Though there were numerous delays, setbacks, and disappointments during our first years in Uganda, there was one new aspect of our lives that proved to be an immeasurable blessing, both at that time and throughout the years to come.

During his Ugandan travels in 1985, my dad met several members of an indigenous group of churches known as the Deliverance Churches. When we first arrived in Uganda as a family in 1986, we began attending one of the Deliverance Church congregations and were impressed with their commitment to the Lord, their sincerity, and their faith. Little did we know then of the life-changing effect our affiliation with this body of believers would have on our family, New Hope as a whole, and the lives of countless others.

My parents first arrived in Uganda tired, spiritually empty, and completely unsure of their own competency for the task ahead of them. For some time before we had left, our church in the United States had gone through very difficult times. It closed three years after we arrived in Uganda. My parents desperately needed to be refreshed and equipped for the work ahead of them through strong biblical teaching and the rejuvenation that comes from godly fellowship.

Matthew 6:8 states that our Father knows what we need before we ask Him. Indeed, the Lord knew their needs, and He had already prepared a body of believers that would not only give them the spiritual nourishment, fellowship, and guidance they needed, but that would also lead us into relationships with people all across the world who would later play vital roles in New Hope's unfolding vision.

The Nakasero Deliverance Church (DC), the congregation we attended, met in a nursery school each Sunday. After the singing, Josiah, Jamie, and I, and all the Ugandan children, would pick up our benches and head outside for Sunday school under the trees. It was here that we met some of our very first Ugandan friends, learned our first Luganda songs, and began to pick up what is often the trademark of missionary kids – the ability to speak English in the exact accent of the locals. (For years, this was how we communicated to the Ugandan children in Kampala, most of whom were fluent in English, but we would switch immediately and subconsciously to our American accents whenever we spoke to a Ugandan adult or a foreigner.)

There are many memories that spring to mind when I think of our early DC days. I'll always remember the red mud that seemed to leap onto our Sunday shoes the minute we would step outside for Sunday school. The Ugandan children never seemed to get mud on their shoes, but ours were always filthy by the end of the day. I remember being elected a Sunday school "prefect," which meant I got to help collect the offering. I remember sitting among all the Ugandan children and having them pull my long blonde hair out of my head one hair at a time. They had never seen a muzungu (white man) so up close before, and they could not resist touching Jamie's and my hair, pulling out a couple of strands, and then tying it into their own hair. I remember, during the times we children stayed in to listen to the sermon, sitting and trying to figure out which man was preaching and which one was interpreting. I remember the nursery school paintings on the walls in the room where the main congregation met, numbers and letters, children and toys, a soldier carrying a machine gun.

Well, those are the silly childhood memories I have – hardly noteworthy or of value. I was too young to understand the depth of the messages we received at every Sunday service and every Wednesday night at our "cell group," but I do remember that it was a time of fellowship and encouragement for my parents. The pastors and elders preached biblical messages that fed my parents. They spoke of covenant and commitment, of accountability, of the work of the Holy Spirit. The times of worship were also inspiring and uplifting. We learned DC favorites such as "The Devil Didn't Like It When I Came Out of the Wilderness Walking with the Lord," and "We See the Government of God in Our Lives." I remember how I loved it when Pastor Titus would lead singing. He loved to sing songs in Swahili and would get so animated that he occasionally stood on his chair and danced as the congregation echoed his enthusiastic choruses.

At the front of the building all of the elders and pastors sat in a row behind a table facing the congregation. Standing to sing and dance with animation and hand motions, wearing black suits, they looked remarkably like the sixties singing group The Temptations! The joy on their faces as they sang spoke of the depth of faith that comes through trials and testing. The unity and friendship they had with each other had clearly been weathered and aged to perfection over the years.

During the late sixties and early seventies, these same men, then just high school students, had started a Bible study together that eventually grew to become a church. Their commitment to each other and to the Lord had withstood the severe testing of Idi Amin's persecution and the danger that accompanied the underground church movement. Now, as the country began to piece itself together, they remained strong in the Lord and devoted to each other as they gave pastoral oversight to the planting of new churches across the nation.

On our first Sunday at Deliverance Church we could not help but notice the only other white face in the entire church. Annie Crowe, a British lady, had been living in Uganda for several months already, and was working and living at an orphanage in town. However, we soon found out that, while she enjoyed her work, her living conditions were far from ideal. Not long after,

Annie moved in with our family and became an immediate favorite with the three of us children. Soon "Auntie Annie," as we children called her, began to speak of her home church and the group of churches, Salt and Light Ministries, which were affiliated with it and with the Deliverance Churches in Uganda. She shared about Salt and Light's commitment to care for its missionaries; to bring pastoral care and accountability to every member of the congregation – both local and abroad; their commitment to community; the work of the Holy Spirit; and the need for strong biblical teaching. Again, my parents' tired and overwhelmed spirits yearned for such fellowship and care and began to be excited to meet the men and women of whom she spoke.

In addition to speaking of Salt and Light, Annie told my parents of the organization's head pastor, Barney Coombs. She spoke of how God had used Barney in so many ways; what a wonderful man of God he was with his tremendous insight and wisdom; he was very pastoral and fatherly. Having not received much pastoral oversight for many years, my dad knew it would be good for him to speak with Barney and, hopefully, to receive some guidance and counsel for the fledgling organization and our family. Although my dad knew the Lord had called him and my mom, he struggled greatly with doubting his ability to lead and tended to focus on his own inexperience.

"On the one hand, I knew God had given me this responsibility," my father explained, "and on the other hand, I felt completely unworthy to keep my position of leadership. I waffled between solid conviction and a lot of self-doubt. Consequently, I tried to hand over my role to several people at different times, and it never worked." He thought that perhaps what he needed to do was speak to someone with more wisdom than he.

In March 1987, a pastor's conference was scheduled to be hosted in Kampala. Pastors from England and Canada would be flying in to join the Deliverance Church pastors for several weeks of meetings, training, and outreach throughout the country. Would we mind hosting Barney Coombs and several other pastors? My parents were very willing to get involved this way, and they looked forward to getting to know people who were so important to Annie and the Deliverance Church pastors and elders.

"I knew the time would come when Barney would ask me about what we were doing here," my dad recalls. "I figured I would tell him everything, but I knew what he was going to say. 'Jay, this is a very good idea, but it is not of the Lord.' I didn't know what I was going to do when I heard those words."

Not long after, Uncle Barney (as we children came to call him) came to stay with our family for a week. And, of course, the dreaded question did come up: "What are you doing in Uganda, and what is your vision for the future?"

"I carefully told him the whole story," my dad continued, "the whole plan and vision. Then when I was finished, his response was 'This is wonderful! This is certainly of God!'"

"My first thought was, *Is he really a man of God? If he has so much wisdom, why didn't he see through me and discern that I don't know what I am doing and I shouldn't be here?*" my dad said.

Instead, Barney's excitement for the vision continued to grow. He traveled with my dad out to Kasana to see the land he had been speaking of. There was almost nothing there but some land that had been cleared, bricks being made, trees being cut for lumber, crops growing, and the formerly impressive Mukubira home, now gutted and destroyed, which we had leased for two years on the condition that we would renovate it for the family. We still had no children, no staff, and very little funding. Indeed, all there really was to show was a plan on paper. Yet despite all of this, Barney continued to be very enthusiastic and willing to help. Soon, Deliverance Church pastors too began to catch the vision and see how they could pray and be involved in the work.

It is impossible to measure the influence that both the Deliverance Churches and Salt and Light had on New Hope Uganda, the organization that later grew from the work my parents started. It was through DC that we met Uncle Jonnes, Auntie Gertrude, Peter Kiyimba Kisaka, Anna (Nyadoi)

Okello, and Joseph and Evelyn Ruyondo, key early staff members that helped lay the foundation for what New Hope is today. It was through DC that New Hope Uganda's first board of trustees was formed, with DC's head pastor, Pastor Nicholas Wafula, being its first chairman. Other key members of the original board included Pastor Titus Oundo, James Ameda, and Ben Oluka. Through the years many other staff and board members have come from DC churches all over the country.

Salt and Light has also made invaluable contributions to and investments in us as a family and the ministry as a whole. After our original organization (WorldCare) unexpectedly abdicated their position as both our sending board and the financial support source for my family and the children's center, my dad approached Uncle Barney to see if we could come under the umbrella of Salt and Light Ministries. Convinced that a "courtship period" would be the best way for such a decision to be made, it was decided that our family would travel to Winnipeg, Manitoba, for three months to become a part of Salt and Light's Gateway Christian Church. Our time in Manitoba was indeed a turning point spiritually for my parents.

My dad recalls, "It also helped us become a part of Salt and Light by the advice, direction, encouragement, rebukes, and corrections we received from the pastors and elders in Winnipeg. Once we and they had agreed that we would join with Salt and Light, the churches also became for us a source of financial support as well as a source for foreign staff."

Annie Crowe soon became the headmistress of our primary school, and David Freeman, from a Salt and Light Church in Witney, England, came and began to train our new teaching staff in Christian education.

On a trip to Uganda in 1987, Barney introduced us to a man who had traveled with him to Uganda. Dr. Ian Clarke of Northern Ireland was very interested in working in Uganda. He asked my father to show him around. After his brief visit to Uganda, the plan was for Dr. Ian and his family to move to Uganda where he would oversee a clinic in Kapeka, a village nearby, and help with the World Vision clinic in Kiwoko. He would also serve as the doctor for our children's center. It was through Salt and Light that Kiwoko Hospital, started by Dr. Ian and another invaluable blessing to New Hope, exists today as well.

———————————————— ⚜ ————————————————

As I look back at the tapestry of the New Hope story it is so evident how the Lord's hand was at work in the early days. He truly orchestrated our "chance" meetings with people and brought us into relationships with men and women across the world that have helped bring the Fatherhood of God to the fatherless.

Indeed the Lord has been good to us! He called my parents from a folding church to a brand-new organization to take a step of faith to serve Him in Uganda. All they knew was that He who called them was faithful. While their step of faith did lead them into a war-torn nation, it also led them to a spiritual spring of refreshment and fellowship. The Lord took our family from uncertainty and loneliness into a time of being surrounded by both Ugandan and foreign brothers and sisters in Christ who shared the same vision and were willing to do what it took to help us see the vision succeed. Indeed, "My thoughts are not your thoughts, nor are your ways My ways," declares the Lord. When we trust in Him, He is faithful to do all that He has promised and more!

Pastor Nicholas Wafula, one of the
Deliverance Church's founders and his wife Betty.

Salt and Light pastors visiting Kasana, 1990.

# Chapter 6

## *Entaandikwa*[16]

_____ ❧ _____

*Instead of putting the beginning stages of New Hope in my own words, I wish to give you the experience of "hearing" it from Uncle Jonnes' perspective. Although his voice intonations, excitement, and laughter cannot be written down, his honesty, humor, choice of words, and insight will give you a firsthand account. I hope you enjoy the story that he narrated to my parents, his wife, Gertrude, and me over dinner one night. Periodically, one of us will also step in to comment, but overall, here is Uncle Jonnes' story.*

"Well," Uncle Jonnes began, "I remember you coming up to me and saying, 'So, do you have an answer?' AAAAHHH," he groaned, "I was frightened, because I really didn't want to say yes to working with you, Jay. My mind was in turmoil: *What if I say yes, and then end up changing my mind? What do I say? I've got to think of an answer, quickly!* But while I was trying to find a way to back out of making a commitment, I was at the same time feeling so compelled in my heart to say yes.

"So, I said, 'Aah, yes, I have an answer. I'm afraid it's a yes!'" My dad smiled, remembering when he had first asked Jonnes if he would like to join him in establishing the Farm Home Project.

"So, that's when he took me to Nateete to tell me about the whole thing. He sat me down and he started telling me about his vision and plan (and by the way, this was the first time I'd really heard about it in any kind of detail!).

_____

[16]"The Beginnings"

71

As he talked, my head became confused, but my heart started warming up every minute! My heart was saying, 'Yes! Wow! Isn't that so true!' But my head was saying, 'EEEE! This is not real. Jonnes, you are being fooled. What *is* this?' Jay had nothing tangible yet to show me that could make me believe all the ideas he was sharing!

"I was being told nice stories, and very convicting ones, too, but I was still confused. I said, 'Lord, this looks like it is what You are calling me to do, but I'm afraid!'

"Then Jay took me to show me the kind of work he had started in Makerere – a timber-cutting project to earn income for the new organization. He showed me machines, saw mills, chain saws."

Uncle Jonnes was thoroughly confused. He had been asked to join WorldCare as project coordinator and assistant to my dad. But he had not realized that the beginning stages would require manual labor, a negative amount of prestige, and very little job security or security of any kind. The plans were to begin raising money by cutting and selling timber. With this money, building and planting could begin before the first children were brought in. But as Jonnes soon found out, my dad's method of working is not to simply delegate and wait for the results. He steps in and does the work himself, showing how it should be done and giving an example of how he wants others to follow. Once he is satisfied with the quality of workmanship and the competency of those working, he will gladly step aside and delegate.

As he began to realize the type of work that this new ministry would require, Jonnes' mind raced back to all that he had been involved in since high school.

"I went from being a spy for the government while I was studying industrial chemistry to a job of preaching and full-time ministry where I had a secretary, a car, a telephone, and all sorts of things," he recalled.

"Then I had a very good job offer with Pepsi Cola, and at the same time was faced with this change of plans to begin working with children.

Now, I'm being presented with chain saws and Wood-Mizers[17]! *This is crazy!* I thought. But for some reason, I decided to keep on."

Here my dad broke in to Uncle Jonnes' narration. "You seemed to be very excited about the sawmill. From my perspective at least."

"Yes! I was fascinated. I had never seen the thing!" Uncle Jonnes replied.

"But you weren't expecting to have to *run* the machines!" my mom laughed.

"No way!" he exclaimed. "I was saying (and hoping!) that this must be what *some* guys are going to be doing. I certainly didn't think *I'd* be doing it! Especially since I'd been given a big title... what was it again? Project coordinator! MY!!! Such a big title! Whatever *that* meant! Certainly not much at that time! I had thought it meant a big office.

"So, I kept listening to Jay and waiting to see more. Maybe the office and big position would be explained soon. So we talked and talked. Of course, Jay was busy trying to envision me. You know," he stopped himself and turned to my dad, "I don't think you used to like to talk to people a lot, but you talked to me!"

"Yeah," my dad admitted. "I wasn't very confident about 'selling' my vision to certain groups of people back then!"

"Wow, we talked!" Jonnes continued, "often until late into the night. Then the day came when we went to Luweero. We entered this big exotic jeep!" he laughed, grossly exaggerating the size and state of our tiny car. "I had to sit with my legs all crunched up like this," he demonstrated to all of us at the table. "We traveled forever. My, it took so long to get there! There were bumps and potholes, and the bush was so high you couldn't see over it. I remember we ate some sandwiches that Auntie Vicki made for us, and still we kept driving. I had never seen Luweero before. The roads were ugly, the buildings along the road were destroyed, and the few that were in Kiwoko had no roofs. Where you can buy bananas now, there were piles and

---

[17]The brand name of the saw mills my dad worked with.

piles of skulls and bones that had been gathered after the war! *Where on earth are we, and what on earth are we doing here?* I asked myself.

"When we finally 'landed' in Kabbubu, there was the introduction. Jay said, 'This is my assistant, and he'll do this, and I'm so and so, and so now let's get to work!' Meanwhile, I was just looking around. Everything was terrifying! I don't know whether you ever looked at my face," he said to my dad. "I must have revealed my fear!

"Right away we went to where they were cutting things. And you started setting up the equipment, Jay. People had already been cutting down trees, and we were supposed to cut it into timber. Remember we later found out that the ones we had cut were too young for making timber?" he chuckled.

"But I stood with arms on my hips.[18] 'So, where's my office?' That was what was in my mind. I looked down at my shoes and thought, *I hope there is something more profitable for me to do than work in this bush!* But while I was standing saying these things to myself, Jay grabbed two branches, one on his left and one on his right, and started carrying them away. Then he came back for more!

"I just stood watching and thinking, *I hope he doesn't think I'm going to follow suit! Let him not think so!* But as I stood there watching, I started to get tense inside. I felt God say, 'Behold My child, serving Me gladly in your country.'"

As he narrated these memories to those of us at the table, Uncle Jonnes' demeanor changed, and he became very serious.

"That really hit me," he said, "because I thought I loved my country. I thought I really loved it; I had even risked my life for it many times. I would do anything for my country. But it hit me that I was standing there not even being willing to carry branches. I thought I was too special to do such a thing. Convicted, I said, 'Lord, forgive me,' and I started picking up branches. Soon, we had cleared a place near the house.

"As we finished the first job, I got so inspired. Actually, I got saved! No

---

[18]Jonnes oftern has a very unique way of using the English language! We have termed his expressions "Jonnesisms"

longer did I think about my shoes! One of them soon had a hole in them, but I didn't care. I was wearing my Wood-Mizer hat, and I was excited. I picked up the chain saw, which I had never held before, and I started working. It was exciting! I was really released to start doing serious work!

"That day ended, and we spent the evening talking. I think every night of that week we would sit and talk and talk and talk. I would ask so many questions. We talked about everything, my life and his life. And I would ask him questions like, 'Are you the kind of person who gets excited about things, or are you not?'"

At this, the three of us women listening to his story erupted in laughter. This was precisely the difference between my dad and Uncle Jonnes.

"Jay said, 'I think I'm more level,' and I said, 'I get pretty excited!'"

What an understatement!

"We stayed in the two-story house that was owned by the Mukubiras. It was still bombed out and a mess then, but Jajja Nalongo[19] took good care of us. I remember the things that were the most common in that house were the big fat rats. My, I'd never seen such big ones! They weren't even scared of us!" he laughed.

The Mukubiras had once been a very wealthy family with many cows, twelve square miles of land, and ample provisions for whatever they needed. However, during the war, their huge two-story home in Kabubbu had been completely gutted by looters. All that remained was the building's shell and a few pieces of furniture that the looters had been unable to carry away with them. The doors and windows had been removed by vandals, and consequently, the family members who still remained lived crowded into the servants' quarters behind the big house. My dad and Uncle Jonnes were allowed to make themselves at home in the big old house wherever they felt would be the most comfortable. Using pieces of rusted iron sheets for doors to provide some sort of privacy, they joined the rats and swallows and attempted to sleep.

---

[19]Jajja Nalongo was the wife of the late Daudi Mukubira who donated the land to us in 1986. She became like a mother to my dad and Uncle Jonnes, and she cared for them whenever they came to Luwerro. She passed away in 2004.

"There was a table and two chairs still left," Uncle Jonnes remembered, "and we would use the table at night to hold the iron sheet against the door frame. I remember one night the rats disturbed you so much, Jay! You were sleeping on the floor and the rats came. I could hear you fighting with them from where I was! The house had been used as a place to store coffee beans, so the rats kept coming to find out what was there.

"Meanwhile, as you were fighting with the rats, I was fighting with swallows. I had lit the paraffin[20] lantern so I could read, and the birds kept flying and hitting me. I would grab one and throw it out of the window, but as soon as I'd pushed it out, another one would come in the other window. My, it was very exciting!"

The next day was another stretching experience for Uncle Jonnes. While my dad was off meeting with someone in the community, Jonnes had been left to begin working on the sawmill. Several men from the community had been hired to cut trees that would be made into timber and, while my dad was not around, were under the supervision of Mujengo, a member of the Mukubira family.

"The next morning," Uncle Jonnes said, "Kamili[21] came to work at 9:00 – an hour late. So I said, in my very broken Luganda, 'Hey, where are you going?' He said, 'I'm going to work. What do *you* want?'

"Trying to keep the upper hand in the conversation I said, 'Where are you coming from?' He said, 'Home.' I said, 'At *nine?*'

"'Why do you ask me that?' he said with disdain.

"'Don't you know *me?*' I answered angrily.

"'*I don't know you,*' he said, 'I only know Mr. Dangers and Mujengo.' And he walked off.

"'Come back here!' I demanded, "Tell your foreman to come talk to me!" Kamili just turned around and said, "I won't! And I don't care."

---

[20]Kerosene

[21]A community worker, who was part of the New Hope work force from its beginning and later became a member of the Kasana Community Church and a good friend of Uncle Jonnes until his death.

"Oh, I got angry!" Uncle Jonnes confessed. "How could this person speak to me that way? Doesn't he know who I am? Does he not realize that I've been trained to fight and could tear him to pieces if I wanted to? But as he went, I felt God speak to me and say, 'You are angry with him, and yet you don't even care that he doesn't know Me. It is not you he is disobeying; it is Me. Why are you here, Jonnes? You think about it. Are you here for yourself or for Me? Since you are here for Me, he's disobeying Me, not you, and there is no reason you should get angry with him. You should feel sympathy for him instead.'

"Humbled, I actually had to go to Kamili and reconcile things with him. From that point on, I started working to try to become friends with him, and we did become good friends eventually.

"At first, people's attitudes toward us and toward our goals were very skeptical," Jonnes recalled. "They knew it was just an idea that wouldn't last. They were interested in making as much money as they could from us while we were there, and then they would return to their former ways once we realized that the project was destined to fail.

"And so, over the next few months as we continued working, people from the community continued coming. Some came sick wanting to be treated, and we didn't know what to do with them! Others came looking for help, asking for money. I remember one man in particular coming and asking me for money so that he could take his wife to the hospital many miles away. So, I told him, 'We don't have extra money, but we have work. If you work, we will pay you!'

"'Eh, my son,' the man replied, 'do you know that I have never worked since I was born?' The man was a cattle keeper and had never done manual labor before. From a cattle keeping tribe myself, I replied, 'You look at me! I've also never worked. I also grew up on milk.'

"'Yes,' he conceded, 'I can see you are a man of milk!'

"'But my cows got finished,' I reasoned with him, 'and I had to learn how to work. You look at me. I'm working with my hands!'

"Skeptical but willing to give work a try, the man walked up next to me and took the branch I handed him. He worked with me for the rest of the day, and in the evening, I gave him the money he had earned. To my surprise, the next day the same man appeared, only this time his back was tied with a sweater because he had hurt it in the previous day's work! 'I've come to work so that I may get more!' he said. And so he did!"

The Ugandan civil war, which had for many years been centered in the Luweero District, had rendered the people of the area hopeless, lethargic, and indifferent to the poverty around them.

"In what is now the town of Kabbubu," Uncle Jonnes continued, "the only businesses that were there were bars, drinking places. People would tell us, 'For us, there is no hope; we have lost everything. We would rather drink, and if we die, that's OK. Do you think we can ever have hope to work and restore the things we lost?'

"No one wanted to invest in anything or to put forth the effort to build houses or improve their land. They would rather live in small grass-thatched houses that would blow over in a strong wind than exert the effort needed to build a more permanent structure. The prevailing mentality was, 'We are here for a short time. Either we will die, or whatever we have will be destroyed or taken from us.' The sense of apathy was overwhelming.

"Kamili himself was one of those almost finished from alcohol abuse. He would have died within the year, but we prayed for him. I remember as we prayed for him, he began to shake uncontrollably, and we felt we needed to cast out the demons that were controlling him. As we did, his shaking stopped, and he was restored. Almost immediately he gave up drinking completely! It was such a breakthrough, one that gave me so much joy and a desire to persevere despite the hopelessness around us.

"As time progressed our relationships with the community began to grow. As we shared the gospel with those around us, we saw people begin to change both spiritually and in their work ethic. I felt that God was starting to really stir up people's hearts. The begging mentality that was so prevalent slowly began to change as people realized that they *could* work and improve their situations. In less than two years those drinking places in Kabubbu were changed into shops because the lives of the people who used to drink there had been changed. A real openness to the gospel became more and more evident in the people we came into contact with."

Mamma Flo, the wife of one of the local witch doctors, was the first local convert. Her faithfulness to the Lord has remained strong to this day. Yusufu, another man whose life was nearly finished from alcohol abuse, also came to the Lord and is now on staff at New Hope and a deacon in the Kasana Community Church! But the change in the community did not take place overnight.

"One of the prominent members of the Mukubira family himself was disgusted with what had become of his life. 'There is no way we can improve things,' he said hopelessly.

"But," Uncle Jonnes had told him, "you don't realize that you still have the most precious thing – your life.

"His response was, 'Ah, but you don't know what we lost. This place was full of cows and wealth. We had everything here.'

"I said, 'Yes, but that just shows you how these things are for a short time. But you still have your life. You still have something that will last. What will you choose to do with your life?' He didn't give me an answer then, and I am still waiting for him to realize the truth."

Junju and Johnny, Kamili's drinking friends, were also ones who never broke free from the despondency that controlled them. Despite the continued witness of Kamili and Uncle Jonnes, and other members of the Kasana Children's Centre, these men continued in their ways, and several years ago we attended their burials.

Though there were encouragements such as Kamili, Mamma Flo, and Yusufu, there was still so much work to be done. Indeed, the battle to free the hearts and minds of the people in the area had just begun. Had we known all that lay in our path, we may have become fainthearted and given up. But the Lord remained faithful and walked with us each step of the way.

Dad and Jajja Nalongo not long before she passed away.

Jonnes Twebaze Bakimi.

Dad and the newly cleared land from the Mukubira Family.

# Chapter 7
## *Lungujja Days*

### DECEMBER 1987–MARCH 1988

With three children to home school, a baby on the way, six dogs to feed (and no instant dog food!), seven bedrooms and four bathrooms to keep clean, a continuous stream of visitors and teams to host, two single men and one single lady living with us, sporadic electricity and water, groceries difficult to obtain, another home-schooling family arriving in the country and needing help, street boys coming for lunch and work, the Kasana team spending weekends at our house, sick team members from Kasana coming back to the city to be cared for, a twenty-foot container of used clothes emptied into our garage to be organized and distributed, the baby finally arriving, and Dad in England for two weeks, my mother endured a hectic time during our three months in Lungujja!

In 1987 we had the excitement of my grandparents, Calvin and Dorothy Young, moving to Kampala to live with us and join us in the work for a year. Later that year, Paul and Jodene Kessel also arrived from North Dakota. And soon we had the addition of Peter Kiyimba Kisaka to the ever-growing staff. Annie Crowe lived with us, and a fourth child was about to join the Dangers' home. The three bedrooms and two "servant's quarters" in the Nateete home simply could not continue housing everyone (not to mention our continuous flow of guests)! The Kessels and Uncle Jonnes spent much of their time in Kasana; still they needed a place to live when they were back in town.

Living space was becoming a fairly urgent issue. The Lord's provision in this area came when we were asked to housesit for a missionary family on furlough. This would allow us to leave the Nateete home to my grandparents, and they could host part of the Kasana team when they returned. That would allow us to have more space to accommodate the rest of the team and the increasing number of visitors we found ourselves hosting in the new house.

The house we moved into in Lungujja was enormous – at least in comparison to anything my family was accustomed to occupying. Although it belonged to a family of five (not to mention their countless dogs and puppies!), they had rented it to serve as a guesthouse for short-term mission teams. While we children loved having so much space to run around, both inside and outside, it was nearly impossible for my mother to keep up with the dusting and cleaning that is so necessary in homes along dusty Kampala roads.

"I moved to Jay's place in Lungujja near the end of 1987," Peter Kiyimba Kisaka reminded me as he spoke of the early days. "Being at your dad's place certainly causes one to get into the thick of the work! At that time your parents and Jonnes and the Kessels had begun working with street kids – Allan, Kasim, Andrew, Samuel, Tomusange, and many others. Each day, many of the boys would come to our place and work in the compound in exchange for a good meal. I'll never forget the time your mom wanted to make something she thought they'd appreciate and that they seldom got. They hardly touched it! I guess it seemed like strange muzungu food, and they were afraid of it! So much for being nice! So, the next day, we made posho and beans,[22] and they inhaled it!"

Then there was the time one of the street boys thought the grape Kool-Aid was alcohol and wouldn't drink it. "I guess we won't try to do special

---

[22]Most of Uganda's staple meal – associated with being very common and not special. Posho is a dish made from cormeal, cooked to a mush. Usually served with beans or peanut sauce over it.

drinks, either," my mom concluded. It seemed best to stick with the tried and true!

On the weekends, Uncle Jonnes, Uncle Peter, and the staff from Save the Children would go and pick up as many street boys as wanted to come and could fit in the vehicles and take them to a football field on the outskirts of Kampala. There they would organize a football game, present the gospel, spend time with the kids, and then give them something to eat.

"The whole thing was a learning experience," Uncle Peter recalled. "While I really wasn't sure what to make of it all, I really enjoyed what we were doing. I never knew what each day would bring, and I wasn't sure I had the skills for what I was doing."

We kids loved having Uncle Peter and Uncle Jonnes living with us. They brought music and laughter to the home, and they were so good with us. We loved having the street kids come as well, and often worked with them in the compounds or traipsed along with the gang to cheer at the football games. We also loved the weekends when the Kessels would come and stay with us, or when a team would camp out in our home. And when the Clarkes (the missionary doctor's family) finally arrived in town, we were thrilled to move over and have another family join us in our school work and afternoon games. It was all so exciting for us! Little did we realize all that was being required of our amazing mother!

Our second Christmas in Uganda was a foreshadowing of Christmases to come. In fact, there were to be no quiet family Christmases for another seventeen years! In addition to our family, Christmas day was celebrated with the Kessels, Uncle Jonnes and his fiancée, Gertrude, Uncle Peter, Auntie Annie Crowe, and my grandparents. The more the merrier, we kids always thought!

———————————— ❧❧ ————————————

The night's silence was suddenly broken by the sound of a cry. I sat up in the darkness, my heart pounding. To the ears of a nine-year-old the sounds coming from my parents' room were terrifying. My mom was crying out in pain, and my dad was coaching her.

"Keep breathing out, honey. Don't push!"

While I've been told time and again since that night that my mom was *not* screaming, it certainly sounded that way to me at the time! I was terrified. I knew what was happening, but I also knew that moms weren't supposed to be in pain. They were the strong ones who *comforted* those in pain! My world was shaken! Too terrified to move, I sat in my bed and listened. Lights were on in the hall, and Auntie Annie and my dad were talking.

"Would you please go and get Auntie Betty?" my dad asked.

"Yes, right away."

Soon, the front door slammed shut, and I heard Auntie Annie's car engine start.

Auntie Betty was Pastor Nicholas Wafula's wife and was also an excellent midwife. It had been arranged that she and Dr. Jan White, a British missionary doctor, would deliver the new baby. We children knew this would be happening at home if all went well. For Mom to have the baby in a hospital would mean that Dad could not be with her, as that was not allowed in Ugandan hospitals. Reservations were made in two hospitals (one that Auntie Betty was registered in and another that Dr. Jan was registered in) in case of an emergency. But it would have to be a *real* emergency for Dad to send Mom in alone!

Dr. Jan had come to our house the night before to check on my mom.

"I think I'll just stay here, tonight," she said. "You never know what might happen, and I don't want to travel in the night if possible." And so she had stayed with us, adding to the excitement we children were already desperately trying to suppress! Our new little baby brother or sister *could* be here by morning!

For what seemed like an eternity, but was probably only a week or so, we children had joined our parents on several long walks around the neighborhood with the hopes of inducing Mom's labor. But to no avail. We walked and walked, to the amusement of the locals! "What on earth was this crazy white family doing making their poor pregnant mother walk for such long distances?"

Often on these walks, we children would become convinced we were lost. We had been walking for what seemed like forever and we *knew* there was no way anyone could figure out how to get back home. All these paths looked the same! So, to convince us, Dad would squat down in the middle of the path, take a stick and draw a map in the dirt.

"Here is where we are now. Here's the mud hut we passed five minutes ago. Here's the road to Grandma and Grandpa's house, and here's home." He never ceased to amaze us! And so, we would begin walking again.

"Any contractions, Mom?" we would ask.

"Not yet! But keep praying! It's bound to happen sometime soon," she would answer. Still we had our doubts.

And suddenly it was here! Yet instead of being excited, I was terrified! What could I do to help? My typical first-born tendencies had kicked into high gear. If I didn't do something, there could be trouble! I reached over to shake Jamie who was asleep next to me in the double bed we shared.

"Jamie, you *have* to wake up!" My whisper was more like a shout. "Jamie, Mom's in pain, we need to pray."

Jamie rolled over and looked at me, confused and dazed, "OK, you can pray," she yawned. At just four years old, Jamie was one of the deepest sleepers ever, and I knew there was no way I could wake her so as to have a serious time of prayer with her. So, I began to pray – to beg the Lord for mercy for my poor mom.

I don't know if I fell asleep again, or if the time really was that short, but what seemed like minutes later, my dad opened the door to our bedroom.

"You have a baby sister!" he shouted.

We were out of bed in a flash! And so the fourth "little J" Dangers arrived into the world. Just under six pounds, Joyanne Michelle Dangers came at 1:00 in the morning on January 4, 1988. We children bounded ecstatically into Mom and Dad's room. There were Dr. Jan and Auntie Betty holding the newest edition. And, look! Mom was smiling! She had survived! My prayers worked!

Following family tradition, we took turns having a specific role at the birth of the next child. This time it was Josiah's turn to be the first "little J" to hold the baby, and I would get to announce the name I had the privilege of helping choose. (Jamie got her turn with numbers five and six!)

The stories of the busyness and excitement of life in Lungujja would not be complete without the account of how the Lord brought us our first ten children, and how it was from Lungujja that we sent out the first team of staff and children to become the first Kasana family. However, that will have to be a chapter all its own!

Josiah, Jennie, Jamie and Joyanne,
in Lunguija just days after
Joyanne was born.

Jamie and Auntie Annie.

# Chapter 8
## *The First Ten*

### FEBRUARY 1988

"I was young and single," Peter recalled. "I was looking forward to life and to new things, and I knew I wasn't headed back home again. When I moved in with the Dangers at Lungujja, I knew my childhood was behind me and I had my whole life ahead of me."

"We were just so green!" Paul Kessel, one of our American staff members, recalled. "I remember the days before the children came - they were filled with great anticipation but also with fear and trepidation. 'Do we really know how to do this? What are we doing?' Looking back now, we *didn't* know! But we learned!"

The first team of staff headed to Kasana was made up of Paul and Jodene Kessel of North Dakota, Peter Kiyimba Kisaka of Kampala, Jonnes Bakimi of Kabaale, and my parents. What were their qualifications to work with children? Honestly, there were none! Some builders, a nutritionist, a homemaker, and an industrial chemist - certainly not a team you'd expect the Lord to choose to counsel, train, and educate children who had been orphaned and abandoned. Other than my parents, who would be remaining in Kampala for a couple more months due to lack of housing in Kasana, none of the other staff had even had the experience of raising their own children. And yet, fully aware of their shortcomings and inexperience, the team had an undeniably common goal, a common vision and passion. The unity that was there in that first team was tangible, and the Lord's blessing was so present. They knew the Lord would work through them, answer their questions, and give them grace. For indeed, it is in our weakness that He is strong! It is in our ignorance and inexperience that He shows His wisdom and guidance. And in our mistakes and failures His mercy and grace covers us.

The big day finally arrived: February 8, 1988. The bunk beds had been purchased and taken to Kasana, but they still needed to be assembled. The shopping and planning had all been done, and the evidence – mattresses, lanterns, cooking pots and pans, food, hoes, and more were piled up in the driveway at the Lungujja house. It was the day everyone had been waiting for. We were bringing our first children – two girls and eight boys – to Kasana. This was the real thing!

Once the men had loaded everything into the back of Paul and Jodene's pickup, we gathered around in a circle to pray. Then the ten children, Peter, and Daniel (a short-term missionary) all climbed up onto the pickup and perched on top of the mattresses and amidst the other supplies. (Obviously, traffic rules in Uganda had not yet been established!) Uncle Jonnes would join the group two weeks later. The Kessels would continue living in the Kabubbu house but would spend much of their time at Kasana, and Uncle Peter would be in charge until Uncle Jonnes arrived. How Josiah, Jamie, and I wished we could join them as we ran after the Kessels' pick up waving goodbye!

Through our work with the street kids, we had chosen five street boys who wanted to come and be part of the Kasana family – Samuel, Kasim, Andrew, Tom, and Allan. The government had also brought us a family of five children – John Bosco Kakooza, the oldest, followed by Kiwanuka Joseph, Katongole Wilson, Namata Gloria, and Namaganda Sylvia. These were our first ten. They were all definitely used to the city and had no idea where on earth they were being taken as the pickup drove deeper and deeper into the bush.

The road seemed to go on forever with elephant grass taller than the vehicle on every side. As the boys chattered away, the two little girls, just eight and nine, sat silently. Their world was certainly changing. We had done our best to begin a relationship with the family of five, who did not know us as well as the street boys did, but their eyes still had a blank stare, they were so insecure and afraid. "Who are these white people? Where are they taking us?"

The first night in Kasana was certainly memorable. Bunk beds needed to be assembled, rooms chosen, the pickup unloaded. Then of course, there was the issue of food. With eight boys, this was certainly a priority!

"I remember looking for firewood as soon as we got there," Peter reminisced. "There was no Jajja[23] there at first, so I got firewood and stoked the fire and cooked tea immediately." Peter had also never lived in a village setting, and although he was a Muganda,[24] due to the schools he attended and the fact that he was raised in the city, he neither spoke Luganda nor knew much of the village culture.

"It was almost like boot camp for me," Peter said. "It was the first time I'd lived in a mud hut, the first time to cook on an open fire, and I had to begin learning Luganda. The first night we stayed in the hut it rained and rained, and the rain came through the new grass roof. My bed was soaked, and I remember sleeping at one end of the bed, curled up to stay away from the water. This was all so new to me! I immediately knew I had to die to the 'old man' and just adjust to this."

After just a few days, the new "family" settled into a routine. While Peter and Jonnes were the main staff always there, the Kessels also spent much of their time with the new family, joining in with the chores, the fun, and the discipleship times. And the days were full! There was land to clear, gardens to cultivate, firewood to collect, water to fetch, food to prepare, laundry to

---

[23]Jajja is the term used for grandparent, and also has become the affectionate term for the women and men who cook for the children – regardless of their age or relationship to the children.

[24]A member of the most prominent tribe in Luweero

wash by hand, and general compound upkeep. Then, of course, there was time for devotions, Bible stories, and much time spent just laughing, talking, and singing. With three guitar players on the team (Peter, Jonnes, and Jodene), much time was made for singing with the children – whether they were sitting on mats under the big tree outside the house, huddled together in the "living room," or in the back of the pickup driving to and from football games in the community.

Football[25] is a favorite Ugandan pastime! Practice or just kicking a ball around for fun occupied at least a portion of nearly every afternoon. Not long after their arrival, a few of the boys also joined a local team, the "Kasana Rangers,"[26] and of course, the family thoroughly enjoyed outings to cheer on their brothers.

"We really didn't have time to formulate a specific vision or method of taking care of the children *before* they arrived," Paul recalled. "So, once they were there, we just had to focus on their immediate needs." With no set programs, school calendar, or structure, there was a lot of time to just *be* with the children, to be a family.

"Every morning, I would begin the day by going running with the boys," Peter smiled, "and then we would all walk the half mile to Kabubbu where we would collect water in jerry cans[27] for washing and cooking. After breakfast, we would then head out to the work in the garden. Every day there was so much work to do! I learned very quickly that you had to have a separate pair of work clothes and that my shoes were not appropriate for the work we were doing, which meant I had to go barefoot for some things!"

"At the end of each day," Peter continued, "I would fall into bed and think, *Well, Lord, I finished another day. I hope I have the strength for tomorrow!* But, at the same time, it was a joy to see we'd actually done something that day, and I looked forward to the next day and all the work we had to do in it."

---

[25]Soccer

[26]Due to the fact that my dad gave them a football, a local team decided to name themselves after him. However, they couldn't believe his name was actually "Dangers" – it must be "Rangers"! And so the name stuck!

[27]Plastic water containers that, when filled, weigh about 45 pounds.

"For the first few days, Namata and Namaganda kept asking me if they could help me cook, but I thought they were too young to prepare the food and cook over the fire, so I kept telling them no. But I soon found out they were better than me! I remember a time when the boys and I were all out in the field, and when we returned, the girls had cooked a very good meal wrapped carefully in banana leaves, exactly as it should be! I realized they weren't so little after all! It was a relief to me, as I'd been trying to carry the load of cooking in addition to my other responsibilities, and it was also an eye opener – they were small, but they could do a lot!"

In addition to learning about village life, living in a mud house, using pit latrines, and cooking over an open fire, the staff was faced with the overwhelming reality that they were responsible for children's *lives*. Not only was it important to make sure that they were fed, clothed, and medically cared for, but there was also a seemingly limitless list of other dimensions to the children's lives – their emotions, their spiritual life, the hurts and fears they had, and the fact that they had never been disciplined in a loving way or trained in godly behavior and character. There were five teenagers, hardened from life on the street, orphaned and abandoned, and a family whose mother had died and father had abandoned them after their mother's death.

"While I was there," Peter continued, "I was like an apprentice. I had no clear understanding of how kids should be treated or raised. I felt like I was learning more than I was giving! I remember disciplining Kasim badly one day, and having Uncle Jonnes come up to me and say, 'That is not a good way to discipline a child. You must never punish them when you are angry. You must wait until you are certain your emotions won't get in the way, and then you can deal with the situation calmly and in love!' I was certainly learning on the job!"

While the team did feel so inadequate, their love for the Lord and love for the children were truly all that was needed.

"I just remember being so impressed with Jonnes and Peter," Jodene Kessel reminisced. "They were so filled with joy and enthusiasm. They were such good role models for the children and for us, and we learned so much from them and from their teaching."

One of the clearest aspects that the new team faced each day in Kasana was the sense of spiritual darkness everywhere. Kasana had been the center of some of the worst fighting during the war, and many lives had been lost on and around our land. In addition to what felt like the spirit of death that hovered nearby was the almost tangible presence of evil that comes from witchcraft. There had been a couple of demonic shrines on our land as well as witch doctors on and near our land in the recent past. Needless to say, the presence of evil was strong. From the beginning, prayer was the major "weapon" used to combat this. And the battle remained intense for several years, with many key lessons learned along the way.

It had been a good day – early morning "athletics" for the boys, school for a few hours for everyone, lots of work in the garden, a football game in the afternoon. As the sun slowly crept toward the horizon, the Kasana family began to prepare for the night. As soon as everyone had bathed, it was time to gather together for supper and devotions. "Where is Bosco?" Uncle Peter asked as the family sat down to enjoy the evening meal.

"He said he wasn't feeling well and needed to rest," was the reply. Not suspecting anything serious, Uncle Peter prayed for the meal. He would go check on Bosco after supper.

But after the meal Bosco was nowhere to be found. Immediately sensing something was wrong, Uncle Peter spoke firmly, "Everyone, get the lanterns lit and put on your boots. We've got to find him."

Instantly, fear gripped the hearts of little Namata and Namaganda. Their older brother had been known to struggle with different things – spiritual things. He often talked to Uncle Peter about the voices he heard in his head. He talked of demons and spirits that would come to him and haunt his mind, spirits of the people who had been killed calling to him. Every time he would speak of this, their skin would crawl, and fear would grip their hearts. Did the spirits take him? Where was he? Was he OK?

"Spread out, everyone," Uncle Peter shouted directions to the boys, who were already shouting Bosco's name and peering through the darkness with the dim light of the kerosene lanterns. Throughout the gardens, the compound, and then into the bush the boys moved quickly.

"Bosco!" they screamed. "Bosco, can you hear us?" But there was no answer.

Crashing through the bushes and into the clearing that was the main road, Samuel and Kasim came to a sudden stop. There was Bosco, lying on his back in the middle of the road. But as soon as Bosco realized he had been found, he sprang to his feet and took off running.

"By that time, I'd heard the commotion from their direction," Uncle Peter recalled, "and ran to find out what was going on."

Down the road and then through our neighbor Hadji's plantation, Kasim and Samuel followed close behind. The night was pitch dark, and the lanterns had been discarded along the way to make for an easier chase. Running through the darkness, the elephant grass and banana leaves beating against his face, Samuel tried to ignore the sound of his heart pounding so he could focus on the sound of Bosco's footsteps not far ahead of him. He had reached a clearing – a potato field. However, the unevenness of the ground and the irregularity of the spacing of potato mounds caused Samuel to slow his speed as he stumbled through the field. Finally, Samuel's athletic abilities and continuous training paid off. He overtook Bosco and grabbed him. Not too far behind, Uncle Peter and the other boys reached Samuel, who was now struggling with Bosco – silent and obviously not himself.

After a long struggle, "I put him over my shoulders," said Uncle Peter. "He was tough and very hard to hold down. And, other than a strange grunting noise, he was almost completely quiet. We carried him back to the hut and prayed with him, and then I told the boys to keep an eye on him."

Hopping on his bike, Uncle Peter raced through the darkness to Kabub-bu to find Dr. Ian, who had recently moved into the kalina[28] with his fami-ly. "I told him about Bosco's condition. 'This is more than sickness,' I said."

Different ones took turns watching Bosco all night, unsure of what he might try to do.

"In the morning, he woke up and was immediately violent," Uncle Peter continued. "Banging his head on the wall, he kept talking about his head and asking for a knife so that he could cut it off. I knew I was dealing with a spirit and not a person."

Finally, Bosco calmed down and lay back down in his bed. As he slept, Uncle Peter and the rest of the boys decided to see what work they could get done. But the peace did not last for long. Soon, Namaganda and Namata came running to find them. "He's trying to kill himself!" they screamed.

When they arrived at the scene, Bosco's eyes had rolled back into his head, and he was violent.

"We had to tie his feet to the bed," Uncle Peter continued. "I didn't know what to do. I knew *I* couldn't do anything for him, and I knew he needed prayer. I felt he needed to see a pastor."

Still unsure of how to deal with such issues, the staff decided that it would be best to take Bosco to the pastors in Kampala for prayer.

"So, we put a mattress in the back of the pickup and lay Bosco on it for the long trip back to the Dangers' house in Kampala," said Peter. The pas-tors did come and pray for Bosco, and he quickly returned to his normal self and was able to return to Kasana.

While the presence of evil continued to feel oppressive, the Lord had truly begun to penetrate through the darkness and train His children to com-bat the demonic forces. He filled their hearts with His peace and the knowl-edge that even though they walked through the "valley of the shadow of death," they need not fear any evil, for He was with them.

---

[28] "Kalina" means a two-storied house, referring to the Mukubira's house that had been remodeled for the Clarkes and eventually my family.

"This situation with Bosco really opened our eyes to the spiritual dimension we'd not been fully aware of before," Peter continued. "I became aware of the battle we were in. We were not just dealing with children. I also then remembered that someone had told me that we'd built our house on the same place where a witch doctor had once had his shrines. This certainly played into what we were experiencing. With all this in mind, I began praying and fasting regularly."

Not long after the situation with John Bosco, Allan also was attacked.

"I remember the children shouting for me," Peter said, "'Uncle! Allan has the same problem as Bosco! Please come quickly!'" The scene was similar to what had occurred with Bosco – a horrible demonic presence: gurgling, and bile coming out of Allan's mouth. However, strengthened from his times of prayer and confident that the Lord who had answered the prayers for Bosco would also answer his prayers for Allan, Peter called the children together.

"I remember that time saying, 'Let's get our guitars, and let's just praise God.' We sang and sang and just worshiped the Lord, and he was cured right there! He never had the same problem again."

From the beginning, the Lord's hand was at work in and through His children in Kasana. But it has not always been easy. To this day the Kasana staff is still learning how to best love, encourage, discipline, and disciple the children the Lord brings us. With each lesson we've learned the hard way, we've wished we could go back and undo the mistakes made in the past. But praise God for His strength that is made perfect in our weakness! Praise God that He is greater than our mistakes and is sovereign over every situation! Praise God that though His Word may be spoken by an imperfect staff member, it will not return to Him void, but one day *will* accomplish all that He purposed for it in the life of His precious child!

There *have* been heartbreaks along the way when we did not see fruit develop in the lives of some of our children. In fact, one by one, our first ten walked away from the Lord and from the New Hope family, leaving gaping holes in the hearts of their Kasana parents. But, as has happened with a couple of them already, we are eagerly awaiting the day when the rest of the dear ten will stop resisting and accept the love of their heavenly Father. When we bump into them in town or see them at the funeral of a mutual friend, they still speak of "home" and their family in Kasana. We know the seeds the staff planted were not in vain. They know they are loved, and when they are ready, we'll shout for joy when we see them coming!

As the ten children and the staff at Kasana were slowly but surely being melded into a family, the Lord was preparing another key figure that was so necessary for the parenting of the children at Kasana.

Dad, Jonnes and Katongole, Kiwanuka, John Bosco, Namaganda, and Namata.

Moving in!.

Kasana's first family (Jonnes far left in the back, Peter tallest in the back, Sarah in the white dress, Paul and Jodene Kessel the 'Muzungu' couple).

# Chapter 9
## *Kasana Kids*

&#x223F;&#x2183;

"One night I had a dream," said Sarah Muwanguzi, one of my closest role models growing up and currently a dear colleague. "I dreamt that I'd gone back home to Entebbe, but there was no space for me there. I couldn't find a place to live, and no one, not even my closest friends, would let me stay with them. As I searched and searched for a place to stay I kept asking the Lord, 'Where can I go?' and then He answered, 'Luweero. I want you to go to Luweero.' Luweero? The heart of the bush war? I'd never even been to Luweero before.

"Not long after my dream, my church organized a mission trip to Luweero, and I was able to join it. While I was there I was so moved seeing little kids walking very long distances to get to school. Many were even crying as they walked. I felt so touched, and I started praying that the Lord would send His people to care for those in Luweero who had been suffering for so long. After we returned home, I continued praying regularly, and one day I heard God say, 'You could be one of them.' 'But how can I begin?' I asked. 'How can I step out? Should I go where we went for the outreach?' As I continued praying for an organization to come and help these people I did not hear any clear answer from the Lord of *how* I could help, but God continued to bring the message to me: 'You can be part of them.'"

Through her desire to help others, Sarah heard about Youth With A Mission (YWAM) and enrolled in their Discipleship Training School (DTS) in hopes of being equipped for service. And, as the Lord would have it, when the time came for the three-month service assignments to be given, Sarah found out she would be traveling to Kasana, Luweero.

"The leaders told me they'd put me where they felt the Lord wanted me, and that was in Luweero! I had never shared my burden for Luweero with anyone!

"When we arrived in Kabubbu, I was so touched to see foreigners – the Kessels, Dr. Ian Clarke,[29] and the YWAM team from Netherlands who'd arrived before us – welcoming us in our own country! I felt the Lord say to me, 'See, My children are serving Me in your own country, and you didn't even know about it!' I had been praying for His people to come to Luweero, and here they were! My eyes just filled with tears. I saw them suffering with things like jiggers[30] and the hardships of the living situation here in my country, and I was so touched by their love for the Lord. From that first moment, the Lord touched my heart and I knew that if He called me, I would also come here and serve.

"Not long after we'd arrived, Uncle Jay came and shared the vision of New Hope with us and showed us what he had on paper about Kasana. As we looked around us at the poverty and the bush that surrounded us, we really wondered if this dream would ever come to pass. Questions filled my mind. 'Could he really be serious?'"

During her three months at Kasana, Sarah became thoroughly involved in the medical work that Dr. Ian was carrying out in Kiwoko.

"But I felt I needed to work with children," Sarah recalled. "I had been translating for Dr. Ian, and while I loved the work, I kept saying to the Lord, 'God I'm not a nurse; I'm a teacher.' But I was willing to do whatever He called me to, and when I returned to YWAM, the Lord continued to speak to me about coming back to Luweero.

---

[29]During the early days, the Kiwoko medical work and the work with children in Kasana were intertwined and included many of the same people.

[30]Jiggers are small fleas that burrow into ones skin and lay their eggs. If not dug out, the eggs hatch and burst through the skin.

"I finally joined the Kasana-Kiwoko team on July 19, 1988. And while my role was still not clear, the Lord began to speak to me about prayer. I spent a lot of time each day in prayer, and this helped me do whatever came my way. I saw God's blessing and really felt that God was with me in whatever I was doing. I was satisfied helping at the clinic, until I saw the kids at Kasana! I soon began visiting them any time I was not at the clinic in Kiwoko, and I felt myself being more and more drawn to them. I felt God wanted me to mother them.

"Eventually, it was decided I didn't need to go to Kiwoko any more, but that I could be of help at Kasana with the children."

And so Kasana gained one of its most influential and loving mothers, a mother who has left a permanent impression of love, compassion, and self-sacrifice on everyone she has touched.

The rain was coming down in torrents as the van slipped and slid along the tortuous dirt road. The new double mattress tied to the roof of the van was drenched from the rain. The trip from Kampala to Kasana had never seemed longer. It was August 8, 1988, and Jonnes and Gertrude, married just five months before, were moving to Kasana.

"We're moving to Luweero," they had told their friends and family, and the responses ranged from rebuke to laughter.

"You're crazy," people had told them. "How dare you take your new wife into the bush, Jonnes? Why doesn't she stay in town and you come and visit her on the weekends?"

"We're moving to Luweero in obedience to God's call on our lives," they responded. "And we're moving to build a family and to be a family."

As they slid from side to side down the narrow dirt road it was easy to see why others had said they were crazy. The house they were moving into, just across the road from the land we had been given by the Mukubira family, had survived the war – barely. In hopes of providing a relatively comfortable home for his new bride, Uncle Jonnes and others had done all they could to give the dilapidated old place a face-lift. But there's only so much that a paint job and few bits of plaster can do to a crumbling building!

"It was actually good it rained when we got there," Uncle Jonnes said and he laughed at the miserable memory, "because that way, there were no surprises later! We knew exactly what we were in for!"

"When we arrived at the 'State House,'[31] as we soon jokingly termed it, we found lunch already prepared for us," Auntie Gertrude recalled. "But we could hardly find a place to sit down. The whole house was flooded because the roof was filled with holes!"

"Ah, yes!" Uncle Jonnes continued. "You could see more 'stars' from inside through the roof than you could see outside at night! As we ate lunch, our bowls got soaked with more 'soup' than we had put in at first!"

The first night they were to spend in their new home, the Bakimis and their adopted daughter, Judith, were rained out. They had to go stay with the children and Peter in their home. Later, when an attempt was made at putting new iron sheets on the roof, that task was quickly halted after the builder nearly fell through the roof because a rotten crossbeam gave way.

"So we erected iron sheets inside above our bed," Auntie Gertrude smiled. "That way we at least wouldn't get rained on in the night!"

When their first little boy, Joshua, was born on February 14, 1989, they erected a polythene canopy over his crib to protect him from the elements.

"But we were optimistic," Auntie Gertrude recalled. "I knew this was just the beginning, and things would continue to get better and better." Well, they certainly couldn't get much worse!

In August of 1988 the Kasana staff began what has become an annual task at Kasana – the selection of new children from the village. The staff members are forced to determine which of the many that come seeking a place in our school or a place to live are actually genuine. Are these actually

---

[31]The State House is the Ugandan version of the White House.

orphans, or is a deceptive parent making up a story to get their child free education? And then there was the overwhelming sense of need absolutely everywhere! During those days especially, everyone was needy.

Ravished by the war, the inhabitants of the area still struggled to provide the basic food and clothing for their own children, much less the thousands of orphans created by the war. And so the process of interviewing, visiting homes, and speaking with local authorities began. We knew we could take in a limited number of day students, but these needed to be the most desperate cases. However, as we began going into the community, accepting requests for positions in the school and preparing to take in new children, the rumors also began.

"Most people began saying these white people had come to steal our kids," said Paul Kusuubira, one of the children from that first local intake, as he remembered the early days. "They said they were going to eat them, to make money out of them, or to take them to America and sell them as slaves."

"When Uncle Jay and Uncle Jonnes first started coming to Kasana," recalled Kimera, another of our first children and currently the head of our childcare department, "I was going to school at the Catholic school just across the road. We would see bazungu[32] come and go, and we would hear the chain saws they were using to cut down trees and clear land for building. We really didn't know what was going on, but I was very curious. Soon, everyone in the village began asking, 'What are they after?' And all sorts of rumors began."

Following years of violence, broken trust, and suffering, it only made sense that the community was so suspicious of these newcomers. Indeed, it would not be until our first group of students had completed their final year of primary school in 1994 that the negativity, verbal abuse, accusations, and lack of trust would, for the most part, be silenced throughout the community.

---

[32]White people

Kimera continued, "When we found out that they were taking care of orphans, I was immediately interested. I had been taking care of myself, working to pay for my own school fees and living with people that I was not even related to. But then I began hearing the discouragements from the village. I remember people telling any of us who were interested in joining, 'These bazungu are coming to recruit you orphans. After they've recruited you, they will make life wonderful for you, but it will just be a trick. Once they have you, they will carry you wherever they want and they will sell you.' Within me, I thought, *I was held at gunpoint five times when Obote's soldiers attempted to kill me, and by God's mercy I survived, I think I will survive this!* And when I began to see how the people at Kasana really treated their children, I thought, *I would rather be treated this way and then sold by this kind of people than to be sold by the kind of people that caused me to suffer during the war.* I think because I had learned to stand firm under a lot of torture, it really didn't bother me that people thought these whites might sell me."

"I remember seeing a bearded man show up at our home one day," Paul continued his recollections. "It turned out to be Uncle Jonnes, but I didn't know who he was then, and I was scared of his beard and wondered why he was coming to our house! I began to remember the rumors I'd heard about the new people coming to take orphans, and my mind was filled with fearful thoughts. Looking back, I know that there were many kids who would have desired to be in this place who didn't come because of that fear. But one thing I was sure of was that I needed help. I had to overcome my fear and shut my ears to what people were saying. I know that it was not an accident that Uncle Jonnes came to our home that day. My father had died more than two years before, in February 1986, and my mother died later in August of that year. My little sister was about three or four when Uncle Jonnes came to us, and she, my brothers, and I were just living on our own. I know God was working out His perfect plan when Uncle Jonnes came that day. And so I decided to take a risk and come with my younger brother, Machumi, and my little sister Anna Maria."

"People didn't know about Kasana and didn't expect good things from the start," Betty, one of the girls from our first local intake and now an enrolled nurse, shared. "I actually still had both parents living when I joined, but neither of them were taking care of me, and I had been left to be raised by my grandmother. My grandmother deceived people here and convinced them that I was an orphan so that I could be accepted. When my father heard that I was here, he was furious. He thought that they had given me away, that I'd never appear again. Then and there, he disowned me and for many years said I was not his child."[33]

And so, after several months of investigations and preparation, in October 1988, forty bare-footed, poorly clad orphans (and some whom we later found out were not orphans!) arrived, fearfully and quietly, for their first day of school at Kasana. Some, though they were in their teens, had never held a pen or a pencil, had no idea how to read their own language, or even say a basic greeting in English, the national language.

Many of the younger children bore the obvious signs of malnutrition – protruding stomachs, bowed legs, and reddish brown hair. Their feet and hands were filled with jiggers, their faces were distant and withdrawn, their hearts hidden behind the walls of self-protection they had carefully erected after the abuse, neglect, torture, and abandonment they had experienced during the most formative years of their lives. But they were some of the very ones the Lord had knit together in their mother's wombs,[34] whose names were engraved on the palms of His hands,[35] and whom He called His own. Indeed, of the many names He could have chosen for Himself, He chose to be called *their* Father—"a father to the fatherless."[36] Unaware of their Father's love for them, these children had no idea what to expect, no idea what their

---

[33]Years later, after the deaths of Betty's grandmother and mother, her father came to find Betty at the boarding school she was attending, and he asked her to forgive him for disowning her. The Lord truly brought reconciliation to their relationship.
[34]Psalm 139:13
[35]Isaiah 49:15-16
[36]Psalm 68:5

futures held, but each one knew that it was hard to find a situation worse than they were already in. Maybe - just maybe - this place would be a safe place.

"From when I first arrived at Kasana," Scovia, another of Kasana's first daughters shared, "I saw the parenting that was offered here. When I began to see how the aunties and uncles[37] treated us, I would just cry and think of how badly I'd been treated before. But here I was handled in a different way. I was loved and handled with care."

"When I first arrived, what I really had in mind was getting help," Paul shared. "I saw this place as a means of getting material things: food and clothing. But I did not even think it would be a place I would come to see as home. But the most interesting thing I found was that it was a place of *comfort*! I realized that these guys really loved us! It didn't take long for me to start getting used to things. Uncle Peter used to pick us up and hug us a lot. We would read books and try to do some school work with Auntie Sarah and Uncle Meekson, and of course on Sundays, we would go to Sunday school. Every Sunday after Sunday school we would go straight to the Dangers' house to ride bicycles. Oh, we had fun! My first time to ever be in a car was also at Kasana! I remember it was the small Suzuki, and I happened to be sitting behind in the trailer. I was holding on as tightly as I could and was amazed to see the trees running by!"

"Auntie Sarah was always with us," Betty continued. "She cared for us as individuals, not as a group. If I were to speak of what she did for us, it would not be enough! When they found out that I was not an orphan, she pleaded for me, and they let me stay. She became my parent. I would come from the village each day very dirty because the path was very narrow and the dew would make us all wet. But she would take my uniform and wash and iron it, and then I'd come the next morning and she would have it ready for me to wear that day! She took care of us when we were sick and would wash us when we were dirty. She was really a parent to all of us! I remember Uncle

---

[37]Kasana staff are referred to by the children as aunties and uncles.

Peter would always have us sing, but we didn't know English, so we would just laugh and make up words! Talking to white people was also hard, and we couldn't understand their accents. But Uncle Peter kept working with us, and we soon began to learn!"

"We really didn't have a normal routine as we do now!" Auntie Sarah shared her memories. "The early days were really focused on just building relationships. From the beginning, we also used to spend a lot of time with the kids studying God's Word with them. Different staff members, and then the teams that began to come, would take time to teach about the Lord, teach songs, and do skits for the children. School wasn't really normal, either! No one would ask for lesson plans or curriculum. We had far too much to do than to sit down and do real lesson plans! I would just think of something, write it down, and then that's what we would do the next day!

"When the school first began," Auntie Sarah continued, "our Jajja had just left. So I used to work with the kids and we'd prepare our own lunch. We would peel the food in the evening, leave it covered, and then in the morning we'd put it on the fire with the porridge and go to school. Early in 1989 we would be in the classroom for an hour, and then they would come and tell us there was maize to harvest. So we would leave class and go to harvest maize. Sometimes it would be harvesting beans or weeding potatoes. Since we didn't have many hoes, if it was time to weed, we'd use our hands to remove the grass. We were also divided into groups where we did gardening. The children were happy to do it. They had a very good spirit about work."

"When people began to hear that we were working hard," Kimera added, "they would say, 'Aah, they have taken you just as slaves, so you are going to *work*, and then after you have worked, they will sell you!' But for years, I'd been living in the community and had been working for local villagers who often would not pay me or give me food for my work. Here, however, I was eating, I was getting clothes, and I was getting help and love. People cared enough to take time to talk to me, so I didn't see any problem here! Some of us older boys even used to do small contracts for the staff members in their personal gardens, and they would *pay* us! In other schools in the village children would fight and hurt each other, and the teachers would never do anything to stop them. But here, if you attempted to beat up your friend, you knew you'd be in trouble because the people here cared!

"The villagers also soon began to say that we were just at 'school' to sing and do no real learning because they would hear us sing and drum very loudly. Well, we were very happy because it was time to express what God had done for us! We had never experienced any thing like this before! It was so good! So I decided to close my ears to what the villagers were saying."

---

During the early days, there was never any certainty that comes from past successes or experiences. This was completely uncharted territory, and the staff was forced to rely utterly and completely on the Lord.

"I thank God for how He'd made me prayerful even about relationship issues that were there," said Auntie Sarah. "When I prayed I saw a difference. In mid-1989, when Uncle Jay came back from his six-month furlough in the U.S. and Canada, he also came back with a real vision of prayer. He would come early in the morning and wake up the staff so that we could pray together. We would take the blueprints of the plans for the children's center and would pray over them. We would pray and pray and pray – for the children, for the land, and for God's will to be done! And soon we began to see very many breakthroughs and the Lord working on our behalf."

Though we would suffer from the effects of rumors and mistrust for years to come, the Lord continued to show us His favor despite what others had to say about us.

---

"It was a sunny day," Auntie Sarah began. "The older boys were out working in the gardens. I had given the middle class some work to do on their own, and I was teaching my little class. Uncle Emmanuel and Uncle Peter had gone into Kampala, and I was the only staff member there."

Auntie Sarah was all alone with over forty children. Though this was far from an ideal situation, she had everything under control.

"Thankfully, Kimera had already emerged as a leader among his fellow students," Auntie Sarah recalled. "I couldn't be everywhere at once, so I instructed Kimera to keep an eye on the children while I went to check on the porridge they were to have at break time."

And then they came. A vehicle filled with the head teachers of other schools throughout the area and the district school inspector. Could the timing have been worse? Not a single teacher was in sight, the children were all alone, and some were working in the gardens and not even on their lessons!

"For a long time," Auntie Sarah explained, "the other schools around had been speaking negative things about us to the District School Inspector. 'They don't really study; they just work in the gardens, read the Bible and sing. Sir, you must close down this school!' they would say."

Their arrival on a day like this seemed to guarantee that the rumors might be taken seriously and that our fledgling school could be closed. But God had other plans!

"Thankfully the inspector found that work had been left on the black board for all the kids," Auntie Sarah smiled remembering the relief she had felt. "The middle class was working quietly, and the little kids were kneeling on the ground using their benches as desks and copying things off of the board into their notebooks."

Up the hill, where the porridge was being cooked and oblivious to all that was going on back at school, Auntie Sarah looked up to see Kimera leading several straight lines of children along the path toward the outdoor kitchen. Behind him walked a smartly dressed stranger followed by several head teachers she recognized from the surrounding villages. Realizing who it was and that most likely the reason he had come was to see if all the rumors about our school were true, Auntie Sarah's heart beat faster. Expecting him to be very upset that the students were alone and that there was only one teacher with so many students, she was instead surprised when he greeted her pleasantly.

"I was standing near a very nice garden the children had planted with Uncle Jonnes," she continued. "It was filled with beautiful carrots and tomatoes. He looked around, saw the garden and the children, still with no adult supervision, now praying together before they began eating their porridge, and said, 'So, what do you teach?' I told him English, social studies, science, math, and agriculture. 'Where are the other teachers?' I explained that they were away for the day but would be returning that evening."

"May I sign the visitor's book?" the inspector asked. As he signed it, Auntie Sarah picked some carrots for him to take with him.

"He was so impressed with the orderliness of everything," Auntie Sarah laughed as she remembered the situation that could have been so detrimental to Kasana.

As he drove off with all the other teachers, Auntie Sarah thanked the Lord for his positive response. She later found out that the purpose of his trip was to drive from school to school picking up the head teachers and taking them to a mandatory meeting where he was going to rebuke them for the poor jobs they had been doing at the schools they each oversaw.

As soon as the vehicle disappeared into the elephant grass, Auntie Sarah opened the book to see what he had written. "This is good! Keep it up!" was all it said. As He would continue to do time after time in the future, the Lord gave us favor in the sight of government officials, and we were free to continue what the Lord had called us to do!

Bukenya, a former child soldier and member of the Kasana family.

Kasana kids.

Kasana kids sing!

# Chapter 10
## *Kabubbu Days*

### 1988–1989

It was March 1988, and Josiah and I were perched comfortably on the gate of the open bed pickup that nearly overflowed with boxes, chairs, mattresses, and our other earthly belongings. Abby, our faithful black Labrador dog, was tied carefully to one of the pieces of furniture and lay quietly on the floor of the truck bed, her head barely visible among all the boxes. The day could not have been more exciting for my brother and me. We were leaving the city and moving to our favorite place, the village. And oh, the plans we had! With plenty of land around us, village children everywhere to play with and no fence to hold us in as we rode our bicycles, we dreamed of soccer games, gardens, chicken houses, forts, visiting the Kasana kids, Uncle Peter, and Uncle Jonnes at their homes whenever we pleased, and more. There would be no more gunfire at night, no more lonely nights with Dad gone to work in the village, no more smelly and crowded city. The Clarkes would live just upstairs. Our heroes, Paul and Jodene Kessel, would live with us, and life was going to be good!

We drove along bumpy roads, and the wind couldn't drown out our voices as Josiah and I sang at the top of our lungs and waved and shouted to everyone we passed. We made faces so Jamie would laugh as she looked longingly at us through the window from inside the cab. Oh, the unashamed joy of a nine- and seven-year-old!

I'll never forget our first night in the house the Kessels and others had remodeled for us in the village of Kabbubu, just a mile from our land at Kasana. It was the big two-story house that formerly had been the beautiful

*111*

home of the Mukubira family. The house had been gutted and destroyed during the war, and my dad had offered to restore the "kalina"[38] if we and the Clarkes and many other Ugandan and foreign missionaries could live in it for two years. Because we had a home in Kampala to live in, priority had been given to repairing the upstairs for the Clarkes who had just arrived from Northern Ireland. Finally, after what seemed like years, the downstairs was relatively complete, and we were able to move in.

As the sun dipped down below the tall elephant grass and banana trees, we children became aware of noises to which we had not been accustomed. The drone of crickets, croaking of frogs, and the scream of the cicada bugs seemed to close in on us, getting louder every moment. We had learned to sleep through the sounds of "lorries"[39] rumbling along the bumpy roads, people shouting, discos on nights when there was electricity in the city, and gunfire in the distance. But these natural noises certainly would take some getting used to!

Life in Kabbubu proved to be one adventure after another, and we children loved it. After our school work and chores each day, we spent hours doing what we had so hoped to do – planting peanuts and beans in a plot of land Jajja Nalongo had allowed us to use, creating a clubhouse with the Clarke kids out of an old goat shed, riding our bikes into the village, carrying water from the "bore hole," and building a lean-to fort with Sennyonjo and Paul, two of our new village friends.

Abby, sometimes bringing grief to us all, also had the time of her life. There were chickens and goats to chase, monkeys and wildcats to hunt, and drunk men passing by on their bicycles to pursue. Unfortunately, due to their drunken state, these men (often regulars) failed to realize the danger of swerving along on their bicycles ringing their bells and shouting nonsense as they passed our house. Our dog had no tolerance for such foolishness. I can't count the times we would hear a bicycle bell in the distance and frantically run out to *attempt* to coax Abby back into the house. At times, we were

---

[38]The Luganda nickname for a two-story house.
[39]The British term for large trucks.

successful. Other times, the poor man was terrified out of his intoxication. One time, my parents had to promise a furious and embarrassed drunk a new pair of trousers as Abby proudly marched away with several square inches of material in her teeth.

In an attempt to maintain peaceable relations with our neighbors who all owned livestock, my father would frequently take Abby outside to the chicken houses behind our home, hold her by the collar and say repeatedly, "Abby, NO CHICKENS!" Then, he would march her to where the goats were tied: "Abby, NO GOATS!" She was a fast learner, and, except for a few times when her "doggish" ways got the best of her, she did amazingly well.

Abby also loved to run alongside us children as we rode to and from Kasana. When we passed one house in particular (a home with three hunting dogs), we would shout, "Abby, NO!" Her hair would bristle and her eyes would turn toward the pitiful looking dogs in the compound. We realized how we had affected the children of the community when we rode past the house one day without Abby. Thinking our regular reprimands to Abby were English greetings, the little children of the home came running out excitedly, smiling and waving and shouting "Abby, NO! ABBY, NO!"

Wildlife, both inside our house and outside, was another interesting aspect of life in Kabubbu. Monkeys in the trees behind the kalina, snakes, and wildcats were not uncommon. My sister Jamie, who was five at the time, always seemed to be the target of the animals around. I'll never forget how one of the missionary's pet monkeys seemed to wait for Jamie and pounce on her when she would walk by. We later found out that the monkey had been abused by the little kids in the community and Jamie's size made her an easy target for the monkey's vengeance. Poor Jamie was also chased and butted in the stomach by the goats behind the house.

Then there was always the usual household wildlife – lizards, mice, rats, swallows seeking their former homes, and a myriad of insects. Once Jodene heard a scratching noise in the bathroom. After searching for a while she finally found the source of the noise – a rat had fallen into the toilet bowl and was doing its best to climb up the slippery, wet walls to escape. Any time a mouse or rat was found there was a loud shout, and all the men and boys on both floors would come running. Late one evening, those of us on the ground floor heard bangs and crashes upstairs in the Clarke's house. Not long after, the Clarke's youngest son Michael came running down stairs yelling that they had found a nest of shrews, and baby shrews were running all over the house. Up Paul, Josiah, and Dad ran, armed with sticks and whatever else they could find, to take part in the hunt!

I'll never forget the time we thought Abby had lost control of her senses. She was frantically digging through an open drawer of clothes and grasped one of Joyanne's small dolls in her mouth. The more we tried to rescue the doll from her grip, the more she would growl and back slowly away from anyone who came near her. Finally, Abby dropped her hostage onto the ground, but kept her nose close to it, and continued to growl. Peeping out from the doll's flannel night gown alongside the doll's blonde head was a pointed brown head with glistening and terrified eyes. Down near the doll's two white feet, a long grayish brown tail protruded from under the innocent doll's dress. Unfortunately for the rat, its seemingly brilliant hiding place was not quite sufficient for deterring our rodent-hunting black Labrador!

The story of the early days in Kabubbu would not be complete without the perspective of Paul and Jodene Kessel, who lived there for several months before we arrived. Natives of North Dakota, Paul and Jodene had joined us in the early and precarious stages of the ministry. Their enthusiasm, dedication, and perseverance did much to keep our hopes alive that the children's center would one day amount to something.

"I remember with great fondness the evenings once it got dark," Paul began. "We ate quite late, sometimes with the Mukubira family and sometimes just those of us who lived there at the time – Jodene and I, Daniel

Hulls, and Len Wright, two volunteers from Salt and Light churches in England. The house had a big flat roof, and I remember going up there many times in the evening and just sitting and visiting with a lot of the Ugandans or just Daniel and me. I have very good memories of that."

But while the evenings were quiet and usually undisturbed during the early months, the days were always full. There was building to be done – renovations on the kalina and the new children's house up the road in Kasana – villagers to assist with medical care, teams to organize, and the first ten children to care for.

"Transportation in those days was so different from now as well," Paul continued. "There were no boda-bodas[40] or taxis. I remember making many trips to Kasana from Kabbubu (a round-trip of two miles) with wheel barrows or bikes with as much cement and tools as we could carry. Everything was so difficult at that time. When supplies ran low, or we couldn't purchase the materials we needed for construction, we had to be creative. I remember a time we needed rebar, so we rummaged through the scraps left from the prewar years to find what we could. Years later, Daniel and I were working out in the bush behind the first children's house and found one of the pit latrine slabs we'd crafted. We laughed as we broke it apart and inside found old car parts and 'what not' that had served as rebar!

"I would leave out a very important part of my memory if I didn't say I remembered with very great joy when the Clarkes and the Dangers came out to live at Kabbubu with us. It was a very fulfilling time, and it became a lot of fun as we watched the two families setting up their homes. Jodene and I had a bedroom on the main floor next to the Dangers' two rooms, and the Clarkes were upstairs."

In addition to our two families and the Kessels, we had other staff living in the kalina. The two Johans (from Holland) had a makeshift room under the stairwell. The tiny room off the front porch was occupied by Benoni, a Ugandan staff member, then later Elizabeth, an American nurse.

---

[40] Bicycle "taxis" that years later were upgraded to "piki-pikis" moped "taxis"

"From the start I remember watching Dr. Clarke racing around getting things done," Paul continued. "It was unbelievable. I wondered if something might be wrong with me. I had lived there quite contented in our little room and really hadn't made very many provisions for our living conditions. I guess I didn't have the insight to see needs very well for my wife. Dr. Clarke, on the other hand, in a matter of hours had lights being strung, a generator set up, and shelves being assembled. I stood and watched in amazement!

"I remember also being very fond of the little boys," Paul smiled, "Josiah and Michael and Sean. Josiah and Michael especially were very eager little beavers that always had swords crafted out of something! I fit right into that!"

From the beginning of our time in Kabubbu, visitors – both expected and unexpected – were an ever-present aspect of life. While many of the visitors stayed in our homes, others, like the YWAM teams, stayed in tents and cooked for themselves over open fires. We soon realized a need to have a guesthouse somewhere nearby to host teams. An abandoned church, the roof of which had been stolen and whose walls were riddled with bullet holes, was soon remodeled to house teams and short-term missionaries. While the builders began to clear away the rubble and erect papyrus mat walls for the inside of the guesthouse, my mom began to train Mama Daisy, a local villager who spoke English, how to cook American food. Soon we were fully equipped to house the many visitors the Lord began to bring along.

Our first official team was from Westmont College in California. Ten guys who had recently graduated and had come out to serve for ten weeks became the recipients of Mama Daisy's experimental cooking. Now known for her excellent cooking abilities, Mama Daisy's beginnings were often cause for much laughter!

There was one time when a recipe called for vanilla and Mama Daisy used vinegar instead. The result need not be explained! There were also frequent times when zucchini and cucumbers switched roles and the zucchini was served raw while the cucumbers were cooked. One day, in an attempt to bless the Westmont guys, Mama Daisy asked them what food they missed the most from home. The next morning, the guys woke up to the sound of popcorn popping in the kitchen – for breakfast! Well, popcorn had been their reply to her innocent question!

Mama Daisy's small mistakes did make us all laugh, and she loved to laugh along with us! Her cheerful disposition, quick wit, and growing cooking skills made her a favorite among the teams, and she served faithfully as our guesthouse cook for many years.

Life in Kabbubu was not all fun and games. There was also schoolwork to be done! Each morning we children would wake up, have breakfast and devotions together as a family, do our chores, and head to the living room for school with Mom. Later, Josiah and I "graduated" to taking several classes with Auntie Gertrude, who lived a mile away in Kasana. However, this trip to school was not a mere hop on the bus with one's backpack. Our "bus" *was* yellow, but it had only two wheels, a banana seat, and U-shaped handlebars! Each morning, I would climb onto my bicycle with my backpack on my back, hook a large thermos of drinking water onto one of the handlebars and a 2' by 2½' chalk board on the other. Balancing as best I could, I would then pull up to the front porch and Josiah would climb onto the handlebars carrying his own backpack, our lunches, and another small chalk board! We would then ride the one mile of bumpy dirt roads to Auntie Gertrude's house in Kasana.

While I peddled hard downhill to gain enough momentum to climb the long hill at the end of the ride, it was Josiah's job to make sure everything stayed on the bicycle and to keep an eye out for the occasional lorry that would come barreling down the road. Once we had reached the Bakimi's home we would spend several hours studying science, English, and social studies using a combination of Ugandan and American textbooks. However, our lessons were often interrupted by workers asking for water, villagers coming to visit, or torrential downpours that would cause us to pack up our books and dodge the water streaming through the holes in the roof as best we could.

Our favorite distraction was the Bakimi's new little baby, Joshua, who sat on a mat next to us as we studied. He was far more interesting than anything we were working on at the time. After our morning lessons, we would head home the way we had come and return the chalk boards to our mom and grandma, who would then use them for Jamie's lessons and our math and history lessons.

When we first moved to Kabubbu two years after the end of Uganda's civil war, many of the vivid scenes of war were still obvious. It was common to see a small pile of human bones here or there throughout the bush. Kiwoko town, three miles from Kabubbu and today a bustling trading center, was the site of several bombed-out buildings, a few dilapidated shacks, and several large collections of skulls and other bones. In an effort to create an ever-present reminder of what had taken place so that it might never happen again, the villagers had collected bones strewn throughout the countryside and stacked them on makeshift shelves along the side of the road both in Kabubbu and Kiwoko. Most of these bones remained a grim reminder of the war's atrocities until 1990, when they were removed and buried in a mass grave.

Our land and the surrounding villages had been the center of fierce fighting, raiding, and killing of thousands of innocent people – indeed, the center of Museveni's bush war. The large abandoned army tank on the side of the road leaving Kampala served as yet another constant reminder of how recently this quiet area had echoed with the sounds of war. Even several years after we moved to Kabubbu, we would hear occasional explosions somewhere in the distance – land mines left from the battles. Fortunately, most of these mines were found and disposed of properly before injuring an unsuspecting passerby. Others, however, left war's gruesome fingerprints on innocent children who happened to step in the wrong place at the wrong time. Some of these children survived; others did not.

Uncle Jonnes recalled a time when the Lord spared his life from war's aftermath. The plan had been for him to use the tractor to plow a piece of our land that had lain fallow throughout the war. But for some reason he still does not know, he chose to first burn the weeds and bush on it before he began to plow. Suddenly, it was as if he had stepped into a war zone! As the fire began to spread across the land there were explosions everywhere, as if a machine gun was being fired! The land he was burning had been scattered with land mines and live grenades just waiting to be set off. Had he chosen to plow first, it would have been him on the tractor, instead of the fire's flames, to set off the deadly weapons.

Even before Dr. Ian Clarke arrived in Kabubbu the word had gone out into the village that a doctor was going to be moving into the Mukubira's kalina. Needless to say, in an impoverished and destitute postwar community such news spread like wildfire, and the front porch of our home became Dr. Ian's new hospital. Malaria and other such diseases were treated, wounds cleaned and often stitched closed, and immunization clinics held.

I'll never forget opening my curtain one morning only to shut it again as quickly as I could. The night before, in a drunken brawl, a man's head had been cracked open with a panga.[41] Members of the community found him unconscious on the road and brought him to Dr. Ian. I happened to open my curtains and look out just as the poor man's head was being sewn back together just outside my bedroom window.

My parents did their best to hide their struggles from us children during this time and to allow us to enjoy our new home. However, there were some things we did experience – exposure to sickness and pain with the clinic on our porch; the days when Dad had to return to Kampala to sit and wait for a phone call from our organization, only to return discouraged saying he

---

[41]A large, machete-like knife used for cutting wood.

must go again the next day... and the next; seeing the bones piled high and hearing the occasional land mine explode in the distance. There was also the news that one of our favorite staff members, Henry, was actually not a good man and had stolen from and lied to our parents and many other people we knew.

Dad and Uncle Jonnes were sometimes threatened, and rumors circulated about their *real* motive for being there (to exploit children, use them to make money, and then either eat them or sell them as slaves in America). There were also "prophecies" from a local, self-proclaimed prophetess who said both my dad and Uncle Jonnes would run mad within a very short amount of time after our arrival and *then* the truth about them would be seen. Needless to say, these situations and the stories we heard brought confusion and fear into our hearts. Our parents faithfully talked to us about each one as we brought our concerns to them and prayed that the Lord would take away our fear.

All in all, though, our time in Kabubbu was one we children will always look back at with fondness. However, we had no idea the depth of the struggles and pain my parents and the other staff members were really going through. For my parents, our two years there were perhaps the most stretching, painful, and faith-testing of our years in Uganda. Day after day, month after month, my parents, Uncle Jonnes, and the other staff members would wonder if this fledgling organization would survive. Daily there was the temptation to give up and leave, but the Lord's grace remained and carried them through.

Mom and the "Kalina."

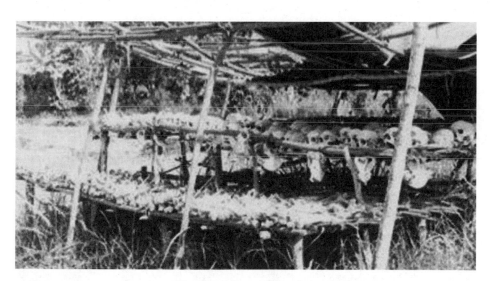

Skull racks in Kiwoko.

Skulls found on our land.

Josiah, Dad, Jamie, Jennie, Mom, and Joyanne
outside the guesthouse, 1989.

# Chapter 11
## Giving Up Is Not of the Father!

❧

### 1988–1989

*"These were refining processes that God had to take us through. They are not things I like to look back to and say 'I wish they could come again.' But I feel like they are really situations that God used to keep us humble. Because if things kept sailing through with no trials, we would not have had to rely on the Lord as we did..."*

*– Uncle Jonnes*

❧

"How much do you trust Henry?" Tom Rodgers asked one day.

"To be honest, I don't," was Uncle Jonnes' reply.

For months a growing uneasiness had been spreading in the hearts and minds of the rest of the team members. Where *was* all the money going? Would we ever get the land signed over to WorldCare, or was it possible that such a presumption was too good to be true? But Henry's answers were always so calm and assuring.

Problems had also continued with our organization back at home. The troubles in our church at home mushroomed, and eventually our pastor resigned. However, we were hearing nothing from the church leaders or even many of our friends, and my parents felt alone and disconnected. When we finally returned for a furlough, we found out the new pastor thought we had left the church with nearly half of the congregation and hadn't even realized we were still missionaries sent primarily from his church!

Relational problems had developed between us and another organization with which we had partnered, and many of the local people and our staff were caught in the middle of several misunderstandings. Rumors were flying throughout the village about our motives and character, and though there was nothing upon which the allegations could be based, the effects of the rumors were draining, confusing, and destructive.

Struggles continued with the people we hired to build and to cultivate the land. The land was never plowed or planted in time, and often the workers would just not show up. The roof of the home for the children took months longer than expected to build, causing us to have to continuously put off bringing in our first children. When it was finally completed, it leaked like a sieve.

Once the first ten children were brought into the home, there was also the realization that now we were responsible for their lives, and bailing out now was even less of an option than before.

Then, after four months of the grueling process of registering WorldCare as the non-government organization we were under, we found out that the new government's laws had changed and every organization was required to re-register. Beginning the whole process again, it took us a year to secure our registration. Not long after we had rejoiced with this success, we were dropped by WorldCare and were forced to first create a new organization, New Hope Uganda, and begin the registration process a third time.

In addition to these and other struggles was the ever-present realization that the team the Lord had gathered really was not qualified in any human sense of the word to carry out the task laid before them. There was no past experience, no appropriate training. "We were declared unqualified," Uncle Jonnes reminisced, "and it was true!"

"I hadn't been at Kasana for very long when I quickly began to realize that Jay and Henry were thinking very differently than each other," Peter Kiyimba recalled. "It wasn't something you could pinpoint, but it was definitely there. Jay was there for care; Henry was there for business. I'll never forget walking through the office we shared in Kampala one day and hearing one of Henry's friends say to me, 'Muzungu mulye,' or 'eat the Muzungu.'[42] I began to wonder about people's motives and was concerned."

Henry was responsible for any of the business-type issues with the new project – exchanging money, purchasing equipment, and much more. Based on our confidence in Henry, other organizations and expatriates also began to use him as a contact for purchasing vehicles and channeling funds. On a fund-raising trip to Northern Ireland he told people, "All I need is small capital to get things started. My family has many square miles of land. We will not need to be continuously receiving funding; we just need help to get started." This type of talk certainly impressed people used to being asked for constant funding and help. His whole message seemed so honest and trustworthy!

"He was one of the most charming, likeable persons I've ever met," my Grandma Dorothy recalled. She worked daily with Henry for eight months. "His smile convinced anyone that he was a nice person. It said, 'I care about you, and I'm here to help you. Trust me.' He was such a smooth talker, so sincere and convincing, and always made us feel indebted to him for all he was doing for us. We just believed anything he said and felt so blessed to have someone like him looking out for us!"

And the more he spoke to people, the more money and supplies came in. But we began to realize that almost nothing seemed to go to the people for which it was intended.

"We were all just so blind to all that was going on!" Uncle Jonnes recalled. "Ah, but Henry had flowery language! He would offer you heaven, and people would believe he could keep his promise!"

"But the more I worked with him," Uncle Jonnes continued, "the more my concern grew. However, I still felt new enough in the organization that I didn't really have the right to question Henry. I didn't know how to explain

---

[42]A common Luganda phrase that basically means "milk the muzungu for what you can get."

what I was feeling to Jay because I didn't want there to be a competition for Jay's favor between Henry and me, for I came in when there was already an existing relationship. I also heard many of the foreigners say things like, 'He's a Ugandan and a person from this area; he *knows* what the people want.' No one wanted to question Henry, and he was trusted implicitly.

"But what scared me the most," Uncle Jonnes recalled, "was that we continued to build and cultivate the land but still we had no ownership of it."

Henry had assured us that his grandfather had promised us the ownership of the land and that he was working toward getting the paperwork completed to transfer ownership from the Chairman, as his grandfather was called, and WorldCare. It was in his hands; don't worry! But the more my dad and grandmother pressed Henry for the paperwork, the more the excuses came.

"Every week or so I would say, 'So how does it stand?'" my dad recalled. "And he would say something like, 'I went to my grandfather, but he was very tired, or sick. I'll try again next week.'"

"You man, what is wrong with your head?" Henry scowled at Uncle Jonnes. "Do you have no brains to understand that I'm the one who brought WorldCare here, and it is me who can stop it or continue it? You must have that understanding!"

"Yes sir," Uncle Jonnes had responded, but in his heart he replied, "But you didn't bring me into WorldCare. God brought me here." Yet something inside him would not let him respond any more to Henry's threats.

In addition to Henry's dislike for Uncle Jonnes, many people in the community took little time in rejecting him as well. Now living among a culture where "saving face" was the most important thing in relationships, Uncle Jonnes' Mukiga-style openness, bluntness, and refusal to cover up sin did not go over well.

"People would say about me, 'This man has come to stop us from getting our "food."' We are interested in the muzungu's pocket, and this is the man stopping us."[43] This was not familiar ground to me," Uncle Jonnes recalled, "I was feeling hostility at all levels, and I did not know what I should do."

In addition to struggles within the camp, relationships were strained with an organization we had partnered with. One day Jodene Kessel, who worked for both organizations, came to Uncle Jonnes distraught. "I dread going to work because all I hear is how bad Jay is. I'm so torn between both sides!"

On top of relational troubles and rumors flying, there was a realization that the new project was very understaffed. "I had been praying that year that God would send more people," said Uncle Jonnes. "We desperately needed more people, and I began complaining and saying, 'It seems God is no longer calling people into such work.' But at the end of 1987 I felt the Lord say to me, 'At the right time, in the right time.' I knew then that He would bring them."

While there was that assurance, many outside voices began to question whether or not Uncle Jonnes and my dad were the ones to lead such a project.

"This type of ministry needs a businessman as the main leader," they would say. "Jay even admits he's not a businessman. He is a pioneer. He got this started; now it's time for him to go start something new and leave this to a manager. And then there's Jonnes. His gifting is in evangelism, not discipleship. He should return to Kampala."

My dad recalled, "I was also so unsure of myself during those days, that I felt I was not in a position to argue with any of these suggestions. In fact, I agreed with them! I knew how unqualified I was, and I was more than willing for someone who really knew what he was doing to take over. For several years I tried many times to hand the project over to more qualified people, but each time the board or our pastors would insist that I continue in my position."

As was mentioned before, in addition to all the other struggles, the early years in Kabubbu and Lungujja were times of real spiritual warfare. We were

---

[43] Had they realized how little was actually in those pockets, they may not have hated Uncle Jonnes so much!

battling "not against flesh and blood, but against the rulers, against the authorities, against the powers of this dark world and against the spiritual forces of evil in the heavenly realms."[44] Reclaiming enemy territory is never easy, and there were many spiritual attacks on the children, health problems, and a constant feeling of spiritual heaviness and darkness that did not begin to subside for a couple of years.

# JULY 1988

"Jonnes," my dad's face was strained and confused, "*what* is happening? I have no way of finding out what is going on!"

Uncle Jonnes and my dad had already made the six-hour round trip to Kampala several times over the previous two weeks to try to receive a phone call from Bill, the WorldCare director. But each day they returned saying they had heard nothing. The time for our scheduled furlough was drawing near, but still we heard nothing from Bill letting us know if he was taking care of our tickets or if we were to work on things from our end (a near impossibility). The ministry was also virtually out of money, and we needed to know if there was any news on the financial end.

For months we had been receiving promises such as, "I am working on such and such a business deal, and as soon as it comes through, there should be at least a million dollars that can go toward the project." But there still was nothing. Well, nothing *financial*. Bill had been able to send us three containers, but they ended up only adding to our problems. One was a twenty-foot container filled with seeds. By the time they arrived nearly all of them were expired, and many were not designed for tropical climates. Few ever germinated. For years, we had seeds "coming out of our ears" and just had to find ways of disposing of them – often giving away boxes of them to anyone willing to take the gamble of planting them to see if anything would grow.

---

[44]Ephesians 6:12

Later, we received a forty-foot container of used clothing from World-Care, much of which was clothing that was not appropriate for the culture in which we lived or were things like winter coats and gloves! And then there was the question again of storage. Where on earth could we safely store everything? While it sat in the container waiting for us to figure out what to do with it, much of it seemed to "walk away." Our final shipment came – a twenty-foot container filled to the brim with American public school textbooks. Needless to say, textbooks on "Pop Stars of the 80s" and "California Drivers' Ed" were useless in the middle of Africa, and once again just provided our staff with one more thing to figure out how to dispose of. (They served as kindling in the wood stoves and other such things for several years!)

"Ah! 1987 and 1988 were difficult times!" Uncle Jonnes recalled years later. "That day when Jay expressed his confusion to me, I remember thinking, *What's wrong? Are we going to pack up and leave? I can always walk back to Kabaale, but what is this muzungu and his family going to do? He can't walk back to America!* But one thing that I will always remember was how Jay never let himself stop even when things were looking hopeless. Up to that point, I don't think I'd ever heard him sound discouraged when he talked to me."

The biggest trouble with communication was in trying to contact Bill. "I would send him a telex saying, 'I need to talk to you on such and such a date, and I'll drive in from Kasana and wait for you to call,'" my dad recalled. Week after week, my dad would drive in to Kampala to wait for Bill to call. In those days, it was extremely expensive to call the U.S. from Uganda, and when one did make the attempt, the chances of getting through were slim to none.

"I would drive in to Kampala every three or four days, to where there was a phone. I'd always first pick up the phone to make sure it was working that day," Dad laughed as he recalled the reality of communication difficulties of those days, "then I would sit down to wait for him to call." I would wait for a couple of hours and then give up and send Bill a telex saying, 'I missed your call; I'll be back in town on such and such a date at such and such a time. Please call me then, or telex me and let me know if there is a better day for you.' I did that for several weeks and never did get a call."

Finally, the silence was deafening, and my dad sat down to write a letter to Bill explaining the situation and how he was struggling. He would go into town and try to call Bill. If he could not get through, he would mail the letter and wait. (And remember, during those days, mailing a letter meant waiting at least a month for it to arrive at its destination!) To his amazement, his phone call finally went through!

"When I did finally get a hold of him, I was so surprised!" my dad recalled. "I'd been trying for so long, I think I just assumed I'd never get through!" So, instead of mailing the letter, Dad began to read it to him on the phone. "The letter stated that I was really frustrated because he could have at least sent me a telex saying he couldn't call, and I would have gladly tried to call him at a different time," my dad explained.

He was part way through reading his letter when Bill interrupted him. "Jay, your problems are all your own fault," he said. "I've been getting bad reports about you and about things you're doing, and it's over. You are on your own. And if you're not careful, I will inform the Ugandan government that you are no longer under WorldCare and are therefore in their country illegally."

My father was stunned. For months, we had heard nothing but silence. We had heard nothing of bad reports or Bill's displeasure with us. This threat and rejection came, at least in our minds, out of nowhere. Just that year, we had had friends deported from Uganda because their organization had turned on them and declared them there "illegally," and my dad knew that his next decisions would be crucial in determining what our family's future would be in this country.

"Thankfully, though, I was the one who had registered the organization," my dad shared, "and the Ugandan government knew me and not him. While we tried to pick up the pieces and decide what our next steps should be, I figured that if I kept my head down and didn't rock the boat, nothing major would happen."

After promises of millions of dollars from Bill to support the work, when we were finally abandoned by WorldCare, other than the three containers and two portable sawmills, our family and the project had yet to receive a single coin from them beyond the original $8,500 that brought our family to Uganda and paid for our 1971 Suzuki jeep, trailer, and brick machine. To this day, we still do not know who was feeding bad reports to Bill about my dad, nor do we know what any of those bad reports were! In fact, when we finally did return to the U.S. for our furlough, Bill invited us to his home and welcomed us warmly as if nothing had ever happened. He mentioned nothing of the phone call or of any of Dad's failures or the allegations against him!

————————————————— ❧⋆❧ —————————————————

# JULY 1988

*Before WorldCare pulled out on us, "Jay had been assured of money coming, and there just was none. Bill turned out to not be living up to his promises. I have heavy memories concerning that time. The WorldCare meetings were difficult, and everyone wondered if this work was to go on. I even remember one member sharing the Scripture that states, 'Who can make straight what God has made crooked,' and suggesting that maybe we shouldn't be going ahead and forcing something to work that God had said would never succeed. Along with the organizational, financial, and relational difficulties, there was the difficulty of being in a postwar country. In retrospect, it is unbelievable how God worked in those days. I would venture to say that corporately we were within a hair's width of packing up and leaving. I guess God gave us what we needed to continue trickle by trickle."*

*– Paul Kessel*

He was sitting under the big tree outside our house in Kabubbu with his guitar. It was a common sight. Uncle Jonnes and his guitar. Often he would make up songs as he went; other times he would belt out his favorite tunes from the Deliverance Church days. But today there was a seriousness about him that was unusual. The strains of the past few months were beginning to take their toll, and there was heaviness in the air. As he began strumming, he started singing. It was a new song; a desperately needed song.

Its words were simple:

There are times when darkness seems all around you
There are times when there seems no future for you
Remember the words of Jesus, He says to you,
"I will never leave you nor forsake you."
*"Giving up is not of the Father;*
*Giving up is of the devil,*
*So keep on looking unto Jesus,*
*The Author and Finisher of our faith."*
Our Father is a faithful God I know
Our Father is so loving a God to me
Our failures He will turn to victory
For the honor and glory of His name!
*"Giving up is not of the Father;*
*Giving up is of the devil,*
*So keep on looking unto Jesus,*
*The Author and Finisher of our faith."*

My dad walked over to Uncle Jonnes and said, "Sing it again, Jonnes." Others nearby came to hear the new song and quickly picked up on the tune. "Sing it again," Dad said with a smile this time, "and keep singing it!"

"It was like God came and gripped us as we sang," Uncle Jonnes remembered with a smile. "We sang it over and over! It was as if everyone already knew the song and had been trained to sing it. We've never sung it again like we did that day. Its message pierced our hearts."

At a time when everyone was ready to pack up and leave, at a time when things seemed like they couldn't get worse, the Lord's message came loud and clear. He said "No! Don't give up! For giving up is not of your Father!"

⟡

# SEPTEMBER 1988–APRIL 1989

Near the end of 1988 we were finally able to secure tickets to fly home for a six-month furlough. My dad had left Tom Rogers, a friend from Southern California who had come on a short-term team, in charge of things for the first half of our time away. Another couple would take over for the second half. My parents were tired and ready for a change of pace. It was during this time away that we had our "courtship period" with the Salt and Light Churches to see if we wanted to come under the umbrella of their ministry. The three months we spent in Winnipeg, Manitoba, Canada with Gateway Christian Community, the Salt and Light Church there, remains one of our family's happiest memories.

Coming from a time of struggle, doubts, and fears, my parents were immersed in care, input, and prayer. While our church in California had not even known we still considered ourselves part of their congregation and had given us a half-hearted and confused welcome, the entire congregation in Winnipeg, complete strangers to my family, reached out to us with arms open wide. It was here that my dad received the pastoral input and accountability he had been craving for years.

"We were encouraged, rebuked, corrected, prayed for, and blessed," my dad recalled. "The Lord also began to deal with my self-doubt and how I'd despised who He had made me." Men such as Pastor Ron MacLean and Harold Sawatzky spent hours with my dad, encouraging him in the truth of the Word of God. "I finally realized that if God had called me to this work, He would give me all I needed to carry it out. I didn't need to doubt His plan or look at my own inability, but to trust in His grace."

"We left Winnipeg feeling revived and refreshed," my mom reminisced. "We were excited to return to what God had for us, but at the same time were torn leaving people who'd become so special to us in such a short time."

⧂⧃

# MAY 1989

"You know what, Jay? I think Henry is the problem, not his grandfather." Despite months of promises to get the land title signed by his grandfather, Henry had still failed to produce it. "Why don't we go directly to the Chairman and see what happens?" Uncle Jonnes suggested.

Without Henry's knowledge, my dad and Uncle Jonnes procured a new set of ownership papers from the land title office, went to the Chairman's home, presented the paperwork to him, and asked for his signature. Within minutes they walked out with the document Henry had failed for months to have signed.

Concerned that Henry might discover what they had done, they rushed back to the Bukalasa Land Title Office to begin the transfer of ownership. During a time when many government officials were hard to find (and if they *were* available they were not in a hurry to push papers through the necessary bureaucracy), the Lord miraculously placed a man from Deliverance Church in the office to which my dad and Uncle Jonnes went. The man was there when they needed him and was very willing to help in any way he could. Rejoicing in the favor the Lord had shown them, my dad and Uncle Jonnes presented the signed document to the man. Already, this signature was basically all that was needed to secure the land, but they wanted to get the paperwork through as quickly as they could before Henry could find out and possibly try to undo what they had done. When the problem arose that our school was still not registered, and there was no ownership of it yet by a Ugandan board, they knew that any other person would have seen this as a roadblock requiring a bribe to cross over. But the man's answer was quite different.

"Don't worry," he told them. "I'll just write this out to 'the proprietors of Essuubi Eppya Vocational Primary School.'" When my dad and Uncle Jonnes walked out of the office with the registration process well underway and at a no-turning-back point, there was no doubt that the Lord had shown Himself strong on their behalf.

Just a couple of weeks later, when Henry found out that they had gone behind his back and obtained the land ownership, he was furious. Later, it was clear that his plan had been for us to build on and develop the land, then to convince his grandfather to put the land in his own name, not that of the ministry! Heading straight to the land title office, he begged the man who had helped us, "Please, sir," he pleaded. "There's been some sort of mistake. The land was supposed to be leased, not given."

Holding up the paper Mr. Mukubira had signed freely giving the land, he asked, "Sir, is this the owner's signature?" Henry could not argue. "Sir, the papers have been signed and everything is official," he continued. "There is nothing I can do."

It was during this time that Henry's true colors began to be seen more and more clearly each day. "Indeed it was terrifying," Uncle Jonnes said. "I felt like anything could happen. He could do anything. I also saw Jay very troubled those days, and I knew his relationships with people were being strained."

The many people to whom we had recommended Henry were also now realizing he was not all he had said he was. Now they came to us asking, "Where is he? Is he genuine? What is going on?"

A letter from my mom to my grandparents, who had returned to the States, gives a clear picture of what was going on:

> "You asked about Henry. The problems that had started
> to surface while you were here concerning his honesty
> have *mushroomed*. Some things happened even before you
> came, but many have happened since. He's told *countless*
> lies and misused thousands of dollars of people's money

with nothing to show for it. The project didn't lose near as much as individuals, including ourselves, and our friends the Clarkes, David and Sandra Kemp, Nick DeKoning, etc, etc... Reverend Livingstone from Kiwoko never received his motorcycle that was paid for in March or so. Henry also did *everything* he could to prevent us from getting title to the land, but by God's grace and with very timely and *wise* moves by Jonnes, we made it around Henry's road blocks. He is really a master-deceiver.... He sold our matatu while we were away and has never given us a dime of the $2,500 he owed us...."

"Tom Rogers was the one who finally squeezed him out of Kasana," Uncle Jonnes recalled, "because he had begun even pocketing the donations we were given by organizations such as EIL. Tom stood up to him and said, '$7,000 was given to you to build the barn, and I want every coin of it back.' Of course, we never saw one shilling, and I think Tom might have personally covered what was lost."

Once my dad and Uncle Jonnes had seen how upset Henry was that they had gone around him to get the land title, they decided there was no telling what his next step might be. He had already stolen pickups from Alan, an Irish man who had tried to help Henry go into business, and they feared he might try to do the same with the project's vehicles as well.

————————————————— ❧ —————————————————

It was August. They chose their timing carefully: Henry was away for the day, and his secretary had stepped out of the main office. Henry's office was locked tightly, but its walls did not go all the way to the ceiling.

"The coast is clear, Jay," Jonnes said after checking the front room.

As quickly as they could, he and my dad climbed up over the wall and jumped quietly into Henry's office.

"We searched through his desk and found the log books for the Suzuki, the Land Rover, the lorry, and Vicki's parents' van, and then quickly climbed back over the wall and walked out of the office as if nothing had happened," my dad smiled as he remembered the incident.

"Oh, we celebrated that miracle!" my mom recalls. Now there was no way Henry could sell the project's vehicles and the lorry that we shared jointly with the clinic at Kiwoko.

Each day it seemed that more and more of Henry's scandals were being uncovered. He also remained more and more elusive, and my parents and others who had been ripped off by him knew that something serious must be done immediately.

"Jay, Jonnes, and David Kemp went to meet with the Chairman and discuss Henry's crimes with him," my mom wrote to her parents. "They've put it in writing, and David Kemp has receipts to substantiate some of it. This has been a very difficult time, but we've seen God's salvation over and over again."

Still, Henry remained hard to find. When anyone asked to meet with him, he would either refuse to set up an appointment or miss the appointment they had set. So many people tried to pin him down, but no one succeeded.

"So, we decided the only way to find him was to get him out of bed on a Saturday morning!" my mom recalled. At about 7:00 in the morning, my parents, Ian and Roberta Clarke, and Sekatebe and Christopher,[45] members of the Mukubira family and friends of New Hope, drove up to Henry's home and quietly walked up to the house.

"When we knocked on the door, Henry answered it, still in his pajamas," my mom recalled. "He looked shocked, and for the first time he didn't know what to say." The small group invited themselves in and sat down. When he asked if he could be excused to change, their answer was no.

"We thought he might escape out the back door if we let him leave the room," my dad explained.

---

[45]Name changed for privacy.

And so they proceeded to present to him their concerns, asking where the money for Alan's pickups had gone, along with the money for the Dangers' matatu, David Kemp's two tile-making machines, Nick Dekoning's vehicle, and so on.

"I'm so sorry," he said. "I will pay you back. I will return the money."

To ensure this, "We got him to write and sign a statement saying he would pay back all that he owed," my dad recalled, "but we never saw any of it. We also took the things from his house that he'd borrowed and never returned from people: the Clarkes' deep-freeze, a TV someone had paid for but never received, and so on."

"It was so painful," my mom shared. "We all *loved* Henry and felt devastated with how things had turned out."

"Even when your dad told us that Henry was cheating him and us," my grandma told me years later, "we didn't believe it. We just thought he was slow in getting around to fulfilling his promises."

In hindsight, it is so clear how the Lord used this time in my parents' lives and the life of the fledgling ministry.

The Lord used a crook and a thief to bring us to Uganda – yet another sign of how He controls all things and how He even uses the wicked to bring about His plans. Uncle Jonnes and my parents learned many valuable lessons from their interactions with Henry that have given them wisdom in other relationships. God also used the connection with Henry to introduce us to his grandfather, Daudi Mukubira, who gave New Hope the first sixty-six acres for the children's center, served as an honorary member of the Board of Trustees of New Hope Uganda, and remained a friend of our family and the ministry until his death in 2003.

The Lord also prepared a ministry to bring us to Uganda and then allowed the circumstances with Bill to cause us to found a Ugandan NGO that would carry the work in the future. The benefits of having a Ugandan-run and owned organization have been tremendous, and we are so thankful that the Lord brought about the need for New Hope Uganda's creation.

While we were in Kampala the Lord had also been preparing the way for us in ways we had never expected. As soon as we were dropped by World-Care, we were able to gain covering and assistance from Deliverance Church and the Salt and Light Ministries with whom the Lord had already connected us in His sovereignty.

And always, through every difficulty, confusion, and time of seeming darkness, the Lord was at work. He had blessed us with wonderful staff at just the right time – the Kessels, YWAM teams, Peter Kiyimba, my grandparents, Sarah (Ndagire) Muwanguzi, Emmanuel Waiswa, Daniel Hulls, Len Wright, Tom Rodgers, and David and Sandra Kemp. He had kept us and preserved us, and we knew that the future was in His hands.

Indeed, the majority of relationships that were strained during those days have been restored, and we enjoy genuine friendship and fellowship with them. Our God is a God of restoration and redemption! He redeems hopeless situations and restores His children to Himself and each other. While we as yet have not been reconciled with Henry, nor have we even seen him since those early days or know where he is, we pray that the Lord will be at work in His life and, most importantly, bring Henry to Himself.

*"It all comes back to whether or not we focus on Him and on what He has called us to do and refuse to take our eyes off of that. While Jesus was on earth, He kept saying, 'I know My Dad, and I know what He's called Me to do.' No matter what temptations, discouragements, or distractions came, because His eyes were on His Father, He could just say, 'Behind Me, Satan!' and continue with His work! It is easy to kill what you have come to do by focusing on little things. And I think the devil wanted to kill our vision and commitment by bringing all these discouragements. But God used them as stepping stones to go further and to strengthen us, and to even give us a testimony."*

*– Uncle Jonnes, during an interview in 2002*

# Chapter 12
## A Friend Closer Than a Brother

*"I was very concerned and didn't know what to do. But God started doing things in His own way. I said, 'The last thing I want to do is leave Dangers here.' My vow to stay, I think, came as a result of our teaching in Deliverance Church about covenant. I said, 'This is not a relationship of just being together, it is suffering together to the end.' I resolved that come what may, I would stay. I said, 'If it winds up, we'll go together, but I won't run away.'"*

– Uncle Jonnes in an interview in 2002,
referring to the difficult times of 1988

It is 2005, and as I look out of my window, I see Uncle Jonnes pacing. He is talking, stopping to think and waving his hands with expression. Then he stops to lean against the chair my mom provided for him but he had forgotten was even there. A few minutes pass, and he stretches his legs and back, but he is still deep in some sort of conversation. The slow pacing begins again. From where I am sitting, I can't see who Uncle Jonnes is talking to. Standing up, though, I can see. It's Dad, and of course, he's weeding the grass. The conversation continues, and without comment they both simultaneously move several feet to the right. The first patch is weeded; time to move on.

Dad begins to talk now. He occasionally looks up to add to his point, but most of the time he remains squatted in the grass, ever busy. It's a typical, almost daily, sight, and has been for years. They're having a meeting – probably discussing a major policy change, a new children's center, or the design of the newest building on site. I love watching them. They know each other so well there is no pretense.

Uncle Jonnes' bad back makes sitting uncomfortable, plus chairs are inhibiting to expression, so he paces. Dad has no use for being idle or for unkempt compounds, so he's weeding. Some days they're wearing their African-style brightly colored shirts with slacks. Other days they are in shorts and New Hope t-shirts, Dad wearing his cowboy hat to keep off the sun, and Uncle Jonnes his old Wood-Mizer hat. They are grayer now than they used to be, a little rounder around the middle too, but not much more has changed over the years! Some days there's excitement on their faces; others there is a solemnity that speaks of deep concern and the realization that only the Lord can bring a remedy to this situation. Some times you can tell there is a sharp disagreement occurring; other times they are on the same track and moving fast!

Their personalities could not be more different. Dad is consistent and steady; Uncle Jonnes is a Mukiga.[46] Yet because of their oneness in purpose, conviction, and goals, combined with years of working closely together, they are nearly inseparable. In fact, these frequent times of discussion are so ingrained in our family's history that one of Joyanne's first sentence combinations was, "Where's daddy? Talk ta Jonnes?"

It is impossible to adequately describe Uncle Jonnes. His personality is exuberant, vivacious, genuine, hilarious, and random. Indeed, he is one of a kind. However, it is not only his personality that is difficult to give justice to. The impact he has had on New Hope Uganda and on the lives of hundreds of children and staff is impossible to measure. My family frequently wonders aloud, "Where would New Hope Uganda be without Uncle Jonnes?"

Not only is New Hope where it is today because of Uncle Jonnes, but my family is also indebted to this man. He is like a second father to my siblings

---

[46]Those who know the stereo types of Ugandan tribes can picture immediately what I mean. For those not so familiar with Ugandan tribal characteristics, a memeber of the Bakiga tribe, a Mukiga, is excitement personified.

and me. He has walked through every hard time my family or Kasana has had, and he has stuck with us, even when his own reputation or comfort was on the line. He is a man who understands and knows my father as few others know him. They share the same vision and convictions, encourage and correct each other, and have worked successfully together for nearly twenty years. Indeed, to my father and, consequently, to the rest of my family, he is "a friend who sticks closer than a brother."

What is it that has bound these men in such a depth of comradeship? Ultimately it is only the grace of God. Many have questioned their relationship. How can a white man so deeply trust an African? How dare an African man openly correct or rebuke a white man? Many who see them assume, "That African must be in it secretly for the money," or "Obviously that white man is naïve enough to entrust an African with such authority." But their relationship has stood, by the grace of God, as an example of true equality, true brotherhood, and of how two men with such different gifts, backgrounds, and personalities, yet united in the Lord, can work as such a dynamic team.

---

"At the end of 1986, I was ending my contract with the African Evangelical Enterprise," Jonnes recalled. "I had no specific goal, though, and I had prayed that God would lead me to where I should work, earn a living, and at the same time serve Him. I had a very good job offer with Pepsi Cola, an offer to continue working with African Evangelistic Enterprise, and at the same time, a desire to work with children. I really needed guidance."

As he eagerly sought the Lord for His will, Jonnes shared his dilemma at a church prayer meeting. The response he had received was, "It's OK to work professionally. There's nothing wrong with that." But his heart was not settled.

"I had been involved in school evangelism in the Greater Kampala Mission," Uncle Jonnes recalled, "and I loved it. Everyone else didn't want to be involved in that part of evangelism. I think they were afraid of the children.

But I loved them! I loved spending time with them and felt the Lord wanted me to continue working with children. But I didn't know where to start!"

At the time of Jonnes' seeking, my family had begun attending the Deliverance Church where Jonnes was a member. "I was looking for people to work with," my dad recalled. "I had no idea where to begin, so at church one day, I just went and introduced myself to Jonnes. I didn't know anything about him," my dad laughed. "I didn't even know his name. But he was very visible in church. We'd seen him in the choir, and we knew he was single. But other than that, we knew nothing about him."

"What do you do for a living?" my dad had asked.

"Well, I was trained as an industrial chemist," Uncle Jonnes began. Already Dad knew this wasn't who he was looking for. We certainly weren't in need of an industrial chemist! But Jonnes' next sentence drew my dad's thoughts back to the purpose of the conversation.

"But I really feel called to work with children." Now *there* was potential!

Their conversation quickly turned to the work Dad was beginning, and Dad asked for Jonnes to pray about working with him.

"As I began to pray about it, I began to rationalize the situation," Jonnes recalled. "This was not nearly the career change I had anticipated. First of all, this man who was asking me to work for him – I didn't even know him. I knew nothing about his organization! In fact, if I *had* known the organization," Jonnes teased, "I would have been even more scared! As I turned things around in my mind, I thought, *I know* nothing *about this organization. This* can't *be right.*

"I did continue to think about it, though, and took it up in prayer. As I prayed and wrote down what was on my heart, I found eight reasons why I couldn't work with Jay and only seven why I should! Yes, this was obviously not where I should go. But still, the Lord kept it on my heart. Then one day, I felt the Lord say, 'Jonnes, are you going to look at your list, or are you going to listen to Me?'"

Many have asked how a relationship can remain so strong and free of competition and suspicion. One key aspect is certain commitments they've both made to each other.

"Like your mother and I promised each other when we were newly married," Dad explained to me one day, "Jonnes and I also have also promised to always give each other the benefit of the doubt. If one of us lets the other down, the other chooses to remember that this was not done to intentionally hurt the other but was simply a mistake." The "benefit of the doubt" is given until the two can sit down and discuss what really happened.

Second, there is a mutual vulnerability to speak into the life of the other. When one sees something in the other's life, Dad and Uncle Jonnes have committed first to love each other enough to say what they see – good or bad – and second, to humbly listen to what the other is saying. I remember times when either one of them thoroughly disagreed with the other. There were never raised voices or anger, but there was real and open debate. However, there was also an obvious sense of humility on both sides – convinced they were right but willing to be proved wrong by the other, especially if the other had biblical proof for their stance.

The open relationship and accountability between Uncle Jonnes and my dad have threatened many people my dad and Uncle Jonnes have met in the past. "How can you relate so closely with him?" they've been asked. "What about the cultural differences?"

"Well, Jennie," as Uncle Jonnes told me once, "it takes weeks and months sometimes for me to remember that your dad is white! To me, he is just like me. I never notice the color of your family!" My own family has made similar oversights to Uncle Jonnes' nationality. My grandma once said, "Yes, there were three white men there – Jay, Jonnes, and Grandpa." It is the beauty of the body of Christ – the joy of seeing each other for who the Lord has made them and not through the stereotypes our society creates.

"When I was in high school," my dad recalled, "a wise Congolese church leader told me that when I became a missionary I should be sure to be *with* the natives. He told me not to just minister *to* them, but with them. And, more importantly than even ministering with them, he told me to be one with them relationally."

Uncle Jonnes' and my dad's relationship and, consequently, the way New Hope is run, are founded on this advice: Ugandans and foreigners living side by side, equal in partnership, in ministry, ministering to each other and to the children the Lord brings us. It is not a case of the white man coming to serve the Africans, but brothers and sisters in Christ joining hands to serve Him together.

In addition to their relationship bringing many skeptical questions, Uncle Jonnes has often received the brunt of many greedy men's frustrations. "Get out of our way, you African," they've said, "you are hindering us from 'eating the muzungu.'"

"When I arrived in Luweero," Uncle Jonnes reminisced, "it was especially difficult. Since I was not from that area, initially I was not received well. People soon began to say that this outsider has come to stop us from getting our 'food.' They would openly say to each other in my hearing, 'We are interested in the muzungu's pocket, and this man is stopping us.'"

Both Dad and Uncle Jonnes have taken turns being the brunt of false accusations. It is not uncommon for my dad to say to the family, "Well, according to the popularity polls, I'm the bad guy now. At least Jonnes is innocent this time," or another time to say, "Well, now I'm wonderful, and Jonnes is terrible." Sometimes they're in it together – for better or for worse.

Over the years Uncle Jonnes' and Dad's relationship has been like iron sharpening iron. They have helped each other to grow by speaking honestly into each others' lives and supporting each other even when it was the least popular thing to do.

A story my dad likes to tell about his and Jonnes' relationship took place in the early days. As he and Uncle Jonnes began to get to know each other,

Uncle Jonnes' "Mukiga" tendencies began to become very evident. If a Mukiga likes you, he'll tell you. If he hates you, he'll tell you that, too. At least there are no questions and no pretense!

From time to time as the two of them would be involved in making a decision, dealing with a staff member, or planning an event, Jonnes would correct my dad. "Jay, you need to do this next time," or "Jay, you should have done this."

"His corrections could have to do with personnel or the meetings I should have had for various decisions instead of making them on my own, or how I could have solved a crisis better," Dad reminisced. "But it was basically a daily occurrence, and often it would be several times a day. And *most* of the time he was right!" my dad smiled as he remembered. "My mistake was usually obvious, so I had no argument. I just accepted his correction as correct and said nothing."

But one day it was too much. Dad continued, "We were walking out on Kampala Road, right in front of the Mukubira and Sons shop. As he finished correcting me for something again, I stopped right there, turned to him, and said, 'Jonnes, don't I ever do *anything* right?' I was overwhelmed. I really meant that question because I knew he was right. His comments were true, and I had begun to feel like I couldn't do anything right. Jonnes was a bit shocked by my statement. I think he hadn't realized how strong he was coming across. From then on he was more careful about what he said and how often he corrected me! But iron does sharpen iron, and we have both continued to correct each other, and to grow as a result of it."

Dad and Uncle Jonnes have also helped each other grow in areas where they are naturally weak or compensated for the other's weaknesses. One of Uncle Jonnes' weaknesses is speaking in riddles. He frequently tries to explain a new plan or idea to the staff using so many "Jonnesisms." The result is utter confusion. No one knows what the plan really is, when it's supposed to happen, or who is supposed to do what to bring it about. When we've all finished laughing at Jonnes' way of explaining things, we all look to

Dad for the translation. It's his turn to talk, "What Jonnes *meant* was this…" he begins.

Speaking to large crowds was one of the areas Dad had little experience in and little interest in pursuing during the early days. He still would much rather Uncle Jonnes do the public speaking, but, thanks to Uncle Jonnes, Dad is not a novice at it any more!

"I will never forget the day when Honorable Njuba came to visit Kasana," Uncle Jonnes said with a twinkle in his eye. At that time, we had not yet had any other dignitaries visit us at Kasana, and my dad had no idea of the rules of protocol. So, Uncle Jonnes jumped in to organize the function.

"Jay," he had said, "*you* are supposed to address the guests and tell them who we are and what we are doing."

But this was not what my dad had signed up for. "Aaah! Jonnes," he said, "I don't like that kind of stuff! I came to build, not to address people!"

"But you are the *director!*" Jonnes had prodded. "Besides, *I* don't know what to say! This whole vision thing is great, but it's all new language to me."

"I was excited about all we were doing," Jonnes explained to me years later, "but I was excited *behind* your dad! I think he was very happy that I liked talking in front of people, so he was planning to use my mouth. But I didn't have his mind and heart to fill my mouth!" Uncle Jonnes laughed at the memory.

"I remember him going very hesitatingly to address the crowd, first saying to me, 'I really don't like this.' But he made a great presentation! And you know what? He hasn't stopped talking about his ideas since!" Uncle Jonnes laughed. "That must have been the 'anointed' day. He communicated what was in his heart, and therefore he won people's hearts!"

❧

In a country where in most tribes there is an intense fear of authority and overwhelming fear of confrontation, there have been many frustrating times in the history of Kasana. Never, the culture dictates, should a poor person speak publicly against a wealthier one. Never should a leader be corrected. Never should a servant or employee openly disagree with his master or employer – at least not to his face. Speaking behind a leader's back, however, is an entirely different matter. It is not at all uncommon for "underlings" to slander, disagree with, and complain about their "higher-ups" openly to their equals and behind the backs of those to whom they are subservient. When given an opportunity in which most Americans would jump to share their opinion or voice their feelings, the average Ugandan would forgo the opportunity and later simply say to a friend, "I just kept quiet." Therefore, even a godly leader, who honestly desires open feedback – criticism and praise – at least in the beginning, should expect nothing but open praise and hidden disagreement and murmuring from his employees.

As stated earlier, Uncle Jonnes was not like that, and he frequently corrected and rebuked my father, his boss. Uncle Jonnes' and my dad's openness and honesty came naturally, and their prayer was that it would continue throughout the staff. However, though this was the precedent set by the leaders, it has been a constant battle since day one to encourage the staff to voice their opinions – especially if they disagree with leadership.

I will never forget the day my dad returned home from a management meeting with a smile across his face. "You'll never guess what Sam did today!" he told the family.

"I've seen the way Uncle Jonnes and Uncle Jay disagree with each other and openly correct each other – yet they still love each other," Sam Serunkuma, a member of the Kasana Children's Centre's Management Committee, had said. "So I'm going to do the same thing! Uncle Jonnes, I completely disagree with what you've said. I think it is wrong and unacceptable." Uncle Jonnes later told me that his heart had leapt for joy when he heard those words! My dad's eyes filled with tears as he too rejoiced at the situation. It was not that Uncle Jonnes had deserved correcting (he was later found to have been misunderstood), but that Sam, who had worked at New Hope for years and carried increasing responsibility throughout those years, finally had the boldness to speak out strongly against "authority." It was a first – a celebrated first.

"We've made progress!" my dad exclaimed. "Now, maybe the others will see that those who speak honestly – whether or not they agree with the leadership – are actually appreciated, not fired or disciplined." Later, on the day that Sam was appointed as the manager of Kasana Children's Center, making him fourth in command, my dad recalled this story to the staff and laughed. "You see," he said, "we don't fire the people who will speak the *truth* to us, even if it's contrary to what we think. We promote them!"

One evening, I had the joy of listening to my dad and Uncle Jonnes reminisce about the past. "There was a time when I was speaking with a visiting business man," my dad recalled. "I was explaining to him all of the new ideas we had for businesses to help the children's center to become self-sufficient, but was also telling him that we were not qualified to run businesses and we were looking for qualified people. I'll never forget his response. 'God almost never works that way,' he said, 'because if you *were* qualified you would do it in your own strength, but if you aren't qualified, you have to do it in His strength!'"

"I agree," Uncle Jonnes laughed. "If I had been 'qualified' I think I would have begun to act very 'professional!' Oh yes, I keep looking to see if there is any industrial chemistry left in my briefcase for me to use. And I just laugh and see Jesus' grace there instead. Praise God there is grace! In our shortcomings, Jay and I have had to look to Him to train us over the years. When I look back at what I knew then and what I was able to do then, I laugh and say, 'This was crazy!' I wouldn't have employed myself!"

And isn't it just God's way to use the weak to lead the strong and the foolish things of this world to confound the wise? An industrial chemist and a builder are not the most obvious team to begin an ever-growing organization that works with children. Yet, it is through the weak that His strength is made perfect, and when it's all said and done, He alone can take the glory!

Jonnes removing a jigger from Dad's foot.

Deep in discussion.

Jonnes, Gertrude, Vicki, and Jay, July 2005

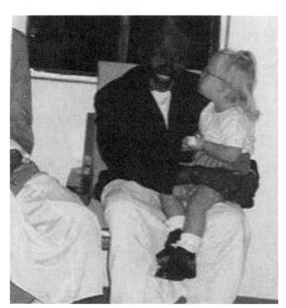

Uncle Jonnes and Julia, 2004.

# Section 2

## The Family Grows

# Chapter 13
## The Heart of an Orphan

Like any other sunny afternoon in Kabubbu, Josiah, Jamie, and I were playing outside – riding bikes, kicking a soccer ball, and chewing on stems of tall grass we had pulled from the bush that grew around our house. Soon a small group of village children began to gather to watch. Too old to join in our childish games, the older children remained at a distance to watch these loud "bazungu." The brave younger children, however, joined us, and between our broken Luganda and their broken English, the fun continued.

Our friendships with the Ugandan village children were based on important things like building forts, playing hand-clapping games, jumping rope, eating ants, climbing trees to find ripe mangoes, and, most importantly, riding bikes. Our bikes, which had been shipped from America with our other belongings, were the only child-sized bikes the children had ever seen. Eagerly, they awaited their turn to ride.

That afternoon, a boy we had seen before but to whom we had never spoken came up to us. "Geevu me mah bayceeko" ("Give me my bicycle") he said, his Luganda accent making the words nearly impossible to recognize. (Determined to get a chance to ride our bikes, he had asked the older children at school how one might make an appropriate request in English. All the way home, he had recited what the older students had instructed him to say. It was one of the first English sentences he had ever known.) There, he had said it, and it worked! Soon, he was off racing down the path on Josiah's tiny silver BMX.

That was the first time we spoke to Paul Nyabenda. Little did we know that this boy would become one of our best friends and that our friendship with him would remain strong even to this day. Little did he know that in the years to come his knowledge of the English language would enable him to translate sermons for numerous people, write several songs, preach countless of his own sermons, and lead many to the Lord.

---

*Thirteen years after our first meeting, I had the pleasure of sitting and reminiscing with Paul over the events of the previous years. During our conversation, I was reminded of Samuel of old. As it was with Samuel, the Lord's hand was truly on Paul's life from his childhood – protecting him, guiding him, and shaping him to become a strong leader and the Lord's faithful servant. Through this conversation and through a testimony he gave at our annual staff envisioning week a few weeks later, Paul provided poignant insight into the heart of an orphan and of the healing that can come about through the grace of the Lord. I would like to give you the opportunity to learn the story in his own words, the testimony he shared with me, and the encouragement and challenges he gave to the staff. May his message speak to you, challenge you, and encourage you as it did us.*

"I first heard about Kasana in early 1988," began Paul, a twenty-five-year-old teacher, family father at Kasana, landowner, and aspiring pastor. "The theory I heard about the place was very funny. I don't know how the rumors started, but they were very threatening. Most people said that these white people who had come were really planning on stealing the village kids, eating them, or making money out of them. I don't know how that was going to happen!" he laughed.

"My first response to these stories was one of fear. I believe there are many other kids who would have desired to be in this place who didn't come because of that fear. For me, taking the step to come to Kasana, to a great extent, required overcoming this fear and shutting my ears to what people were saying.

"There was one thing of which I was sure," he said. "I really needed help." And so, with nothing to lose, Paul chose to ignore the threatening rumors and discouragement that circulated throughout the village. In October 1988 he and his two younger siblings joined the Kasana family.

In 1986, two years before we met Paul, his father and mother both died within months of each other, and Paul and his siblings were left alone in the world. "When I lost my parents," he confessed to the audience, "my heart was broken. I felt that I was left in a complete state of uncertainty and anxiety. Nobody cared. It was impossible for anyone to convince me that he cared because people that I had trusted betrayed me. That fact affected how I was able to relate to others."

As with many other children who have lost their parents, Paul interpreted the death of his father and mother as betrayal – those who were supposed to always be with him and care for him had broken his trust by leaving him alone.

In addition to the rejection and betrayal he felt from his parents' death, at a time when the young family needed them the most, their neighbors and parents' friends quietly slipped away so as to avoid the unwanted responsibilities and inconveniences of caring for orphans.

"The community cannot associate with a child unless he is in a family" Paul explained. "That's what happened to us. We had had quite a number of people, friends to our parents and our family, but after I buried my father and, after a few months, buried my mother, those friends were nowhere to be seen. Why? It is because as orphaned children we had lost identity, and therefore we belonged to nobody. No one wanted to have us. We were, indeed, a misfortune."

Lacking identity, direction, and comfort, yet feeling responsible for his younger siblings, an overwhelming emptiness and pain gripped Paul. His experience had taught him that no one could be trusted – not even his own flesh and blood, much less those he had once thought were friends. In an attempt to protect his broken heart, and faced with the reality of his family's need, he labored to suppress his emotional pain and seek material help.

"I thought Kasana would be a place of getting material things: food and clothing," he explained.

As he had expected, from the beginning of their time at Kasana, Paul and his siblings were provided for and cared for. However, he realized that though his physical needs were being met, his insecurity and emotional trauma remained a constant reality.

"My family had been shattered," Paul remembered, "and when a child's family breaks, he becomes very insecure and his heart becomes very susceptible to danger. So, we children did anything we could to build a wall around ourselves to protect our broken hearts. *If my father and mother are not there to defend me,* he thought, *I will defend myself.*"

Never letting anyone close enough to help him deal with his hurts and pains, Paul did everything he could to survive on his own.

"One method we used to protect ourselves," he continued, "was a defense mechanism: a way of interpreting reality very fast. I used to have trouble when anybody would call me – especially Uncle Jonnes!"

Paul smiled at Uncle Jonnes, who sat among the other members of staff. The rest of the audience chuckled, knowing the deep bond of a father and son relationship that now exists between them.

"If someone would say, 'Uncle Jonnes is calling you,' my first and immediate question would be, '*Why?* What have I done?' I automatically assumed that any call by an adult could only mean trouble. I had interpreted the circumstance quickly. My second response was to then find a way of escape or else somebody might touch my heart."

One other painful characteristic in the heart of an orphan is what Paul refers to as a "mind of scarcity."

"Everything that is there, no matter how abundant it is," he explained, "will never be enough to a child with this kind of mentality. Believe me," he stressed, "you could give everything you have to that child, he can sleep on many mattresses, have more than enough blankets, and have an abundance of food, but he will not be satisfied. When I first came to Kasana I received many things for which I said thank you. But then, I would sit in the corner and say to myself, 'But I'm an orphan. I'm an orphan.' Even when I had food, even when I had good clothes, I knew I was alone; I still had no identity.

"The other day," he reminisced, "I was reflecting on how, when we were still new at New Hope, we used to grab the food we were given, even when it was plenty. It *was* plenty! Served in heaps on our plates! But we still ate quickly, looking everywhere to see what others had. All we could think was, *How can I survive?* and we would eat as if we would never get to eat again. We weren't sure! The security and the assurance were not there.

"Do you know why most orphans are very needy?" Paul stopped and looked intently at the staff, his pause emphasizing the gravity of his point. "It is because their inside is hollow. They are trying to fill the void with anything, but nothing will take away the pain. Their hearts are broken. Until the past is dealt with, until the Lord reaches in and heals the hurts and pains that are there, until He fills that void, there is no way you can truly reach that child."

Just as he had explained, during the first few months of Paul's time at Kasana, the Lord began to work slowly but surely in his heart, and the feelings of insecurity, rejection, and fear that had plagued him for years began to subside.

"I found Kasana was a place of comfort and realized that these guys really loved us! Uncle Peter would often lift us up and hug us. We would have time to read books, do activities, work in the gardens, and spend time having fun with the 'aunties' and 'uncles.' God had brought me into a family – one made up of people of different colors! It was really amazing."

As Paul became more and more a part of the Kasana family, his heart began to soften toward the Lord. But it was not until 1990, two years after he joined New Hope, that the Lord penetrated Paul's heart and drew Paul to Himself.

"God started working in my life differently in 1990," he said, "in ways that amaze me. From 1988 to 1990, I was just going to Sunday school and doing things, but really I had not yet given my life to Christ."

But that year the Lord broke through to Paul's heart, and through a visiting team from Youth With A Mission he met his Heavenly Father.

"I had to make a commitment. I gave my life to Christ and began getting serious with the Lord."

Finally, the deep process of healing and cleansing of Paul's broken life could begin in earnest. And day by day, the Lord's work in his life was evident.

"Pain of the past can be a very big stronghold," Paul explained to us. "People become so bound to the past that they can see neither the future nor the present. As soon as a wounded person experiences a new pain, even if it is very small, it will stir up all the old hurts.

"That was me. I was very fearful and timid, and my heart needed healing. But people like Uncle Jonnes counseled and discipled me, and helped me to deal with my past. I'm not all the way there yet. But my desire is that whatever God reveals to me or through somebody, I should be willing to deal with it until I am completely free.

"Today, when I see what I am involved in now as a family father, I ask myself, 'Lord, who am I to be doing this?' I know it is only because somebody sacrificed his life for me. It is because somebody looked beyond the old Paul, the lost little boy that I was. He saw the product, and therefore he walked toward the product. The process was hard, but I believe whoever touched my life looked past what I was then and saw what I could become.

"You know," Paul continued, engaging the staff's complete attention, "there are some people who cannot talk about certain situations in their past. You might simply mention the name of their father, and they burst into tears. But I want to encourage you to reach out to these children! Use their cries as an opportunity to reach out to them."

His sincere plea and challenge moved many in the room to tears.

"Don't despair! It *is* tough. Having gone through it myself, I know. But now, seeing all that God has done for me, I am able to talk about the past because I'm not a slave to it!

"Pray for the children," he continued with undaunted conviction. "Pursue them. Pursue what is in their hearts and what God's interest for them is. Jesus did not sit and wait for people to come to Him. No! He went to where *they* were and chose a few out of the crowd. He saw what, by God's grace, these men could become, and He pursued them.

"And finally, speak the *truth* to them! Did you know that not all facts are truth?" Paul laughed with excited confidence. "The *fact* is I lost my biological parents. Everybody knows that, not so? But the *truth* is I'm not an orphan! I'm not! God has put people in place as my family, and He is my Father. That's the report I have in my heart! Someone may say, 'There goes an orphan,' but that doesn't bother me now. Because I know I'm not an orphan. And that's the *truth!*"

*After a heartfelt applause from the staff, many weeping with gratefulness for the Lord's work in Paul and all He still could do for the many children they loved, Uncle Jonnes rose to end the meeting. Unable to hold back his tears he said, "Listen to those words, 'I am able to talk abut the past because I'm not a slave to it.' I know how many times I prayed for Paul," Uncle Jonnes' voice shook as he cried. "I said, 'I want to get into Paul's heart,' for my heart had been joined to his. At one point, I felt like I was losing him, but I said, 'I can't lose him. Lord, I can't touch him, but You can.' And I remember committing him to the Lord."*

*Uncle Jonnes turned to Paul, his voice still quavering through his tears, "I'm proud of you, son. Now I can share the same place, the same honor and ministry with you. Not because of what I've done. I'm so thankful that grace was there."*

*Then he turned to us, "People, in looking after these children, we are in the process of making history. But we cannot make good history unless we deal with the past. What Paul is talking about is history. It has happened. It is in his story. It is painful. But there is someone who cares. God cares, and He has brought you here to be a part of that caring."*

The truth of Paul's testimony and what the Lord has done in his life cannot be told without also including the words of a song Paul wrote several years ago. After seeing all that the Lord had done for him, and realizing the depth of the hope he now had, Paul changed his name from Nyabenda to "Kusuubira," which means "to hope." At that time, he wrote this song:

*Thank You, Lord, my God, for Your love for me*
*Yes, Your love for me has brought me from far away!*
*Look at that wondrous love! Look at that wondrous love!*
*Once I was fatherless, but now, I've got a family*
*A beautiful family, with God as my Father*
*Look at that wondrous love! Look at that wondrous love!*
*Once I had no hope, but now I've got new hope*
*The only hope that I have comes from my Lord!*
*Look at that wondrous love! Look at that wondrous love!*
*Once I was lonely, but now I've got my friend*
*The sweetest friend that I have is Christ Jesus!*
*Look at that wondrous love! Look at that wondrous love!*
*When trials come, Lord, I pray, make me stand*
*When trials come, Lord, I pray, make me stand.*
*And make me a witness for Your love!*

Paul Kusubira

Many years ago... Paul and his younger siblings Anna Maria
(who tragically passed away in 2004), and Machumi.

Paul teaching at the Institute of Childcare and
Family on the Heart of an Orphan, 2004.

# Chapter 14
## *Engraved on His Hands*

⤟⤠

*Can a mother forget the baby at her breast and have no compassion on the child she has borne? Though she may forget you, I will not forget you! See, I have engraved you on the palms of my hands.*

– Isaiah 49:15–16

Who are these fatherless we speak of? What are their untold stories? What anguish have they suffered? What dreams and aspirations do they have? Who was with them when their fathers were killed or when their mothers lay sick on the deathbed? Who refused to care for them when they needed care the most?

In this chapter, I would like to "introduce"[47] you to some of the fatherless who are now part of the Kasana family. Many are currently with us; many have moved on. I want you to hear the Father's heartbeat for these children, hear His cries and see the love and compassion He has for each of those He calls His own – those whose names are written on His hands.

*He said to me, 'You are my Son; today I have become your Father.'*

– Psalm 2:7, NIV

Jackson

<u>History in his own words</u>:

"It was one day in 1985 when I was born into a family that was sorrowful. We had no hope at all. My mother had returned to her parents to give birth to me, but before I was born, she and her fami-

---

[47]All names are changed for privacy.

ly had to flee from the soldiers. The bombs were bombing, and my mother and grandparents fled one way and my father fled with other people in a different direction. When my father reached a small town, he met soldiers who shot him to death. The war continued, and soon it was time for my mother to give birth. The name she gave me in my tribal language means 'war.'"

Jackson joined New Hope in 1993.

Kasana parent's comments:

"Jackson has a heart of servanthood. He is obedient, humble, and gentle. He has a heart for God."

Teacher's comment:

"He has worked as a very exemplary student leader."

Gifting:

Jackson is excellent in working with children, and he loves to teach Sunday school.

Future aspirations:

Jackson wants to be a teacher or businessman.

*I have seen his ways, but I will heal him; I will guide him and restore comfort to him, creating praise on the lips of the mourners...*

(Isaiah 57:18–19)

William

History:

His father was Kigozi; his mother, Tereza. His father died during the war; his mother died in 1996 due to illness. For several years, he lived with an aunt who was a witch doctor. While living there he was forced to help her mix her potions and carry out her "arts." Even years later, the influence of witchcraft from his childhood brought him pain and fear. After living with his aunt, William lived on the streets until he was taken in by an old woman who offered to help him.

Hobbies:

William loves to play drums in church and sing in choir. He is a very good goalie and an excellent long-distance runner.

Personality during his early years at Kasana:

He tended to fall into sad, gloomy moods.

Future aspirations:

William would like to be a teacher and/or missionary.

William's prayer requests:

That his mother's relatives will come to know the Lord.

"God may dwell mightily in my life."

After he went through Neil Anderson's "Seven Steps to Freedom in Christ" and really surrendered his life to the Lord, the frequently sad and distressed look on William's face has been washed away. The Lord has truly begun to create praise on the lips of one who had much reason to mourn!

*I will be his father, and he will be my son. When he does wrong, I will punish him with the rod of men....But my love will never be taken away from him.*

(Samuel 7:14–15, NIV)

Nathaniel

History in his own words:

"My father died in 1984 during the war. When the war was over and I was just three or four years old, we left Kampala, where we'd fled during the war, and returned to our home area in Luweero. But when we came from Kampala, we were helpless. Our clanmates were no longer helping us, and we had nothing, not even a grass-thatched house. Each night, we would sleep with neighbors. But when we heard about the center, my mother took us and we registered there. We joined New Hope in 1989. When I came, my feet were blistered from syphilis and jiggers, but I was cared for when I was here; I got treatment and love from the staff. It was there that I started to enjoy life."

Aspirations:

Nathaniel would like to become an accountant.

*A father to the fatherless, a defender of widows, is God in his holy dwelling. God sets the lonely in families, he leads forth the prisoners with singing.*

(Psalm 68:5-6)

Esther

History:

Her parents were together when she was born. Her father was wealthy and owned many cows. While looking for good pasture for his livestock, Esther's father moved their family to Luweero. However, when Esther was just one year old, her parents separated. Later, they found out that her father died. Esther joined the New Hope family in 1989 along with her mother, who worked for the organization for several years.

Hobbies and abilities:

She is very good at sports, loves singing, and spending time with young children.

Her hobbies are playing netball, chatting, and listening to good, godly music.

Kasana parent's comment:

"Esther is outgoing, friendly, and loves to laugh. She is hardworking and cares very much about her family."

Future aspirations:

Esther plans to be a nurse or midwife.

Esther's prayer requests:

"To stand firm in Jesus until I die."

*'I will live with them and walk among them, and I will be their God, and they will be My people.... I will be a Father to you, and you will be my sons and daughters,' says the Lord Almighty.*

(2 Corinthians 6:16, 18)

Jane
History:

Jane was born on the roadside as her mother was heading to the hospital. Her parents were in a casual relationship and were not living together when she was born. Her father died when she was four years old. She first lived with her paternal grandmother, then with her mother for a short time. Following the Ugandan cultural tradition that the children belong to the father and his family, her mother soon took Jane to her paternal aunt. This aunt later brought Jane to live with her cousin in Luweero. She stayed with this cousin for nine months, and then her cousin died. Jane was then brought with her cousin's children to New Hope in 1991. Her mother is still alive, but Jane doesn't stay with her mother because she is a peasant and cannot support her.

Jane's prayer request:

"That I may desire to know more about God and have a serving heart."

*"... for in you the fatherless find compassion,"* (Hosea 14:3)

Jared
History:

Jared's parents separated when he was very young, and each remarried. Jared lived with his father for several years. Then one day, Obote's soldiers came into their village and told everyone to pack up their things because they would be leaving the next day. That next morning the entire village met, carrying everything of value they possibly could, and began the long march to wherever the soldiers would direct them. After they had marched for several kilometers, the soldiers stopped the crowd and separated the men from the women and children. While some soldiers remained to guard the women and children, the others led the men into the bush and proceeded to shoot or hack to death every single one. Jared joined New Hope in 1989.

<u>Aspirations</u>:

Jared would like to adopt and care for many orphaned children.

*I have chosen you and have not rejected you. So do not fear, for I am with you; do not be dismayed, for I am your God. I will strengthen you and help you; I will uphold you with my righteous right hand.*

(Isaiah 41:9–10)

Hannah

<u>History</u>:

Hannah was born in Kampala. She is the first born in her family but is not quite sure if her parents were living together when she was born or not. Her father died in 1987 of an illness, and her mother is still living. However, her mother couldn't afford to care for her or educate her as she was poor and was also caring for three other children. Hannah was brought to Kasana in 1993 by her grandfather.

<u>Hobbies</u>:

Hannah likes playing netball and weaving.

<u>Kasana parent's comment</u>:

Hannah doesn't really trust many staff and can be very closed to them.

<u>Parents' prayer request for Hannah</u>

That Hannah's heart would be healed of past hurts and that she would be able to trust adults.

*He gathers the lambs in his arms and carries them close to his heart.*

(Isaiah 40:11)

Caleb

<u>History</u>:

Caleb is not sure where he was born. He is the first born to his mother but does not know if his father had other children. His parents were married and living together when he was born. His father died during the war, and his mother died of AIDS in 1998. He lived with his grandmother even before his mother died, and it was his grandmother who brought him to Kasana in 1991.

Hobbies:

Caleb loves soccer and is one of the best players on his team; he is also good at masonry.

Cause of father's death:

Gunshot

*Listen to me...you whom I have upheld since you were conceived, and have carried since your birth. Even to your old age and gray hairs I am he, I am he who will sustain you. I have made you and I will carry you; I will sustain you and I will rescue you.*

(Isaiah 46:3–4)

Daudi

History in his own words:

"I was born to a very poor family, which even did not own a bike as some do. We lived deep in the village. My father's job was to dig pits for other people. But if you had come to see us then, you would have seen that we did not have a pit latrine, and yet my father was good at digging them for other people. Finally, because of the terrible situation we were living in, my mother decided to go away and leave me and my sisters to suffer in the village. My father was also an alcoholic. When our mother left, he would go out drinking and come back at night and ask, 'Where is food?' We would just stare at him because we did not have food. People had told our dad that if he was to continue being a drunk he would one time come home and find us starved to death. I tell you, I was really affected in my inmost being. After my father's death in 1994, a lady called Karen came to my village. She began to help us and then took us to New Hope. That is where I even got saved from."

Hobbies:

Daudi likes basketball, reading, and working to earn money.

Staff comment:

Comes to school and does what is required of him, but his heart has not been fully changed. He seems lonely sometimes or deep in thought.

*In the place where it was said to them, 'You are not my people,' they will be called 'sons of the living God.'*

(Hosea 1:10)

Simon

History:

Simon's parents were not married to each other when he was born. His father was a police man and was stationed in another part of the country soon after Simon's birth. His mother could not care for him, so he was passed from one person to another who abused and mistreated him. When he was four years old, someone put him on a bus and sent him to the area where his father was stationed. However, his father refused to acknowledge that Simon was his son, so Simon lived in a box outside the police station and ate the prisoners' leftover food. Each day the other police and prisoners would tease Simon's father and ask him why he was not caring for his son, but each day his response was, "He is not my son." New Hope staff found him at the police station while they were investigating one of New Hope's robberies. He joined the Kasana family in 1991.

Staff Comment:

Simon still struggles with insecurity and rejection. However, in the last year or so he has begun to respond to the love of his heavenly Father in a new way. Our prayer is that in the place of the rejection in his heart, Simon will hear the Lord's affirmation that he is a 'son of the living God.'

Hobbies:

Simon is an excellent football player; he loves music and plays the keyboard, guitar, and drums.

*The LORD your God is with you, he is mighty to save. He will take great delight in you, he will quiet you with his love, he will rejoice over you with singing.*

(Zephaniah 3:17)

Yusufu

History:

Yusufu was born in 1980 in a town outside of Kampala. His father and mother were married and lived together until the father's death in the war in 1985. At that time, his mother left him with his grandmother, who is a peasant farmer. The mother went to Kampala where she eventually remarried and had two children, but then later divorced. Yusufu's grandmother cared for him and put him in school when he was old enough. But by the time he was seven years old, she could no longer pay his school fees, so he stayed at home. One day she was told that Kasana was taking applications, and she applied. He was accepted in 1990 as a day scholar and continued to stay with his grandmother. When his grandmother became too sick to care for him, he joined Kasana as a boarding student.

Yusufu's prayer request:

"That God may continue ruling in me and that His will should be done in me."

Dream:

Yusufu's dream is to build a new house for his grandmother because hers is very old.

Staff comment:

"I pray he will learn to trust, to be more open, and to realize how much God loves him."

*...those who are led by the Spirit of God are sons of God. For you did not receive a spirit that makes you a slave again to fear, but you received the Spirit of sonship. And by Him we cry, 'Abba, Father.'*

(Romans 8:14–15)

Matthew

History:

Both his father and mother died of AIDS and left six-year-old Matthew and his siblings alone in their home. They were soon found by an aid organization that began covering their school fees, but did not feed or clothe them. Eventually, a kind lady began to care for them. In 1991, this lady met Uncle Jonnes, and New Hope began to help the children. Matthew and his siblings moved from their parents' home to Luweero to join the Kasana family in 1994.

Hobbies:

Matthew enjoys football and badminton.

The list could go on of boys and girls, sons and daughters, who lost the most important people in their lives and suffered pains so deep that they cannot be described. So often the world looks at them and sees a burden or a nuisance, sees them as unimportant and useless. But the Lord sees them and knows them. He identifies with them for they are His. Their names are written on the palms of His hands. And He calls Himself their Father.

*You are the children of the LORD your God....Out of all the peoples on the face of the earth, the LORD has chosen you to be his treasured possession.*

(Deuteronomy 14:1-2)

# Chapter 15
## The Family Grows

*"So many times we've stared at problems and have only been able to say, 'Lord, save us.' We are in an area in which Satan has had so much past success in destroying lives. Now, in a way that this area has not experienced before, the kingdom of God is being established. God has been and is continually seeing us through, and His work moves on. We know that there are many of you that pray for us regularly. Those prayers make more of a difference than you realize. Please pray on!"*

– From a newsletter Dad wrote in October 1989

After our second intake of children, which took place in October 1988, life began to fall into a routine. We gradually began to be able to add new staff members to the ministry team – Meekson and Grace, and Joseph and Evelyn Ruyondo. We were still struggling financially, so the buildings built after our first mud home had cement floors, tin roofs, and papyrus walls. Later, these were upgraded to brick walls on the outside with papyrus walls dividing the separate rooms. And then, finally, buildings with walls completely made from brick became the norm.

Near the beginning of 1989 the children and staff moved "up the hill" into the first relatively permanent buildings. There was one home for the girls and one for the boys. Although it had never been part of our plan, necessity forced us to first house the children in dormitory-style quarters – or the "General Paddock," as the children termed their dorms. Before long there was a new home for the Bakimis, one for the single ladies, two more for the boys, one more for the girls, and then one built for the Ruyondo family. Things were looking up!

Our school was also beginning to look more and more like an official school. Instead of the "big kids' class" and "the little kids' class," children were able to be evaluated and placed in the appropriate primary level class. Annie Crowe began traveling to Kasana regularly to help us establish curriculum and within a short time became the first headmistress of our new school – officially registered in 1989 as "Esuubi Eppya Vocational Primary School."[48] Along with Annie came excellent training for our teachers, more school supplies, and support from Christian schools in the UK. Still, she is most remembered by many of the children for the special bread she used to bring them as a treat each time she had come! Consequently she earned the title, "Auntie Mugati."[49] Her former Kasana students, now grown men and women, still use that nickname as a term of endearment each time they refer to her and those early days. David Freeman, or "Uncle 1-2-3"[50] as our children called him, the headmaster of a King's School in Witney, England, also began to visit Kasana regularly to give guidance, encouragement, and training to our teachers.

During those days, the feel of a tight-knit family permeated New Hope. While we had begun to grow, we were still small enough that everyone knew what everyone else was up to, how they were doing, and where they were.

"I remember when Uncle Jonnes or Uncle Jay would go to Kampala," reminisced Kaleera, who joined the family as a nine-year-old in 1990. "None of us would fall asleep until we knew they were home. We would lie in bed, waiting for the sound of the van, and as soon as we would hear it in the distance, we would jump out of bed and run to the roundabout." After the vehicle was surrounded by little ones, Uncle Jonnes and Dad would climb out, hug everyone, and then they would be off to bed again. "Now we could fall asleep!" Kaleera laughed.

---

[48]"Esuubi Eppya" means "New Hope" in Luganda.

[49]Mugati is the Luganda word for bread.

[50]Becasue of the song he taught while he was in Kasana, "1-2-3 Jesus Loves Me," our children soon referred to him as "Uncle 1-2-3"; many did not even remember his real name.

"I loved the early days," Kaleera continued. "I came when I was very young, and I started receiving love from so many people. My whole life started changing. I had been so lonely when I was at home and didn't have any love, but when I came here, I found there was a lot of love around, and I started getting hope and joy for the future.

"I remember wishing we could be sick so Auntie Evelyn, our nurse, would take care of us," Kaleera laughed. "Auntie Sarah and later Auntie Julie would bring all of us little ones to their house in the evenings and bathe us and then give us tea and ground groundnuts. They were real mothers to us."

"I joined New Hope in 1989," said Sebuchu Nathan, who is now in university studying to be an accountant. "My family and I had been in a desperate situation, and when I came to Kasana I was cared for and received love from Auntie Sarah, Uncle Peter, Uncle Emmanuel, and Uncle Jonnes and so many others.

"I remember in the old days we had groups; there were no families yet. Each group had about eighteen children. We were each given a piece of land to cultivate, and we would have competitions to see which group could do the best in gardening! I remember our group, group four, was led by Auntie Gertrude. We won 50,000 shillings because we were the second best group growing groundnuts, peanuts and potatoes!"

While we Dangers lived in Kabubbu until March 1990, we were at Kasana almost daily, taking part in as many things as we could. We children would finish our school work as quickly as we could and then ride our bikes to join whatever activities were taking place at the time – gardening, a football game, Duck-Duck-Goose...anything! Each Sunday, we would ride our bicycles to Kasana for Sunday school in the mornings. During those days, church was held in the barn in the afternoons, and only the older children and adults had to go to church!

"We never attended Sunday services," Kaleera recalled. "We would just go to Sunday school and then ride bicycles for the rest of the afternoon!"

Each day Dad made several trips to and from Kasana on his bike. There were very few vehicles in those days, so everyone used bicycles. Abby would run to and from Kasana "protecting" Dad from anything or anyone that came too close! Then, finally, on March 1, 1990, our family moved into the house that Salt and Light had funded and my Grandpa Jack had built for us on site.

# "Running" Water!

We had all gathered down at the barn, and there was excitement in the air. "The Lord has blessed us, children," Uncle Jonnes began. "Our friends Jerry and Yolanda White have worked hard and have generously sacrificed their money so that we can have an 80-meter deep bore hole!"[51] Cheers and clapping erupted as each of the children (whose usual job had been to walk the half mile to Kabubbu to the public bore hole each day to collect water for drinking, bathing, and cooking) rejoiced wholeheartedly! God had provided once again! No longer would they have to spend hours each day just getting water. No longer, during the next water shortage or drought, would we have to stand in line for hours on end at the only bore hole for miles around, hoping that there would be enough water to fill the jerry cans ahead of ours and ours as well. And even better, no longer would the children have to hear the jeering of villagers who gathered at the public bore hole and took pleasure in mocking the "orphans from Kasana."

"Imagine," we all said to ourselves, "a bore hole *on site!*" It was almost as good as having running water!

"Kamya, come here!" Uncle Jonnes called excitedly. Kamya, one of our "little guys" who had suffered for years with a serious heart and liver problem, had been chosen to hold the bucket that would receive the first water from the bore hole. After a prayer of thanksgiving to the Lord for His wonderful provision, Uncle Jonnes began to pump the handle up and down. As the clear, clean water came gushing out into the little bucket Kamya held,

---

[51]A bore hole is a deep well from which clean water can be pumped. Unlike open wells, water from bore holes is protected and therefore kept clean.

cheers erupted again! Following the formalities, each child took turns pumping water, taking a drink, and, of course, splashing as much as they could on those near by!

## A NEWFANGLED MACHINE

At the sound of the engine starting, children began appearing out of no where. What *was* that noise? It was 1991, and in those days the only engines we ever heard were those of the tractor, an occasional vehicle, and my family's tiny generator. This new noise certainly needed to be explained. It was Kasana's first lawn mower that my parents had purchased at an amazing price from some missionaries in Kenya, and it turned out to be one of the most amazing things the children had ever seen!

"Uncle!" the children shouted over the noise of the engine, "what *is* it?" Within moments all the children were there, ready for a demonstration of this newfangled piece of machinery. Dad turned off the engine and lifted it up for the children to look underneath. "It's like a helicopter!" they decided as Dad explained how the blades go round and round to cut the grass. Then, each wide-eyed child got to hold onto the handle and push the mower while Dad carefully directed them. It cut the grass with precision and ease they simply could not believe! Once a good portion of the lawn was cut and the children had each taken a turn, they began walking slowly and carefully on the freshly cut grass. Some even lay down in it because it felt so soft and even!

Not long after, several mischievous boys, their eyes twinkling, grabbed a handful of grass and stealthily walked over to their Uncle Jay. Their aim was perfect! Almost instantly the air was filled with grass as the staff and children grabbed handfuls and threw it at anyone they saw! For the next twenty minutes there was a colossal grass fight – the most fun we had had in ages!

# THE FIRST THANKSGIVING

"That was the horn!" the news spread through the crowd. "She's almost here!" Our hearts were pounding fast as we children made sure the lines of our choir were as straight and orderly as we could make them to welcome Uganda's First Lady, Mrs. Janet Museveni. We had thought this day would never come! Uncle Jonnes and my dad had invited the wife of Uganda's president to join us for Kasana's first annual Thanksgiving Day and to open our new classroom block, but we hadn't thought she would actually accept an invitation from such a small and insignificant organization! Yet, the air horn Kakonge blew from his lookout point signaled that our doubts were unnecessary and she was almost here!

We had been preparing for days. Every single bedroom, every cook house and firewood pile were in impeccable order. Then, the day before her arrival, several carloads of soldiers had arrived. They had searched every house she was to visit and spent the night walking to and fro throughout the bush, ensuring that the First Lady had nothing to fear during her visit to Kasana. For weeks, we had been practicing our songs and presentations time and again, the new song especially. Uncle Jonnes and Dad said it was going to be our anthem. Uncle Peter Kiyimba and his wife, Dorothy, had come several days before to help Uncle Jonnes write the song and teach it to all the children and staff. Its words were simple, but they tell the story of Kasana, and since July 11, 1991, they have declared our purpose and hope.

The sun is rising again –
A sign of new hope today!
Jesus the Light, Light of the World
Shining His light in Kasana![52]
Arise now, shine in my life!
Arise now, shine in Kasana

---

[52]Kasana means sunchine in Luganda. This was the name of the village before we arrived.

180

Arise now, shine over Uganda
J~sus the Light of New Hope Uganda!
Emmambya esaze nate
Ng'elaga esuubi lyaffe!
Yesu yakka munsi zonna
Kitangala kya Kasana!
Yakka, yakka musana ggwange
Yakka, yakka wano mu Kasana
Yakka, yakka, yakka mu Uganda
Yesu Musana ggwa New Hope Uganda!

Sennyonjo and Betty stood by the roundabout in their carefully washed and ironed "New Hope Kids" t-shirts and welcomed "Mamma Janet"[53] as she climbed out of her vehicle.

"Welcome to Kasana!" they smiled. "We are so glad you have come!" Their job for the next several hours was to introduce her to the different staff at Kasana and take her on a tour of the site. In an area that had suffered so much from the war, President Museveni was more than a hero. He had ended the war that had claimed the lives of most of our children's parents and had allowed the next generation to begin life again in peace. The children couldn't believe that the wife of their nation's president was now here, visiting them, in their own homes!

After her tour of the children's houses, gardens, and classrooms, Mrs. Museveni came to my parents' house for refreshments and a visit, and then it was down to the new classroom block for the real purpose of her time at Kasana.

"What you see, you see because of what the Lord has done," Dad said with emotion. "We felt we should stop and thank God for having established the work of our hands."

After Dad spoke, Mrs. Museveni stood to address the crowd. Her words of encouragement and thanksgiving were exactly what we all needed to hear.

---

[53]Because of her reputation for concern for orphans, many call the President's wife, Mamma Janet.

"It is exciting for me to see that the ideas I've always had have been fulfilled," she said. "And I liked what I see here at Kasana even more, because when they came, the leaders of this place didn't have so much money, but they didn't go away. They started on a very humble beginning which they could at that time, and now they can build more ambitious structures. I pray that this lives as an example to you and that it grows into a bigger thing and that we can come here again and again and see living children both in body and spirit. And it is now my pleasure," she concluded, "to officially open and commission the first block of classrooms of the Kasana Children's Center."

As my dad wrote in a newsletter after her visit, "It was a great day! God once again blessed us in many, many ways. He blessed us with great weather. It poured all around us but only sprinkled at the site for fifteen minutes before she came – just enough to keep all the dust down! She is a wonderful, gracious lady who spoke kindly and with great love and care to the children, and provided us with *very* encouraging comments."

From that day on New Hope has held a Thanksgiving Day in either July or August of each year. And each year, we are reminded of the Lord's love and faithfulness. Years later, Mrs. Museveni joined us again and rejoiced with us in the work our heavenly Father had continued to do at Kasana.

# ANIMAL TRACTION
- from newsletters throughout the years by Richard Casebow

"One of my main goals here is to change the perception of agriculture from one of subsistence drudgery to that of a viable, even enjoyable, living. Currently, this is not the case, with all the heavy digging being done with a hand hoe and a very small reward from the effort put in. Over the last few years, my apprentices and I have been developing ways of mechanizing the local agriculture using oxen and one basic tool, the plough. We can now plough the land, put in planting furrows, weed the crops and make ridges for sweet potatoes. With the addition of a harrow and a card, both of which we have made on site, we can be even more efficient."

❧

"In September we ran an ox training course for some of our older children. It started off as a bit of a wrestling match and a battle of the wills, with broken yokes, bruises galore, and mud and dung everywhere. It was, however, good fun, and it wasn't long before we had pairs of oxen meekly pulling weights and going right and left to the tugs on their halters.

"My ox training career was temporarily halted by one particularly stropping beast who dragged me through a heap of old barbed wire with his halter rope wrapped around my ankle and then proceeded to turn around and tenderize me with his hooves. I must add that this was not supposed to happen! I was supposed to be showing the bullock who was boss by hanging on when he fled, but I tripped on the wire and got wrapped in his rope. I ended up with cracked ribs and several nice deep cuts, which put me out of action for a while.

"In spite of the initial problems, the oxen really make a difference to the cultivations here. Ox ploughing is much quicker than digging with a hoe and much cheaper than ploughing with a tractor. However, ox ploughing is virtually unknown in this part of Uganda with most people digging their fields by hand. If we can prove the benefits of using oxen here, hopefully others will take up the idea and thereby increase the potential for food production in this area."

# THE FAMILY GROWS

Looking back, 1989 and the early 1990s were indeed times of growth for New Hope. The barn was completed and dedicated in 1989, and new staff and children continued arriving. The first classroom block was also opened, and one classroom was able to be used, though the whole building itself was not completed for several more years. Once the barn was completed, it instantly became used for more than just agricultural activities. The carpentry workshop now had a home, accounts had a new "office," there was a place for Sunday school classes to be held even if it was raining, and our growing congregation, which overflowed the classroom it had been using, could meet in the spacious mid-section of the barn. My dad's parents, Jack and Jeanne Dangers, had also joined us in the summer of 1989. Then in 1990, Anna (Nyadoi) Okello and Berna Waiswa were added to the teaching and parenting staff. In 1991, Richard and Alison Casebow and their six-month-old daughter, Emily, joined the Kasana family from Basingstoke, England. Mike and Anne Imusatlaba, Margaret Musinguzi, Michael and Margaret Ejokedeke, Tonny Muwanguzi, Mabel Nayigaga, Margaret Achengo, and Tom and Grace Mwanje were other invaluable additions that joined us in 1992 and 1993. Those days also saw the first streams of teams that have blessed Kasana for years. Teams from Pepperdine University, Oral Roberts University, YWAM, a church in Northern Ireland, Calvary Chapels in California, and a Baptist church in Camarillo, California, brought refreshment and encouragement to the staff and were sources of excitement and new friendships for the children.

Kasana also had its first wedding – two staff members and teachers, Emmanuel and Berna, who had met at New Hope, were married in Jinja. The wedding was certainly a family event! As many as possibly could crammed into our van to make the four-hour trip to attend the wedding. For many of the children, it was their first time in a vehicle! Our little choir sang at their reception, and little Wasswa Michael, one of the newest members of the Kasana family, was their ring bearer. Because most of the children and some of the staff could not attend the wedding, the couple returned for a festive reception in the main classroom at Kasana following their honeymoon!

However, near the end of 1990, while there was a sense of excitement for all that the future held, while we saw the Lord working in ways we had not expected, bringing staff and establishing the work of His hands at Kasana, there were also many struggles. It was during this time that one of Kasana's sons, Ziwa, died of cerebral malaria.

The rumors once again started throughout the village. "You see, they are killing the children!" and several children left for fear that they too might be "killed by the whites." My family's personal funding also began to dwindle during those years. However, the Lord knew this, too, and though His ways are not ours, they bring about the character He wants in us and the blessing He has planned.

Ox ploughing.

New staff family, Tom and Grace Mwanje.

Kamya holding the bucket while Uncle Jonnes
pumped the water from our first bore hole.

# Chapter 16
## *Please Take Your Gun off My Table!*

It was a normal evening in the Dangers' household. Supper was finished, and it was Jamie's turn to do the dishes that night. Mom was sitting at her desk in the living room typing on her manual typewriter a fax she would send to Kampala the next day with Dad. I was sitting working on a writing project, and Dad was reading a story to Joyanne and Josiah. The constant sound of the generator's engine in the shed outside shielded us from outside noises and kept sounds from our own house from drifting across the bush to the villagers and children's houses around.

Abby had been outside barking consistently for at least a half an hour and seemed completely uninterested in coming inside. However, she finally complied to my dad's commands – her hair standing straight on her back, and her muffled barks stubbornly continuing despite dad's strong coaxing to be quiet. Knowing Abby's hunting instincts, we figured there must be a wild-cat or something of that sort outside. If only we had listened!

With no warning, the door opened suddenly; two men dressed in military uniforms pushed their way through the kitchen and into the dining room. One of them was carrying an AK-47 assault rifle.

"Excuse me, sirs!" My dad was on his feet in an instant, and there was anger in his voice. "What are you doing in my home without knocking?"

"Sir, we are with the NRA[54] and have been given a warrant to search your home. Now please sit down, be quiet, and do what you are told!"

---

[54]National Resistance Army – Museveni's army that had defeated the former regime.

"Museveni's men do not do such things," my dad argued, still standing. "Museveni does not allow his men to enter a civilian's home without knocking and without a proper search warrant."

"Sir, I said *sit down.*" The man's voice, though not raised, was growing impatient.

"Yes, and I said, please show me your search warrant first," my dad insisted.

At this, the man's patience was over. Pointing the gun at my dad, he cocked it and said emphatically, "Sit down, sir, and don't make me shoot!" His uniform boasted a captain's insignia. The other man's uniform was that of an enlisted soldier. While such behavior was certainly against current military policies, the men's uniforms did hold authority – not to mention the gun the captain carried.

My dad complied slowly and carefully – reading the man's face as their eyes remained locked together. By this point, Jamie had already hurried into the living room and sat huddled with my mom, who had joined the rest of us on the cushioned chairs that formed a square around the Indian carpet.

"We have instructions to search your home," the man continued, "as we have been informed that you are harboring Kenyan spies."

*Kenyan spies?* I thought, shaking uncontrollably with fear. *We don't even know any Kenyans!*

"And," the man's eyes grew serious, "please make sure you obey all that we are telling you to do. We have one hundred soldiers surrounding your house and land, and all of the children and staff are under arrest and cannot help you."

My mom gasped. The terror in my own heart intensified as I pictured our dear Auntie Sarah, Uncle Jonnes, Sennyonjo, and so many others tied up outside under gunpoint.

My dad's mind raced as he prayed for wisdom to know what to do – this *could* be an empty threat, but it could also be true. Any decision made must be governed by the Lord's wisdom. "Sir, we have we never harbored spies against the Ugandan government," he assured the man. "We do not even know what you are talking about."

But the captain would not listen. As we sat with the gun on us, he ordered the man with him to search the house. After several minutes, he returned.

"There is nothing, sir," he said to his superior. However, we now knew that even if this was a legitimate search, these men were making as much of it as they could: the pockets of the man's cargo trousers that had been empty when he disappeared down the hall were now bulging with things we knew he'd helped himself to. Dad and Josiah hid their watches between their legs as inconspicuously as possible. Mom quickly turned her wedding ring around to hide the diamond and slid her hand between her knees. I felt like I was going to be sick. We'd heard horror story after horror story of missionaries and Ugandans alike being robbed at gunpoint. Some had walked away unharmed. Others were beaten or killed. Memories of the terrors of our time in Kampala flooded my mind as I begged the Lord for mercy and protection for our family, the staff, and the children.

*It's our turn now,* I thought. *I guess it was only a matter of time until we experienced what many others have...Lord, please spare our lives!*

"Sir, if you do not tell us where you've hidden the spies, we will take you away and put you under arrest."

My dad continued to explain that we had no contact with the Kenyan government, nor any spies against the Ugandan government, and that the answer he was giving now would be the same answer he would give even if he was put under arrest. My stomach turned as I thought of what they might do to Dad if they took him away – or what they would do to us as soon as he was gone. I sat visibly shaking as their discussion continued.

Soon, however, the façade of the search warrant was discarded as the private carried armloads of our belongings outside and loaded them into the unlocked van. This was simply an armed robbery.

As the private continued loading the vehicle with all they could fit into it, the captain remained standing in the dining room, he and his gun facing all of us in the living room. My dad, still unwilling to let this man run his household, noticed that the butt of the AK-47 was now resting on our dining room table.

"Sir," he said, "please take your gun off my table! You are going to scratch it."

I was dumbfounded at my dad's boldness and terrified at what the man's response might be. But, to my surprise, with a passing glare, the man lifted his gun off the table. "People's lives are more important than tables," he said.

After the private worked for a while, the captain handed him the gun and proceeded to do his own searching and collecting of goods.

The private's face was far fiercer than that of the captain, and his conversation was scarce. Walking over to my dad, he leaned closely toward him and said, "Give me your watch."

"I've never seen such a look of hatred and murder," my dad recalled years later. "I knew that if it were up to him, my life would have ended as soon as they entered the house. I've never seen anything like those eyes before."

For what seemed like hours, we sat as the two men searched our home, taking with them anything they deemed valuable. And, of all the nights they could have come, this one was the most "fruitful" possible. Because our house served as the ministry office during those days, the amount of cash that was hidden in our home was far more than we would have had as a family. We had just received a donation from England to begin building a new classroom block. Dad had recently exchanged the money (in those days everything had to be done in cash), and it was ready to be used. In addition to this large sum of shillings was over a thousand U.S. dollars in cash that New Hope had helped a recent team exchange into shillings. They had "hit the jackpot."

When the captain came back into the living room to collect whatever valuables were there, the hair on Abby's back stood straight up, and she growled fiercely.

"Sir! Make your dog keep quiet!" he instructed my dad.

Dad petted Abby's head and audibly said, "Abby, be quiet." Then, under his breath, he whispered, "Good dog, Abby. Good dog." Abby's continual low growl kept the men away from the radio and tape deck that sat next to her – at least for the time being.

"Give us the keys to your vehicle!" the man with the gun demanded.

"My assistant has them," my dad said. It was true; he did have a copy of them. However, the men had been hiding in the bushes and watching our house for over an hour before they came in, and so they knew more than we were aware of.

"Yes, but you also have keys. We saw you drive in an hour ago. Now give us the keys!"

The private walked quickly to my dad and took the keys he handed to him.

Finally, after about an hour of sitting under gunpoint, the captain instructed Dad to stand up. *They're taking him away!* my mind screamed! *O God, please protect my dad!*

"Bring your dog with you, sir!" they shouted. "Follow us!"

My dad slowly complied, looking back at each one of us. Standing in the doorway between the living room and the hall, the captain pointed his gun at Dad while keeping a close eye on us. Then he said calmly, "Now, the rest of you stand up quickly."

We were led down the dark hall and herded into my parents' bedroom where they had sent Abby and my dad.

"Remember!" the man shouted, "The house is surrounded by soldiers, and if you try to escape, you will be shot!"

As he turned to close the door, we heard voices – familiar voices. It was Auntie Sarah and Auntie Evelyn! They too were being ushered into the back bedroom. The staff wasn't tied up after all! We children clung to them as they were pushed into the room.

"How is everyone?" my dad asked them. "Has anyone been hurt?"

No. No one was tied up; in fact, no one was even aware that we were being robbed. Evelyn and Sarah had merely come down to see if they could get a ride to town with my dad the next day.

"Praise God everyone is safe!" we all whispered! Then the engine started, and the van peeled out of the driveway.

"You all stay here, and I'll crawl out into the house to see if there is anyone still there," Auntie Evelyn instructed.

"Absolutely not!" my dad replied. Although Evelyn had lived through the war years in Uganda and was accustomed to such times, there was no way my dad was going to send a lady ahead into danger.

Dad carefully crept through the hall, with Evelyn crawling behind him, and opened the back door. The coast was clear - no one was surrounding the house. It had, indeed, been merely an armed robbery with a small band of men, and nothing more.

It wasn't long before the staff and children were notified and came quickly down to be with us, while Dad and Jonnes and other staff men rode off to Kiwoko Hospital to see if we could borrow their vehicles to track the stolen van. The children and women staff helped clean up the back of the house and assess the losses. My room was the only room that had not been touched. Dad's wardrobe was nearly empty, and the radio Abby had so valiantly protected was gone as well. All the money - both personal and ministry - was gone. As we gathered in the living room, someone began to sing. That was all we could do...sing and pray and keep our eyes on Jesus. It was easy to ask why - why had this happened at a time when our personal support was so low we were living off savings? Hadn't we gone through enough trials and tribulations here? Why another one? But God knew, and He had been there with us. As we focused on the words of the songs and prayed together, our hearts were strengthened with the knowledge that He was with us and that He was working all things out for our good and His glory.

*Dad and Kiwoko and Kasana staff searched for the car until late that night, but they were forced to give up when the rain blurred the tracks at a four-way intersection on a dirt road in the town of Semuto. The next day, a radio announcement was made about the robbery, and the following day, someone called the Kampala Police Station to report an abandoned vehicle on Hoima road outside of Kampala. It was ours, but everything else they had taken was gone. The vehicle had simply been used as a get-away.*

꒰ꕤ꒱

The radio crackled as my dad and Josiah, sitting on the living room couch, tried to find the BBC station on the radio we'd borrowed from Uncle Jonnes. It was dark on the evening of January 17, 1991, the day the United States had begun bombing Iraqi positions in Kuwait. The Gulf War was beginning, and our cousin Jeff, who was in the Marines, was on his way over to the Middle East. As Americans faraway from home with a cousin and a nation headed toward danger, we were anxious to hear what the news had to say.

Mom and Dad had also just returned from Kampala and brought with them stacks of mail – Christmas mail (always nearly a month late in Uganda). My mom went to the bedroom to get cleaned up from the dusty round trip to Kampala. Abby was barking loudly outside, so we brought her in so we could hear the radio more clearly. Phil and Cory Schmidt, our teacher and his daughter, and Jamie, Joyanne, and I gathered on the Indian carpet in the living room, instantly engrossed in our letters from home.

"Everyone lie down!" Several men's yells tore through the excitement. "We said LIE DOWN!" Before we could realize what was going on, five men had burst through our door, three of them carrying AK-47 assault rifles. My stomach turned. *Here we go again,* I thought. *HOW could we have forgotten to lock the door?* It was the first night we'd forgotten to do so since that fateful night back in November.

"What are you doing in my home?" my dad quickly jumped to his feet and demanded.

"We are here for one thing and one thing only, and that is dollars!" One of the men rushed forward and shouted, his gun pointed threateningly at my dad. "We want dollars! Now LIE DOWN and tell us where they are!"

"I'm sorry," my dad said, his eyes scanning the room to evaluate the situation as he slowly and reluctantly obeyed, "you should have come two months ago. We had some then, but they're all gone now."

On top of the letters, with the BBC news now clearly blaring in the background, the rest of us had already found space on the small carpet to lie down. Dad joined us and put little Joyanne facedown and lay on top of her – that way, if there was any shooting, his body would shield her from the bullets.

"PUT YOUR HEAD DOWN, SIR! None of you should look at us!" One of the men pointed his machine gun right at my dad's head as the others surrounded us. My dad complied with the command, but put his head up again just seconds later. As he continued to gather information, his initial observations were verified: one man was wearing my dad's jean jacket that had been stolen in the last robbery, and another man was wearing one of Josiah's hats. The two robberies were connected!

"I said we want dollars!" the man's shouting continued. "Now tell us where they are, or we will shoot!"

Jamie, Cory, and I held hands and prayed silently as we kept our faces plastered to the carpet. My mom, still in the bedroom, heard shouting. Immediately aware of what was going on, she wrestled with her thoughts – *Should I go in and be with my family, or break the screen, climb out of the window, and run for help?* If she were to run for help, she would run the risk of being caught – perhaps this time the house really was surrounded by soldiers. Also, if she did not come out, the family would be terrified wondering what had happened to her.

"Come here, madam," the man said gruffly as he turned the gun to where she stood in the hallway. "Come here and lie down quickly." Her presence was a comfort to us children as she lay down next to us, her face too resting on her arms above her head and facing the carpet.

"Go search the house," the man who appeared to be the leader said gruffly to some of the others.

This intrusion in our home was far less "gentlemanly" than the last one.

Within minutes, we heard crashes and shouts from the back of the house as the ransacking began. Plants were knocked over and the pottery that held them smashed; shelves were emptied and turned over. Tearing sheets off the beds, they began to load our belongings into them, tie the sheets into bundles, and carry them outside.

"Sir, I said we want dollars!" the leader in the living room continued shouting. "If you do not give them to us, we will beat you and your children."

"Sir, I told you," my dad looked up again, "men came two months ago and took everything we had."

"If you will not give us dollars, we will beat you!" He repeated himself, then turned to one of his cohorts, "Go and bring me a stick!" Within seconds, a man appeared with a thick stick from a cassava tree. He raised it high, as if to strike, brought the stick down sharply and quickly, then stopped. Another man came running in from the back of the house with my guitar in his hand. Holding it by the neck, he too raised it over his head and prepared to strike, but stopped...or was stopped.

"I think an angel stopped them," we children whispered to each other as our muscles that had prepared themselves for a beating relaxed. While we will never know if it was the men's intention to beat us or to just intimidate us. I remember sensing the Lord's presence so clearly that night, and I would not be surprised at all if an angel had stood in the way and not allowed the "weapons" to make contact with our unprotected backs. While this evening was so much more violent and potentially fearful than the last one, the Lord's Word continued to echo in my ears.

"Though I walk through the valley of the shadow of death, I will fear no evil."

During the next hour and a half as we lay on our faces, the men continued to ravage the house, demanding dollars and threatening us if we would not produce cash. They yelled and threatened, frequently placing the guns on my dad's and Phil's heads. Braver than us girls, Josiah joined my dad and Phil in continuously raising their heads to gather as much information as possible – what the men looked like, what they were wearing, and more. Throughout the evening, the threats of beatings continued, as my guitar and their sticks continued to be swung above our backs toward us.

But we were never touched.

Then the threats were turned toward my dad and Phil: "If you do not give us dollars," they said, "we will take one of you away." We children lay praying that the Lord would protect our dads and that if they were taken, no harm would come to them – or to us while they were gone. As the terror went on above us, we girls began to pray and recite the verses we'd been learning in school that year. When those were exhausted, we began whispering verses we'd learned from years past. Oh, the comfort of the words of truth during the terrors of the night!

"I was not scared at all during the second robbery," Josiah recalled years later. "I just thought, *We've done this before. Let's wait it out and get as much information as we can in the meantime. It will be over soon enough.*"

I, on the other hand, every time the gun was placed on Uncle Phil's or my dad's heads, felt sick to my stomach. "Keep your heads down!" I pleaded with them silently. I knew what they were doing, but in my mind, it wasn't worth it. "Though I walk through the valley of the shadow of death..." I reminded myself. I knew the Lord was with me, with us...but while my heart was at peace, my stomach still churned.

As we lay obediently on the floor, my dad noticed one of the men pick up his shoes that had been sitting next to the carpet. "Sir, please don't take my shoes," he said. "The men that came last time took my other ones and those are the only shoes I have left."

To our amazement, the man set the shoes down and smiled with sickening graciousness. "Don't worry, sir, I will leave your shoes."

Not long after, my dad raised his head again. "Have you ever heard of Jesus?" he said to the men holding the guns above us.

"Yes!" one of the men glared this time. "Jesus was a rich man, and since you are His children, you should also be rich. Where are the dollars?"

After a few more attempts to share the love of Christ with the men, my dad stopped. They were not interested, and the violence and destruction seemed to be increasing. We could hear things being smashed in the back of the house. Then, the men in the back brought out our crate of glass soda bottles. They would open one, take a few sips, and then smash the bottle on the concrete floor. Glass and sticky soda sprayed everywhere across the room.

"Sir, if you don't give us dollars, then we will take one of your children," the leader said with hatred.

"I knew that if they were going to take one of us kids," Josiah later recalled, "that I had better volunteer to go to save the girls."

But Uncle Phil quickly raised his head and spoke before Josiah had a chance. "Sir, you cannot take any of the children," he insisted, "but I will go with you." Instantly one of the men ran over and placed the gun on his head and cocked it. "Silence! We want dollars! Give them to us now, or you will be shot!"

The now old explanation was given again, and the fruitless discussion continued. A gun was then placed on Josiah's head and cocked, and the men told my dad that if he did not give them what they wanted, they would shoot.

"O Jesus!" I cried into the carpet. "Please protect my brother. Please don't let them shoot!"

The scene continued for what seemed like an eternity. Joyanne, still protected by Dad, had fallen asleep and lay peacefully through the storm. Oh, to have "faith like a child"!

Finally, they'd taken all they were interested in from the house and realized that there really were no dollars secretly hidden anywhere.

"Stand up, sir!" the leader shouted at my dad. "And bring your dog with you!"

"O Lord!" we prayed fervently. "Don't let them do anything to Dad!" As Dad stood up slowly and carefully – observing the situation and deciding what his wisest course of action would be for our safety and his own, he looked at the men. We were very aware that they were taking away our main sources of protection – our faithful dog, Abby (who had continued to growl at the men each time they came near her; and Abby very obviously intimidated them), and our dad, and wondered what they might do next.

As had happened in the first robbery, the men led my dad and Abby out of the living room, a gun on them. Mom quickly moved over to cover Joyanne, who still slept peacefully. Then, as soon as Dad had disappeared into the hallway, it was our turn. "Stand up! All of you!" the men shouted. My mom picked up Joyanne, and we quickly obeyed, filing quietly into the hallway. Josiah's eyes never left the men's faces.

We were herded into my bedroom, and the door was locked behind us. But this time, my room had not been left untouched. Instead, in the darkness, we could hardly find a place to stand. The two beds had been knocked on their sides, the mattresses lying on the floor amidst my now-shattered clay pots that had held my numerous plants. Our feet crunched over dirt and the scattered clothes and books that had been left behind. My wardrobe was leaning forward precariously, held up only by an open drawer.

We heard the engine of our now twice-stolen van start up. At least we are all together, I thought, as I saw my dad and felt Abby brush against my leg. Then, I heard what I'd feared most all evening – the sound of machine gun fire. I muffled a scream and grabbed whoever was next to me... only to find out that it was not machine gun fire at all. My oversensitive imagination had translated the sound of my dad tearing the screen to climb out of the window as gunfire. In seconds, my dad was out of the window, now wearing Phil's shoes (which were too small for my dad, but better than nothing). As he ran through the bushes up to the children's and staff houses to sound the alarm and possibly even stop the thieves, Uncle Phil climbed out of the window in his socks and began helping each one of us out into the flower garden outside my window. Our instructions from my dad before he'd left had been to run to the bush and hide there until someone came to tell us the coast was clear. Phil would stay with us until others came, then he would join in whatever chase might take place.

We ran across the yard, feeling very vulnerable on such a moonlit night, and were grateful for the tall spear grass that hid us from whoever might be still lurking near the house. As we sat huddled together on the ground, my mom began to sing:

"You are my hiding place,
You always fill my heart with
songs of deliverance
Whenever I am afraid I will
trust in You.
I will trust in You
Let the weak say I am strong in
the strength of the Lord, I will
trust in You."
– words and music by Michael Ledner, ©1981 Maranatha Music

As one by one we joined in, the words of this beautiful song brought peace, comfort, and boldness to our hearts. He *was* our hiding place. We certainly were still afraid, but a peace that passes understanding filled each of our hearts. We sang one song after another. At this point we didn't even care if we were discovered. Our voices grew louder and louder as the truth of God's Word strengthened our feeble hearts.

We hadn't been hiding for more than fifteen minutes when we heard shouts coming down from the kids' houses. It was the "big boys"! With no shirts on (to be more camouflaged in the darkness) and armed with sticks, pangas, and rocks, they were ready for a fight. We had never been more excited to see Kimera, Sennyonjo, and the others. Uncle Phil left us with the boys and ran inside to get my dad's shoes the soldier said he would leave. Of course, they were not there. So, in his socks, he hopped onto Jamie's little bicycle and peddled as fast as he could to Kiwoko Hospital where Dad and the others had headed once again for vehicle assistance.

Once again, the children and women staff came down to help us put the house back together. This time, the job was far more difficult than before – there was glass everywhere, and what belongings remained were strewn across the house. Once we had brought some sort of order to the chaos, we all once again gathered in the living room to pray and comfort each other. The Ugandans in the room knew exactly the fear that comes from being at the mercy of gunmen, and their prayers for us, their hugs, and tears brought encouragement to our hearts.

*Again, Dad and Uncle Phil were gone until late in the night. This time, though, the van was discovered and brought back that night. The next morning streams of villagers came to offer their condolences to us. "They have stolen 'our van and our things,'" they said, showing that we were truly part of the community and what was done to us was done to them. We received amazing gifts from those who could not afford to give – sheets from Mamma Rose, a dear friend of New Hope and a member of our church, new plates from Jajja Torofisa, one of the children's caretakers, and more. In addition to the support of our local friends, our support from the West also began to grow again. Before the robberies, our family's support had been the lowest it had ever been. However, the Lord used the news of the robberies to remind people that we were still out here, and once again, we had all that we needed.*

# Chapter 17
## Push-ups, Police Stations, and Missionary Detectives
### ⌀⌀⌀

In the days and months after the two robberies, my mom and I struggled to not allow fear to control our lives. We checked the doors countless times each night, jumped at every unusual sound, and slept fitfully. During those days, our house was so separate from any of the others – with thick cassava plantations between us and the rest of the site – that we were an unprotected target. Consequently, while most children in America do regular fire or earthquake drills, we began to carry out regular "robbery drills." There were different scenarios, each with the same basic beginnings. Every window except for the window near the dining room table and the one in the living room across from it was to be closed as soon as it was dark each evening so that we could choose where the robbers would approach the house. The doors were to be locked by dusk and the keys placed out of sight – never left in the door. An extra key was always kept hanging on a nail in the storeroom. We kept an air horn in my parents' room at all times. The most common drill began with Uncle Phil stepping outside to pretend to be a thief, and coming up to the window of the dining room while we were all eating. He would demand for the door to be opened. My dad, pretending to comply with the "thief's" demands, would send seven-year-old Jamie (not me, because I was too scared, and not Josiah, because they might see him as a threat) to the storeroom to get the key. As soon as she entered the storeroom, Jamie was to hit the power switch to turn off every light in the house. The rest of us, then, would hit the floor screaming (something we never did in the drills) so as to drown out the *threats of the men at the window and to take away their control, and crawl as quick-ly as we could to the storeroom. Dad would grab Joyanne out of her high chair, crawl with her to the storeroom, give her to us, and then proceed on to his bedroom. We were to lock ourselves in the storeroom and continue screaming so as to be heard by the staff and kids, while Dad would blow the air horn in the darkness out of the bedroom win-dow. All the staff and children were told that the sound of the air horn meant a break-in or danger of some kind. At that signal, the older boys and staff men would come running down to our house with sticks and stones, ready to grab anyone running away...For Josiah and Jamie, the drills were thrilling. To me, they were a continua-tion of the terror we'd experienced. I knew they were necessary, but I have been eter-nally grateful that we never had to carry out a drill "for real." However, while our home was not broken into again, the story of the robbers continued...*

## This chapter is by my dad, Jay, a "missionary detective."

The stories that follow are pieces of a much longer story that could fill another book. It is a story of one miracle after another, including the salva-tion of one of the thieves. Since it can't all fit here, I've chosen some of the key stories to share with you. I am telling the flesh-and-blood side of the story, but there was most certainly very significant spiritual activity every step of the way. God was with us, and He intervened again and again. He orches-trated many events and enabled us to do things that we otherwise wouldn't have been able to do. He deserves the praise and the glory – we had the fun.

The "we" who had the fun included Jonnes, Phil Schmidt, and me. Sometimes the action was intense; sometimes the boredom was intense. Often, while we were discussing clues and strategy or just waiting, Phil would relieve nerves or entertain himself – and anyone who happened to be around, such as policemen, gas-station attendants and passersby – by doing push-ups. I tried it a few times, but decided I was conspicuous enough with-out this unusual behavior.

"Jay, that man is wearing your shirt! Stop the car! Stop the car!" These frantic words from my wife were the beginning of a wild couple of months chasing robbers.

It had been a first-class "Kampala day." Those who have lived in Uganda understand that phrase – every thing that can take five minutes takes two hours or more. The city just seems to own you until long after you wanted to be home. While waiting for Jonnes and me for "five minutes" in the Entebbe Road fax office, Vicki had wondered why she had even come, and then thought to herself, *Maybe God wants me here to see someone wearing some of Jay's clothing.* She prayed specifically that God would open her eyes to see it. Now, six hours later there he was!

We were still in Kampala at 6:00 in the evening driving on a rough dirt road we had never been on before. I was very unhappy because our "Kampala Day" had, as usual, taken much longer than hoped and prayed for. I didn't want to be on the road after dark because of bandits, and it would be at least two and a half hours before we could get home now, well after dark.

Jonnes was driving the van, Vicki was in the middle of the front seat, and I was by the door. At Vicki's cry, I shoved my head out the window to see who she was yelling about. In the dust rising behind the car I saw a man turning to run as he reached back for his companion. Before Jonnes could get the car stopped (in the middle of an intersection), the men were disappearing behind a house. Before the car stopped I was after them, but they had at least a forty-yard head start. I rounded the house and crashed through a garden of cassava plants that completely blinded me from what was ahead. Suddenly I was out of the cassava and into a sweet potato field. I slowed down, my mind racing to figure out what I was seeing. What happened next happened so fast I only had time to react and no time to understand.

Near me was a man in a long sleeve blue shirt (not mine), and at the far end of the field was another man squatted beside a sweet potato mound. He had no shirt on. No one else was in sight. Jonnes appeared beside me as a horizontal flash as he crashed his way out of the cassava, hit a potato mound, and nose-dived into another. The man near me started sounding an alarm (a bit like a war cry).

*How does that man know we're chasing a robber?*

Then they were off at top speed. *I don't know who I'm chasing, but they seem to know where they are going.* So I took off after them. They rounded the corner of a long narrow house. The house and a nearby barbed wire fence made a narrow corridor down which they ran.

*What is he doing?* As I had rounded the corner of the house I almost ran into the man in the blue shirt who stood there looking confused. I had never seen him, so I didn't have time to deal with him.

*Why is he climbing the fence?* The shirtless man was halfway up the fence. As he saw me approaching him, he came down. Coming toward me with his hands out in a questioning manner, he said, "What is it?"

Jonnes arrived again.

"He's the one!" I shouted as I grabbed his arm, violently twisting it behind his back. Jonnes grabbed the back of the man's trousers, nearly lifting him off the ground to make struggle difficult. "He was the first man through the door in the first robbery."

"I'm a lieutenant in the NRA."

"I know you're in the NRA, but you were wearing a captain's uniform when you came into my house!"

"I'm innocent! I bought the shirt in Owino Market!"

"So, why were you running, and where is the shirt?!"

"I bought it in Owino!"

"So, where is it?"

The questioning was getting nowhere fast, and a crowd was gathering asking what was going on. It was highly unusual to see a white man in this slum, and even more unusual to see one dragging a man away. But as they picked up that the man was a thief, they were ready for mob justice. As the first blows began to land on the man, he suddenly became cooperative. "I hid the shirt under the sweet potatoes." Sure enough, it was right where I'd seen him squatting as I broke through the cassava.

Fearing the crowd's intentions toward the man, we quickly marched the now-willing lieutenant to the van.

At that point I made a mistake that the soldier regretted for weeks. In my enthusiasm to display our trophy to my wife, I directed the man to the window of the car and asked Vicki if she had ever seen him before. Without warning, the fury of the "mother bear" in the front seat was unloaded in a torrent of words: "You scared my children! You...!" I began moving him toward the sliding door at the side of the van, but just as his head was about to enter the van, a man from the crowd smashed a brick into his face – pieces of brick filling his eyes. Seconds later, lying on the relative safety of the van floor, the temporarily blinded soldier again was pleading his innocence. "Madam, I..." He was wasting his breath. His pleas meant nothing to the woman who knew exactly who he was and could feel the terror he had inflicted on her children.

We didn't get home until nearly midnight. In those days there were no telephones, so the children had no way of knowing about the captured robber, the time spent reporting to the local authorities, the trip to the military police post where there was no facility for incarceration, and the escort by military police to the Luwero District Police Post. The children could only sit at home and pray, wait, and sleep fitfully.

---

Before we caught the lieutenant, we had spent weeks investigating the area around Namusale where our emptied van had been recovered the second time. In order not to raise suspicion, we had sent one of our boys, four-teen-year-old Kakonge, to spy out the land. He brought back interesting information. There was an AWOL soldier living at his father's house near the site, and there was another family with several disreputable soldiers in it that lived a couple villages away. We decided to pay the AWOL soldier a courtesy visit and see if I would recognize him. I didn't. However, our new friend, Lieutenant Charles, proved to be invaluable to us later on. His story was simple. He had joined the army to fight for freedom. Now he had no more interest in the military and was waiting for his highly placed father to pull some strings to get him out. In the meantime he had needed a vacation, which we left him to enjoy.

The District Security Officer (DSO) took our robberies and our investigative attempts very seriously. A few nights after we made our big catch in Kampala, a fifty-man military contingent swept through the area around Namusale. Every house was searched, every household questioned. While no guns were found, two AWOL soldiers were arrested.

The next day I was informed by the DSO that I was needed at the military barracks to see if I could recognize either of the arrested soldiers. The first one I had never seen before, but Lieutenant Charles, the second prisoner, was happy to see me. We chatted awhile about his adventure, and then we told him about ours. When I mentioned Lieutenant Kasujja's name, Charles interrupted, "I know Kasujja; I know his brothers, his father, all of them. I know right where he lives. It isn't far from where I live. I can take you there."

I don't know quite how it worked, but it *seemed* to be agreed by the military and the DSO that if Charles would help us with our investigation, he wouldn't have to be in prison. He liked that, and so did we.

Kasujja was a tough guy. In spite of the ease with which we captured him, he refused to divulge any information. The DSO used some "persuasive" techniques on him, but he kept silent. The mob would have killed him, but he knew the DSO would only hurt him. When we let Charles have a few minutes alone with him, however, he became very talkative. He wanted to protect his family, so he was ready to talk. Often what he said was lies, but at least it was talk, and we had something to begin with.

---

We had been dragged all over the place by Kasujja's lies, and the four military police, two regular police, and the Criminal Investigation Department (CID) officer were pretty fed up with the false leads; their patience was gone. Kasujja finally told us where we could find Ali, the man dressed in a private's uniform in the first robbery. The military police were dead serious when they told him he would pay for it if he was lying. He paid for it. He was slammed up against a tree, and some "corporal punishment" was applied to the backs of his legs. When they brought him back to where I waited at the car, he was sweating heavily and his swollen legs were visibly trembling.

The house he led them to hadn't been lived in for months. Apparently it was where they had stashed the loot, but Ali had run off with it the next day when Kasujja and his brother, Kibirige, were off spending some of our money.

While the police had taken Kasujja aside, Jonnes stilled himself to watch the whole situation. A small crowd had gathered. He noticed a girl trembling. She was about ten or eleven years old. She looked terrified. He called her over. Immediately she started talking. "I'm not the one. I'm not the one!"

"Where is he then?"

"It's the other sister, not me. Her name is called Namakula, and I'm a half sister. It's not me, it's her!"

In no time she had told Jonnes where her sister lived, and we were off again. That little girl's information saved Kasujja from a lot more beating and made finding Namakula very easy. Getting from Namakula to her brother, Ali, was not so easy.

The CID officer "interrogated" Namakula, a flirtatious nineteen-year-old, but her coy ways soon left him "twitterpated" and saying, "She has no information. Let's leave her alone."

Jonnes wasn't convinced and took over the rest of the investigation. He placed himself on the grass with his back to the van parked five yards away. Namakula sat a few feet away from him with a good view of the van, its open side door, and the prisoner sitting in the back. After a bit of small talk, Jonnes asked her gently to look at the man in the van and tell him if she had ever seen him before. He watched as her eyes went toward the van, up over the van, and down the other side, carefully avoiding looking at Kasujja. "No, I don't know him," she said. Jonnes knew she had something to hide.

Again he asked her to do the same thing. This time she did as instructed, but lied smoothly, "No, I've never seen him before."

"Take us to where Ali lives," Jonnes coaxed.

For the next several minutes we got a long list of excuses of why she couldn't do that – she didn't know, she had only been there once a long time ago and couldn't remember, she wasn't good with directions, etc., but Jonnes was unmoved. Off we went to the town she had named. After zigzagging around the town following her faltering directions, she finally said, "I'm sorry; I just can't remember where he lives."

"OK," Jonnes said, pretending to have authority that she didn't know he didn't have, "it is either him or you, but one of you is going to go to prison!"

"Oh, I remember; I have a sister who lives here! Maybe she knows."

Within an hour and a half – 7:30, we had found the sister, the unfindable house, checked in with the local police post, coordinated with a military patrol that was in the area because of the high level of crimes there, and set up an ambush. Phil and I were disappointed that we weren't able to watch the action, but the military didn't want this to turn into an international incident if one of us got hit in the cross-fire. We had to wait in the car hidden in someone's backyard.

Charles was positioned on the porch of the landlady's house talking to the landlady. From where she stood, this cooperative woman could see across the courtyard to the road from which Ali would approach his apartment should he come home that night. Inside one of the empty apartments, the military police were stationed with their AK-47 assault rifles ready. If Ali approached, the landlady would signal Charles, then Charles would signal the MPs, who would step out with guns trained.

At about 9:30 the plan worked exactly as planned – it couldn't have gone more smoothly. By the time Phil and I were called to the scene fifteen minutes later, all of "Ali's" possessions were in the courtyard, Ali was stripped to his underpants, hands tied behind his back, and was squatting in a circle of "adrenalinized" MPs. They asked me if I could identify him. That was easy – the second man in the first robbery – the one with hate in his eyes – he had glared into my face from eighteen inches away as he took my watch from me. Tonight he did all he could to avoid letting me see his face. An MP took care of that by yanking his head up to face me.

"Where is the other man?"

"I don't know."

No further questions were wasted. There was a cedar hedge just feet away, and its branches were quickly turned into painful whips. Just a few good strokes on Ali's bare back and his memory improved dramatically. The man's name was Kibirige, he lived in Makerere, and he was Kasujja's brother.

After collecting our possessions (clothes, shoes, a Vitamix, etc.) from among Ali's possessions we all (Phil, Jonnes and I, Charles, two police, CID, four MPs, and two criminals) piled into the nine-passenger van, and off we went. (We let Namakula stay with her forgotten sister as they obviously needed some family time.)

We arrived at Makerere about 1:00 a.m. The streets of this slum were empty and quiet. We parked the car in front of a shop about fifty yards from the house Ali and Kasujja had indicated. Again, Phil Schmidt and I had to sit and wait along with one of the MPs. Phil climbed out of the car and began doing push-ups. I was happy to have the MP's company because Ali was telling me with his eyes that he would rather kill me than look at me. I had little confidence in the rope with which he was tied.

The rest of the party arrived at the door of the house. With a gun to his back, Kasujja knocked on the door and identified himself to the occupants. The instant the door began to open, Charles and the MPs charged into the one-room house. While Kibirige still lay on the bed with their children nearby, his terrified wife began offering information – the neighbor had the radio. Seconds later Charles was through the neighbor's door just in time to see him shoving our radio under the mattress. A fist to the jaw by Charles ensured that the neighbor knew who was in charge and that the radio wasn't his.

I recognized Kibirige from the second robbery, but both Ali and Kasujja now identified him as the third man dressed in civilian clothes (whose face we never saw) in the first robbery – the robberies were now officially connected. We later found out that the second robbery was staged to get money to bribe Kasujja out of prison – he had been caught during an unrelated robbery.

Minutes later we were off again to the other side of the valley, having added Kibirige and his neighbor to the entourage. Kibirige knew where Kabonge (the one who kept threatening to hit us with the guitar and the cassava stick) lived. We collected Kabonge and our two soda crates and then went to pay his sister a visit at 2:30 in the morning. Her place was amazing. It was another one-room place, and she occupied it with several other women and heaps of clothes that covered every bed and most of the floor. Thankfully she hadn't yet unpacked our suitcases, so identifying our things was very quick and easy.

At this point there was no more room for criminals or anyone else to be added to the van, so we didn't arrest Kabonge's sister. We proceeded straight to the nearest police station to deposit the night's catch before we went after the last two robbers. However, we had to wait for morning to arrest Paulo, Kasujja's younger brother. He had been arrested earlier that day for attempting to destroy a military uniform – government property. In the morning we added him to our collection. The remaining robber, Kanyonkole, managed to elude us entirely.

⊱⊰

Since the day of our big catch some weeks earlier, Jonnes and I had returned to caring for our families and the children back at Kasana. Occasionally we would get an idea and race off to the police station, collect some police to make our investigations official and a criminal or two to answer questions, and head for Kampala or to the village where Kasujja was from.[55] God blessed our efforts time and time again, and eventually we had recovered about two-thirds of all we had lost, including a video camera, sewing machine, bicycle, guitar, clothing, and bedding.

On one of our last days of investigation we had Ali lead us to the man to whom he had sold my camera and camera equipment. The trail led us all over the city and to the car Ali had bought with our money. Finally we had my camera, case, lenses, and flash and were done for the day.

It was about 9:00 at night, and we were moving slowly through traffic with thousands of pedestrians weaving in and out of the cars on Luwum Street by the bus park. In the front seat it was Jonnes at the wheel, the CID was in the middle, and I was by the door. In the next row was another CID officer, one of our staff members, Joseph Ruyondo, and by the door, John, our favorite policeman. Things were quiet, and John had laid his AK-47 on the floor. In the back were Ali and the man we had arrested for trying, knowingly, to sell the stolen goods. Ali's hands *had* been tied.

"He's out!" came a voice from the back of the van.

Glancing quickly over my shoulder, I saw Ali's hands disappear out the back side window. The rest of him was already gone!

What happened next was pure adrenalin and chaos. The door wouldn't let me out because I had rested my arm on the lock! John couldn't get a handle on his gun. Joseph leaped out after John, and his shoe fell off.

At last I was out and running. John rounded the back corner of the van firing two shots into the air. The crowd dropped to the ground as though trained. Military-trained Ali hardly slowed at all as he sprinted away on all fours. He had crossed the street and was moving swiftly through the Caltex station on the corner. John was thirty yards behind Ali, and I was five more yards back.

---

[55]In Uganda, one must provide transport, food, and fuel for the police if one really wants a case to be solved.

Ali disappeared into the darkness at the other side of Caltex and turned up the nearly deserted street by Nakivubo Stadium at full sprint. John was entering the darkness. *What?! The bottoms of both his shoes at the same time? That's his gun I hear on the pavement! He's out of the race; it's up to me!* Then I knew what happened to John. The big black chain that caught him across the thighs bounced, catching me across the stomach. But then I was over it and off again.

I could see Ali fifty yards away and moving fast. I have no idea how he missed the chain. There was more light now, and far ahead I could see a large crowd. Ali was headed straight for it.

Behind me and unbeknownst to me, John had picked himself up off the pavement, looking frantically for his gun. In those short seconds a bystander had grabbed the gun and was running away with it! John caught him with his fist, wrestled the gun from him, and turned to join the race.

Ali entered the crowd and was lost to my view. I was sure I was wasting my time. This wasn't a good part of town, and I wasn't sure what kind of reception I would receive from the crowd. I charged on. Then, just before I reached the sea of people, out from the crowd coming straight toward me was Ali, a policeman holding each arm! I must confess that at that sight my adrenalin got the best of me, and I greeted Ali with two fists in the stomach.

The two policemen had been alerted by the shots John had fired and grabbed the right man as he fled through the crowd. Once again, God had intervened, doing what we couldn't have.

*And so the rumors began...Kasana has great "medicine"! One should never steal anything from New Hope, for they have the ability to find anything that was stolen and even catch those who stole from them! Of course we knew Who carried the source of our success, and with great excitement, we were able to share with the villagers around us of Jesus Christ, Who cares for His children and makes the impossible possible. God also demonstrated His great mercy when Uncle Jonnes, who was visiting the men in prison, was able to lead Kabonge to the Lord! He died just weeks later from AIDS, but we rejoice to know that the grace of God spared him, and we will see him one day in heaven!*

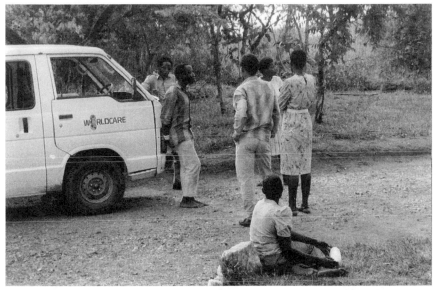

Sarah, Evelyn, Emmanuel, Jajja Torofisa, and the policeman surrounding the thief.

# Chapter 18
## *Family Life*

⋄∼⋄

*It is impossible to tell the whole story of New Hope – the daily laughter, tradi-tions, dangers, and frustrations. This chapter is a collection of my siblings' and my memories, of staff members' recollections, of newsletter clips, and of short stories of life in Kasana. I hope you enjoy reading each vignette as much as I enjoyed putting them down on paper!*

## ENSWERA![56]

"A good critter tale is our Easter Monday snake hunt," wrote Richard Casebow in his newsletter dated August 2000. "Not so much a hunt, I guess, as a full-scale assault on an identified enemy."

"Omusota! Omusota!"[57] At the sound of this alarm, every able-bodied male at New Hope drops whatever he is doing, picks up any "weapon" he can find, and runs in the direction of the cry.

"Josiah!" panted Lutwama, one of our boys who had run to find my brother. "There is a big snake up in the tree by the administration office." Josiah dropped what he was doing and ran with Lutwama up the hill. Already a crowd had gathered.

"Enswera!" people kept saying. A mamba or a cobra. It was in the top of a very tall tree and would require a very careful strategy to bring it down so it could be killed. Several guys with rocks light enough to throw far but big

---

[56]Cobra or mamba
[57]"Snake! Snake!"

enough to do some damage were stationed on one side of the tree. On the other side was a huge group of guys waiting with big sticks to attack the snake once it had been dislodged.

As soon as the signal was given, all the boys with rocks began throwing them as high and hard as they could, hoping to knock the snake out of the tree. However, the tree was so tall and the snake so high that even if the snake was hit, the rock had lost momentum and the mild pelting only served to irritate the snake.

"After an hour of stone-lobbing and catapulting, which must have sent half a ton of rock skywards," Richard continued his narration of the story, "the snake still hadn't suffered a direct hit and was dithering about on a high branch, probably wondering if gravity had been reversed and the ground was falling past him! Assuming that this was, in fact, a cobra, we needed to make sure that this one did not get away, so I (foolishly) suggested that I go and get the chain saw, climb the tree, and cut down the branch that he was on."

Strapping the chain saw onto his back, Richard began to climb up the tree until he reached the snake.

"Richard was able to cut off the branch the snake was on, and we all stood ready with sticks to beat the snake to death," Josiah reminisced, "but as the branch fell, the snake just jumped from that branch to another one. Soon Richard came down with a concerned look on his face."

"There are three things I'm afraid of," he said, "chain saws, heights, and big black snakes that have had rocks tossed at them for an hour! You combine the three, and I can't take it!"

"As we were trying to figure out what the best course of action was now that the chain saw idea did not seem to work," my brother recalled, "Dad said, 'Josiah knows how to use a chain saw, and he's not afraid of snakes or heights.'

"So, I strapped the chain saw on my back," Josiah laughed at a typical "Dangers volunteer" opportunity, "and climbed about thirty feet up into the tree. I got into a safe position and began cutting the first branch that the snake was on. The branch didn't break suddenly, but just gradually swung down and deposited the snake on a branch between me and the ground. By this time, I'd gotten a good look at the snake and knew for sure it was a black mamba about five and a half feet long.

"The black mamba is the fastest and most aggressive snake in the world, and one of the most deadly as well. They are also the only snakes known to attack humans unprovoked – and we had been throwing rocks at this one for more than an hour!

"My situation wasn't looking too promising. The snake was now *between* me and the ground! I half expected that I'd have to jump out of the tree because I thought it was going to attack. Just in case, I had the people below clear out two areas – one where I could throw the chain saw and one to where I could jump. I climbed very cautiously down the other side of the tree from where the snake had been and made my way down to the branch that it was on. It was about fifteen feet out on a branch. So I started cutting that branch. I was sure it was going to start coming toward me and I'd have to jump the twenty feet to the ground. Fortunately, though, it stayed at the end of the branch, and I was able to cut all the way through the branch and it fell to its death. There, on the ground, it was pounded to shreds by the dozens of onlookers."

"It wasn't a cobra after all," Richard concluded, "but, in the absence of a decent snake ID book and a hydraulic platform to get up there to get a good look, he had to go!"

# BUSH FIRES AND WATER FIGHTS – A KASANA CHRISTMAS

Christmas in Uganda, the hottest and driest time of year, is usually right in the middle of the year's longest dry season. Most of the year temperatures range around the 70s and 80s, and there is humidity due to heavy rainfall. December's and January's average temperatures are usually around 95 degrees Fahrenheit. The grass begins to turn brown, the wind is hot and dry, dust whirlwinds become common, and the ground is hot beneath one's feet. One year, my mom decided we must have been in Uganda too long when my little sister Joyanne came running home shouting, "Mommy, look! The grass is getting brown! It's almost Christmas!"

There are countless traditions that make Kasana Christmas times some of my favorite childhood memories. School is out for the year for the Ugandan kids (Ugandan schools follow the calendar year), and while many children go home to visit relatives, those that do not have relatives stay around. When Kasana was still small, all of the children that remained would be divided up to spend the Christmas holidays with different staff families. With excitement, Josiah, Jamie, Joyanne, and I would rearrange our rooms to accommodate as many Kasana kids as possible. Mom would begin planning menus that would feed an army and that would also satisfy both Ugandan and American tastes. Evenings would be filled with Bible stories, games, or Christmas caroling around the site or at a campfire on Christmas night.

During one Christmas holiday, after a particularly enjoyable time of Christmas caroling, someone suggested, "Why don't we all head to Kiwoko to sing?" And so we did! The lorry was quickly driven to the roundabout, where about thirty excited children waited, relishing the spontaneity of the occasion. We all climbed into the back of the lorry and headed in the dark to Kiwoko Hospital. After caroling to the staff there, we were allowed to go into the wards and sing to the patients and nurses and doctors on duty.

Another Kasana Christmas "tradition" is fighting the many wildfires that spread rapidly during this hot and dry time of the year. Often, there is plenty of time to react to the blaze. A small cloud of smoke is seen off in the distance, and a group of men and boys volunteer to jump into the lorry and head towards the fire. However, other times, there is no warning at all. The sound of nearby crackling or an occasional piece of ash floating on the wind communicates imminent danger, and a quiet afternoon can suddenly become a desperate attempt by anyone available to beat out the fire and protect the grass thatched roofs of the children's houses.

One dry season day, my siblings and I were sitting in our little classroom located in our front yard. Auntie Laurena, a staff member from Langley, British Columbia, and one of our teachers, was our babysitter that day. Our parents and many other staff members had gone into town for various missions. It was nearing lunchtime, and we children were having a hard time concentrating. As the heat intensified, we began to think of lunch. But then our daydreams were interrupted by Auntie Gertrude's quiet call for Auntie Laurena.

"I'm so sorry to interrupt," she said. "Could I talk to you for a minute?"

When Auntie Laurena returned to the classroom, she had a concerned look on her face. "Well guys, she said. "Class is over for the morning, and we've got company!"

Poor Auntie Gertrude had just received unexpected guests – an entire carload of men were on her doorstep. From both Canada and Uganda, they had sent several messages letting us know they would be arriving to visit Kasana, but we had not received a single one. (We did receive one of the messages a couple of weeks later!) They were here to visit the site, meet with the leaders if possible, and spend the afternoon here.

During the time when trips to Kampala were few and far between, our grocery supply often varied drastically. We would all stock up during one trip to Kampala, and go again when there was almost nothing edible left in our houses. This was one of those days. The Bakimi household had almost nothing left, and the Dangers' household was not far behind.

"I am very happy to come and help you cook," Auntie Gertrude had said, "but I just don't have enough food to cook at my place for this many people!" Assuring her we would see what we could do, Auntie Laurena called upon the "team" to race into the kitchen and see what we could find.

Each of us was pretty sure what we would find in the house – enough leftovers to feed the four of us lunch and nothing else. We raced into the kitchen and began scrounging around for anything. Amazingly, we found some rice and pounded groundnuts, which we quickly threw together as a makeshift meal to serve our waiting guests (and they were, by the way, extremely gracious). After the meal the men went off for a tour of the site.

Suddenly, we saw *them* – just a few flakes of soot floating on the wind. Seconds later, we could hear the crackle of dried grass burning not far away. Within minutes, the fire was coming closer and closer – heading straight for the generator house! We ran quickly to remove the generator and jerry cans of fuel. It was then that we realized this fire was not just coming from one direction, but two! If something did not happen quickly we would be surrounded. The flames were not just spreading through the dry elephant grass and bush; they were leaping from treetop to treetop and, consequently, spreading far more rapidly than usual. Areas where a well-worn path would break the density of the brush and would have stopped the fire from spreading did nothing to stop the intensity of the flames, which leapt over the bare ground without slowing down at all.

Running into the house, Laurena grabbed our air horn, reserved only for emergencies such as armed robberies and, now, fires. After several short bursts of the horn, the Kasana boys began to appear out of nowhere – and with them our visitors! We suddenly knew *why* the Lord had sent all these men so unexpectedly! On a day when nearly all the Kasana men were gone, we would not have had enough "manpower" to put out the fire. Our all-knowing Father, therefore, had sent a whole team to help us! After nearly an hour of fighting the fire with branches, soil, and buckets of water, the soot-covered group of men we had first seen as an unexpected burden were now heroes! The house was saved, we were safe, and we once again thanked the Lord for His perfect orchestration of every aspect of our lives!

<hr />

The battle lines were drawn. "On your marks, get set, BEGIN!" my dad shouted. But instead of lunging forward, the four groups slowly began inching toward each other, their "weapons" in hand. While some of our Kasana water fights were spontaneous and completely chaotic, others were strategic and intentional! It was New Year's Day and time for our favorite New Year's tradition. We were evenly divided into teams according to age and size, with equal numbers of staff and children. Each team was given the *exact* same amount of water – three small basins full and two large ones. Each child or staff member carried a full cup or small bucket of water – their weapon for the fight! The goal – to be the driest team by the end of the battle!

The excitement in the air was tangible. No one wanted to be the first to be soaked; every drop of water was precious. The boundary lines were clearly marked; then the first brave soul threw his water toward the "enemy." The fight had begun! The air was instantly filled with shrieks of laughter as water flew everywhere! The strategy was always to determine how close one could get to the enemy for your "ammunition" to hit its target while avoiding the opponent's ammunition.

Usually, the first to get soaked were the ones who later went fearlessly into "enemy territory" while their drier team members stayed further behind providing ammunition or quietly stalking an unsuspecting adversary who was chasing someone else. What fun we had! Truly, those who got soaked were not upset – the heat of the day made the cool water a welcomed relief.

When the last drop had been used from the last basins, the whistle was blown and a cease-fire declared. Each team would then line up, and the judges would be called upon to determine which team had come out of the fight the driest. Of course, often as soon as the winning team was announced, a bucket of water from out of nowhere often "happened" to land on the driest person, and what ensued next was pure and hilarious chaos!

"Auntie Alison?" Sande and Josiah tried to make their voices sound as innocent as possible. "Could you come out here and help us with something?" Oh, if only she had remembered what time of year it was and which two boys were asking her to come outside! No sooner had she stepped onto the verandah than she was drenched from head to toe! They had chosen their timing perfectly and knew that their "victim" was one who would *love*

to join in the fight. Soon, nearly everyone on site was involved! Running through the bushes, the entire site was "in bounds." Many staff and children who had hidden in their homes were dragged out, laughing and screaming, and then doused with water! No one was safe, and by the end not a single person was dry!

# CHRISTMAS DAY

From a newsletter by Richard Casebow

"Christmas at Kasana begins at Christmas time. Perhaps a week or so before Christmas Day the realization dawns that something needs to be done, and a committee is hastily rounded to organize the celebrations. We live in community, and so our celebrations are as a community; we are a Christian community, and so our celebrations are all about Jesus coming to earth for us.

"Christmas Day starts in the wee small hours of the morning. Long before the cock crows, the blackness is punctuated by smoky hurricane lamps casting shadows of people heading for the small kitchens built behind the main homes. The night noises of the bush are joined by muffled conversation, the sound of splintering firewood, and the crackle of kindling as the cooking fires come to life. Around the flickering flames, the children bend to the task of peeling sweet potatoes and matooke, preparing vegetables and sorting rice. One or two are dispatched to go and cut banana leaves to wrap the food in before steaming it in the large blackened cooking pots.

"Elsewhere, the young men are up to a more sinister pursuit. Somewhere, off in the darkness, a pig grunts its annoyance at being woken from its warm bed, and then squeals in protest as it is led off. A young bull, bought the day before, is being led to a clearing amongst the trees.

"Church at Christmas is the main time in the year to dress up, so everyone does their best. From the small, dusty children from the surrounding villages in their 'too big' shorts tied together with banana fiber and new t-shirts to newly married couples in their flouncy and fantastic wedding clothes.

Our family makes an effort, too; the girls are beautiful and the boys sport both ties and clean knees.

"The service is packed and boisterous – full of praise and thanksgiving for the wonderful gift of grace, sent to earth as a little baby. We sing and praise and give testimonies. The drummers' hands are a blur as they pound out the rhythm, trickles of sweat running down their faces as the temperature rises. Different families take it in turn to bring the contributions: some sing, some act out a short skit, some read.

"Throughout the service, the women and older girls straggle in, released at last from their kitchens and able to dress up for the occasion. Some of the pig crew, however, are still hard at work, hollowing out an anthill and filling it with charcoal, ready to receive the carcass, now neatly lashed to a pole. The charcoal is lit, and soon the pig is gently lowered into the hole to begin to cook.

"Christmas lunch is served to around two hundred guests in all, under the mango and jackfruit trees in our back garden. Everyone brings a contribution of food to add to the barbecued pig, the beef stew, the kebabbed goat and the chicken. There are potatoes, sweet potatoes, matooke, cassava, peanut sauce, fried cabbage, and chapattis, then to finish up, a small square of cake.

"There are also crates of Coke and Fanta bottles, which are cooled down by tying a rope to each crate and lowering it into our underground rainwater storage tank where each one sits in the cool water until all the guests arrive and the feasting begins.

"The feast is served by the ladies from long tables to a plate-carrying queue. Then we all sit down under the shade trees and eat and talk and laugh together. The fruit of hours of preparation is soon demolished and the remains are cleared away in readiness for the next event – the games!

"The games are a mixture of team games and dancing, but they inevitably include imports from the U.S. and U.K., such as the Chicken Dance and the Hokey Pokey. With laden bellies, but willing hearts, we all do our best, and as the afternoon cools into evening, more energetic games such as volleyball are even played.

"As we fall exhausted into bed at the end of the day, we are surrounded with all the night noises of Africa – the crickets, the tree frogs, the bats, and night birds, all joining the sound of drums from far and near across the bush as the village people celebrate on into the night."

# FIRE!!!

"Two nights ago, Vicki and I were sitting in our living room about 9:00 with some friends," my dad wrote in a newsletter dated February 1995. "We heard the footsteps of someone running up to the house. I knew that there was trouble! Just then, he yelled, 'The chicken house is on fire!' Because we live at the opposite end of the site from the chicken houses, we were about the last people to know. By the time I got to the scene of the fire, the papyrus roof was completely gone, and it was immediately obvious that there was nothing to save. It was only a matter of keeping an eye on things to make sure that the fire didn't spread to the big grass thatched chicken house that was only about four yards away! By the grace of God, the wind was not blowing the direction that it normally does, which would have been directly toward the big house!

"By North American or British standards this would have been a very small loss," my dad continued, "but by our standards, it was a pretty big loss. Richard Casebow, our agriculturalist, has been working to build up our laying stock and get them in a rotation so that every three months a new batch of hens comes into lay and an old batch is 'retired.' What was lost in this fire was ninety hens, which is the main part of six months of the rotation, and four hundred fifty brand-new chicks. Some of these chicks belonged to our staff, who had formed a cooperative to help them get some extra cash on the side. For them, this was a very big investment. The walls are all that remain of that unit. The cause of the fire is not clear. At first we suspected that it would be the brooder that has heat produced by a charcoal fire, but that doesn't seem to be indicated. The only other possibility that we can come up with is arson, but there are no suspects and we don't know of any enemies who would have done such a thing. It seems that we will never know for sure."

# A Sermon Delivered Unconsciously

It had been a routine surgery to repair a hernia Kalera had for some time. The operation had gone smoothly, and another one of our boys, Rukundo, was sitting on the hospital bed next to Kalera waiting for the anesthesia to wear off. Little did Rukundo know he was certainly in for more than just keeping Kalera company during his recovery!

"Excuse me, everyone!" Kalera's voice rang out through the men's ward. "May I have your attention?" To this day, Kalera has no recollection of the events that transpired in the following minutes.

"This is not me speaking!" he announced as soon as he had the attention of all the patients throughout the male ward. "This is the Holy Spirit speaking through me."

As everyone stared, Kalera, who had been speaking in English to a largely Luganda-speaking audience, called upon Rukundo to begin translating for him. Still unaware of what he was doing due to the medication he had been given during the surgery, Kalera proceeded to preach the gospel to his captive audience. Once his message had been made clear, Kalera then went ahead to quote the entire Twenty-seventh Psalm for good measure.

"The Lord is my light and my salvation," he declared. "Whom shall I fear? The Lord is the stronghold of my life – of whom shall I be afraid?...Though my father and mother forsake me, the Lord will receive me...I am still confident of this: I will see the goodness of the Lord in the land of the living."

With confidence and a smile, from his bed Kalera then called out, "Is there anyone who would like to give his life to the Lord today – anyone who would like to be saved?" When hands went up in positive response, Kalera directed Rukundo to go and pray with each person who had been convict-ed!

When the news of Kalera's sermon arrived back at Kasana, the staff not only had a good laugh, but was so blessed to see that the roots of the gospel had gone so deeply into Kalera that they would be manifested even when he was unconscious! The time they had spent investing in Kalera, praying for him and with him, training and guiding him, was already beginning to bear fruit – and he didn't even know it!

# "BLACKBIRDS"

"I want to tell you about one group of children that we have here that we very affectionately call the 'Blackbirds,'" my dad wrote in a newsletter in February 1995. "They got this name because of their size (our littlest boys ages six to ten), their color, of course, and the fact that during the holidays, Saturdays, and other times when they have nothing on their schedule, they would alight on one staff member's lawn, stay there for some time, and then 'fly off' to another staff lawn. Though these 'Blackbirds' are not flawless in behavior, they are a delight and I get very excited to think of the potential that they have to become well-trained fathers and craftsmen and leaders in the community. Please pray for these 'Blackbirds' and for those of us to whom it has been given to raise them."

"I also remember being fond of the slightly older boys," Paul Kessel's nar-ration adds to my dad's memories. "Alex Mwesigwa, Kalera, Rukundo, Wass-wa John, Mulindwa, Mubeezi...so many of them! I really remember just lov-ing after work how they would mill around and do whatever. I just loved vis-iting with them. Saturday mornings were spent cleaning, gardening, and working in the houses. But Saturday afternoons were when they would be listlessly milling around looking for something to do, and I liked that! I just tried to be available for whoever came blundering around. They would meander over and begin playing with our kids, or beg me to tell them sto-ries! They were especially amused that we white people hunted – it didn't seem quite like what white people would do. So they were always prodding me for hunting stories, and they didn't have to prod very long...!"

## FILLING IN WHERE THERE'S A NEED!

"This school year I have been having a new experience!" my dad wrote in a newsletter in 1995. "I'm the new P1 teacher! P1 is the equivalent of a North American kindergarten/first grade combination. I'm just filling in and training our new P1 teacher. It is a great experience that I'm enjoying very much, and actually, word has it that the students are also enjoying it very much! I want to tell you about some of my pupils. Talemwa Kaleb (Talemwa means 'He never fails,' meaning that God never fails) seems amazingly alert and bright considering that earlier in his life he was so badly malnourished that his hair is very thin, straight, and almost blond. Talemwa is different than most of my other students in that most of them have lost one or both of their parents due to AIDS, and he lost his father in the war. His mother, who is still alive, was on the run with other refugees of the war and unable to provide him with the nourishment that he needed. His mother has been unable to provide education for him and lives quite a ways away from here, so he will be a boarding student.

"About half of my twenty children have never held a pen, pencil, or crayon before in their lives. In fact, I don't think they have ever even had a piece of paper to write on. This is in spite of the fact that some of my students are much older than the usual six-year-olds one would expect. I have some aged between eight and twelve, though because of malnutrition, many look like they are the right age for the class. They are all eager to learn and are trying very hard. After I have given them a demonstration on how to make a letter, their little hands often just quiver as they try to get a signal down to it to make it the shape that I've described. I then have to take their hand in mine and repeatedly cause it to make the required shape. Gradually the letters start happening with less and less of my input. Often an 'n' looks like it was run over by a truck and an 'f' looks like a palm tree caught in a hurricane, but there is real progress! I have been interested to see the difference that even one day can make in the quality of their work. New letters begin to come more easily than previous new letters did as they begin to get used to holding the pencil and making small, careful shapes.

"My main aim for them for this year is to be able to read and write their own language, Luganda, even if they don't learn anything else. We cannot always be sure how long a child will be with us, and if they are taken away from us by some relative and they never get a chance to go to school again, I want them to at least be able to leave knowing how to read their Bibles. We are using the 'Writing Road to Reading,' phonogram method, which we have redone for Luganda, and things are moving along very well."

# HAVE YOU HEARD ABOUT
# KASANA'S SPECIAL "MEDICINE"?

Uncle Jonnes was standing in Kiwoko town waiting to purchase something at a local shop. Once again, our generator had just been stolen, and the Lord had miraculously led us to the place where it had been hidden. "I heard they have special medicine at Kasana," the shopkeeper was telling his first customer. (In Uganda "special medicine" refers to witchcraft related potions and powers.) "I think I even know where they hide it." Smiling that he had not been recognized, Uncle Jonnes chose to continue listening in on the conversation instead of revealing who he was. "Are you serious?" the customer asked in amazement. "It must be so powerful to be able to make the generator be found again. It certainly isn't wise to steal from that place. Their powers will make you fail." The conversation went back and forth as the two men speculated about the special medicine "Dangers" must have brought from the U.S., or maybe even Uncle Jonnes brought from Kabaale. Unable to remain silent any more, Uncle Jonnes, still unrecognized by the men who were speaking of him, stepped in.

"Actually, I know what their medicine is – and let me tell you, it *is* powerful!" he said, smiling confidently. The two men stared at him incredulously. Maybe he could tell them where it was; maybe he had access to it himself!

"Actually, the name of our 'medicine' is Jesus! He is the King of kings and the Lord of lords! He knows everything, sees everything, nothing is impossible for Him, and He cares for His children in amazing ways!" And, never needing encouragement to share his faith, Uncle Jonnes proceeded to share with these two lost men the truth of the power of Jesus Christ and all that He had done in his own life and in Kasana.

## THOUGHTFUL THUGS
### – from Richard Casebow's newsletter, dated May 2001

"I was sitting in a management meeting when Chris Sperling, one of our colleagues, came running to find us. Between breaths, he explained to us that he had been held at gunpoint, just outside our main gate, and that the Kiwoko farm pickup had also turned up just at that moment. The gunmen had taken Chris' money and then driven off in the hospital farm pickup in the direction of Kiwoko. Our first thought was to alert the Luwero Police so that they could get word out and set up a roadblock. So (forgetting that wonderful new technology, the telephone!) I jumped on my motorbike and, with another member of staff on the back, rushed off toward Kiwoko to tell the police there.

"We assumed that the thieves would just drive straight through Kiwoko, but as we approached the town, I noticed a couple of people running and a column of black smoke rising into the sky. Those of you who know Africa will know that people don't ordinarily run anywhere, so I got suspicious and stopped the bike just on the outskirts of the little town and asked what was going on. The gunmen, rather than just driving through Kiwoko, had made straight for the police post, shot a police lady in the leg, stole all the guns, and then set it alight. We had turned up just after they had left, traveling in the direction of the hospital. We were just discussing what to do next and what was likely to be happening at the hospital, when all of a sudden, a vehicle started coming from that direction and everyone started running for the bush. Being conspicuously white and on my bike right in the middle of the road, I decided to do likewise, whipped the bike round the back of a building, and ran with the rest of them, taking refuge in the undergrowth until the 'all clear' filtered back to us. Apparently, they had driven on past the hospital without stopping, and the vehicle we had seen was totally unconnected with the incident!

"It eventually transpired that these weren't just ordinary thieves, but were part of a rebel group trying to get guns and destabilize things before the elections. They had hijacked a vehicle further up our road and then done a vehicle exchange at our front gate. As they drove off, they said that the pickup would be left further down the road. Nice of them, I thought! However, when the pickup was found, its contents were missing. The farm manager had been on a shopping trip to buy goodies for the farm Christmas party and was just finishing up by coming to us for some chickens. The gunmen had distributed all the goodies to the local people where they left the vehicle as a gesture of goodwill! I think they were all caught a month or so later, and we certainly haven't heard any more of them and their group!"

## ANOTHER SNAKE STORY!

It was 9:30 at night, and my parents were on their way to the secondary school site to make a phone call. After years of driving to Kampala to make phone calls to the U.S. or anywhere else, we had moved into the phenomenal stage of being able to get a phone signal at the secondary school! It was 1999, and we were certainly moving into the "modern age"!

As they drove up to the gate, the headlights of the car fell across a huge snake lying next to the road.

"I knew right away that it was a python, and I went after it with the car," my dad recalled with excitement. My poor mother on the other hand, in the early stages of pregnancy, was suffering from "morning sickness" at night. But there was nothing else to be done. For the next several minutes my dad, all his boyish hunting instincts fully awakened, raced around the field in the big, heavy 4x4 trying to kill the snake with the car. As the snake slithered to escape the crushing weight of the tires, my dad chased it, slammed on the brakes as soon as the tires rolled over it, shoved the car into reverse, and laid scratch as he backed over the writhing snake. He made dozens of passes over the enormous creature; it certainly was a wild ride!

"Vicki was having a terrible time," my dad recalled. "She was terrified at the thought of this monstrous snake escaping and being a danger in the area, but at the same time was revolted at the sight of its writhing body and its head rising up in the headlights some two to three feet off the ground! On top of that, the wild ride was making her increasingly nauseated."

Finally, the snake, injured but still fully able to move, escaped off of the soccer field, just out of reach of the tires. Though it had been driven over dozens of times, my dad knew that it could easily survive and be a danger to the community if he did not finish it off.

"As soon as I knew I couldn't get the snake with the car anymore, we raced back to the main site where I left Vicki to recover at home," my dad continued.

The phone call would just have to wait! Needing no prodding to join in on the hunt, a crowd of older boys jumped into the car and onto the roof rack armed with machetes, axes, and hoes, whooping and hollering their "war cries."

Stunned from its terrorizing experience minutes before, the snake was still where my parents had left it.

"One blow with an axe by Jonnes and it was over," said my dad, "except for the stir caused when we arrived back home with our excited army and a ten-foot, eight-inch trophy!"

## BOSCO AND THE WHEELCHAIR

"It can't be *that* difficult," Bosco insisted. "I'm sure I could do it just as well!" All the Worcester family children were gathered in the family banda (African style gazebo), and a heated debate was taking place.

"Me too," shouted another overly confident young man. "Bosco, I bet I could even beat you in a wheelchair race."

"No," disagreed one of the younger children. "Uncle Francis just makes it looks easy because he's been doing it for so long! I don't think you could do it, Bosco!"

The debate was about their family father, Uncle Francis, and his wheelchair. At a young age, polio had crippled Francis's legs, and he had been confined to a wheelchair. But his wheelchair certainly didn't limit his movement or his speed. Uncle Francis could do almost anything someone with legs could do. There was almost nowhere Uncle Francis couldn't go, almost nothing he wouldn't do.

*Surely, it wasn't that difficult to race around in a wheelchair,* the kids thought!

"OK," Bosco challenged one of the younger boys, "when Uncle Francis gets home, I'll show you I can do it just like Uncle Francis."

As soon as their family father's wheelchair was seen in the distance heading home, a shout rang out, "He's almost home!" Children began running out of their houses so as not to miss the show.

"So, you think you can race around like I can?" Uncle Francis asked Bosco with a grin. "Let's see it!" Uncle Francis loved a good joke. Soon, Francis was sitting on a bench in the banda, and six foot two Bosco had climbed into the wheelchair.

With a bit too much confidence, he wheeled across the banda and headed toward the ramp that led outside. Within no time, as he headed down the ramp, Bosco lost control and flew out of the chair. The chair, having gained momentum, sped down the ramp and landed on top of him! The howling from the children could be heard everywhere as they ran down to pull Bosco up off the ground! And of course, Uncle Francis's abilities were once again eulogized!

# THE GREAT ELEPHANT HUNT

– from an excerpt from Richard Casebow's newsletter of December 1998

"For quite some time we kept getting reports of a large herd of elephants that were causing trouble in an area about twenty miles up the road from us. Eventually they moved off, only to show up again just ten miles north of us in the bush. This was too much for us, and we decided to go and have a 'look see.' So one evening we loaded up the trusty Land Cruiser with the whole family and Tom, one of my apprentices, and set off.

"Ten miles isn't much on the open road, but it took us over an hour of driving down bush tracks to finally reach a vast swamp where the elephants were supposed to be. (It has to be said at this point that Alison had forgotten to take a tray of brownies out of the oven before we left, only remembering it about half an hour into the trip!) Not seeing anything resembling an elephant in the vicinity, I cautiously followed the track out into the swamp until it became clear that I could go no further. I had no intention of getting stuck, so I reversed back up the track, and, not seeing a hole, promptly slid off and ended up sunk to my belly pan in clayey quicksand!

"Tom and I worked for at least an hour to try and dig the car out, but nothing worked, and, as the sun set over the wild swamp where wild things roam, an hour's driving into the almost trackless bush, and as the frogs turned up the volume from loud to deafening, we finally decided that we were stuck!

"God bless Tom, he volunteered to go for help. As he jogged off up the track into the darkness, we set about trying to turn our predicament into an 'exciting adventure' for the kids. Emily wasn't convinced, but the two boys, being more gullible, were fine! After lighting a fire and running out of sticks and not really wanting to go too far into the dark bush to get more, we decided to retire to the stricken car and feed the mosquitoes. There we sat until around 11:00 p.m. when we heard the beautiful sound of a diesel engine above the frog song. Jay had kindly come out to rescue us and very kindly didn't seem to mind or comment on our standard of judgment! Tom had found a man with a bicycle about halfway home and, for a small fee, was ridden the rest of the way on the carrier.

"We got the car out the following day with the help of my dad's[58] tractor, but not without some difficulty. The bemused cattle herders that we met whilst trying to extract it informed us that the elephants were indeed 'just over there' and told us of a better track we could have taken!

"Needless to say, the brownies were charcoal after six hours in the oven!"

## MISCELLANEOUS MEMORIES

The stories could go on and on! There was the time sixty of us were crammed into the back of the lorry, some seated on benches, others standing and leaning out over the railing to see outside. The air was filled with excitement. Namata and Sarah Nakyeyune kept the songs going, and between shouting out their excited observations and laughing at each other's jokes, everyone else joined in, singing along at the top of their lungs!

We were on our way for our first school field trip – and it was a whole family event! The van led the way and drove ahead of us with the pregnant staff ladies, the very little ones, and some of the older girls. For many of these kids it was their first time out of our area, their first time on a paved road, and their first time to see a two-story building. It was a day of firsts! The airport, the botanical gardens where we had a huge picnic and played games, the agricultural research center, Kampala itself, and a potter's kiln and workshop. So much to talk about on the way home!

---

[58]Richard Casebow's parents, Allan and Jean Casebow, served at Kiwoko Hospital for several years.

Then there were the countless times of sitting on the grass outside one of the houses just singing and singing and singing. Hours of entertainment can be had with several drums, a couple of guitars, and lots of kids! There were the times when our *entire* secondary school would pile into the back of the lorry to go and play sports with another school's team! There were the hours spent playing on the "adventure playground" built by a team from England. There were P7 weeks, staff versus children volleyball and football competitions, times spent with teams and other outside visitors, Thanksgiving days, family feasts, and more.

Oh, the Lord has been good to those of us blessed to be a part of the Kasana family! He has been faithful in His blessings and caring in His provisions. He has continued to fill our mouths with laughter and our hearts with joy!

Andrew and David Casebow with a python trophy.

Paul Kessel and Dad carrying the Christmas pig.

Game Day!

# Chapter 19

## *Kyotera*

❧

"Julie!" My whisper was more like a muffled scream. "Pull the covers over your head right now!" The room was dark except for a few beams of moonlight that streamed through the holes in the tin roof. I could hear the rhythmic breathing of the girls asleep on the mattresses next to us.

"What is it?" Julie whispered from under her covers.

"A rat! A huge rat." I shuddered. Scuffling and scratching could be heard above us and around us.

It was our first night in Kyotera, a small town in the Rakai District of southern Uganda, and already our time had been memorable. I wasn't sure I was cut out for this after all.

Our preparations for the night had been different than our routines at home. The floors in the mud building where we stayed were flea-infested, and, as our Ugandan friends explained, there was only one way to get rid of them: burn them out.

Julie and I and several of the Ugandan girls collected piles of dried banana leaves and spread them several feet thick across the floor of our bedroom. Standing in the doorway, one of the girls struck a match, and within seconds, the bedroom was filled with smoke and the sound of crackling flames. Once the fire had subsided and the ashes were swept out of the room, we brought in another heap of dried leaves.

"This way," Nannyonga explained, "if there are any remaining, they will have to walk a long way before they reach us!" We laid our mattresses on top of the leaves, and soon the five of us girls assigned to that room had settled in for the night.

But then Nannyonga remembered to warn us: "Always keep your feet and hands well covered. If you don't, the rats will come and chew on them while you're asleep. While they chew, they blow carefully on your skin so that you can't feel it. You won't know they've eaten your skin until you wake up."

That was it. I knew it would take a miracle for me to fall asleep now. As I tossed and turned, I soon realized that my four companions were not the only other inhabitants of the room. Back and forth across the rafters ran first one rat and then another, each one pausing occasionally to observe all that lay below. For several hours, I lay tensely under my covers, unable to close my eyes for more than a few seconds.

Finally, I was able to drift into a fitful sleep. Then, half conscious, I reached above my head to rearrange what I thought was one of the folded cloths that served as our pillows. But as I picked it up, my whole body shuddered violently as I realized what I held in my bare hands. It was a huge rat that had found a comfortable place to snuggle down and spend the night: my hair! Disgusted and fearful, without thinking, I hurled the helpless rodent across the room as hard as I could and threw the covers over my head. It was going to be a long week!

❧

There were several purposes for our trip to Kyotera. First, terrible rumors had reached us of the devastation that immorality and AIDS had on that area and of the thousands of destitute children who made up the majority of the town's population. We had been told that the situation in our area was not far behind that of Rakai, and we felt we should begin to prepare for what was coming. We also wanted to see what doors the Lord might open for New Hope to serve in Rakai in the future.

For a long time we had felt the need to send a group of Kasana kids for an extended outreach that would enable them to serve children who were less fortunate than they. Through visits to the area and contact with Molly, a Ugandan Christian childcare worker who had laid down her life to serve the children in Rakai, Uncle Jonnes and my dad organized twenty-two children and staff to make the six-hour drive from Kasana to Kyotera. Molly had arranged for our entire group to stay with a family of orphans who lived alone in the home their parents had left them. We would help the children, play with them, plant crops in their garden, clean their home, and share the gospel with them. We would also spend time with two other families in the area, helping them in similar ways.

As our vans pulled up to the children's home, I was initially impressed by the size of the house in comparison to other village homes and by the fact that it had a tin roof. However, I soon realized that the house's relatively impressive exterior were like a coating of whitewash on a tomb. As we climbed out of the vehicles we were nearly overwhelmed by the feeling of neglect and utter hopelessness that permeated the entire compound. The joking and laughing that had occupied us during the long trip soon turned into a contemplative silence as we were introduced to the inhabitants of the house.

Jessica,[59] the oldest, was thirteen. She had been left with the responsibility of caring for, providing for, and raising her four younger siblings. She and three of her siblings came out to greet us, their smiles unable to disguise the distant look in their eyes and pained expressions on their faces. Then tears sprang to many of our eyes as we noticed Sempaka, a small boy cowering close to the house. His extreme fear of strangers, and particularly adults, was instantly evident.

At the age of four, Sempaka had lost both parents, suffered neglect and abuse at the hands of relatives, and lacked proper nourishment. He also had a severe stuttering problem that created in him a sense of uselessness and extreme insecurity. As we turned to greet him, he quickly looked down and began to shake uncontrollably, completely unable to speak or respond to us

---

[59]Children's names changed for privacy in this chapter.

in any way. Uncle Jonnes reached down and pulled Sempaka close to him. The small boy stiffened, but did not resist. It was probably one of the first hugs he had ever received.

After our sobering welcome, we were given a tour of all their parents had once owned. Their relatively large home was now dark and dirty, and almost entirely empty. The garden's once promising harvest of matooke and maize, now almost completely neglected, had been destroyed by hearty tropical weeds and elephant grass that had grown unchallenged for months. Yet it was not the weeds and elephant grass that stunned and silenced us.

As we made our way through the bush, tripping over the uneven earth, we realized where we really were and what it was that we were stumbling over. Under our feet and all around us were heaps of dirt, some carefully outlined by stones. This was not just the family garden.

"My mother and father are buried here," one of the small children said. The haunting truth was almost overwhelming. Only a few feet behind the home where the children had been raised, and where they now fought alone to survive, lay the graves of their parents, aunts, uncles, and other family members. Day after day, these children were taunted by the reality of their situation: they were alone, surrounded only by the memories and remains of those they once called family. Desolate and abandoned, they were left to face the fears and trials of life on their own, while those who should be their protectors and providers, comforters and guides, lay nearby, silenced by the consequences of their past lifestyles and sins.

Through our interaction with the children, our understanding of their plight became clearer. While they were alive, the children's parents had been wealthy according to village standards. Their unusually large home and well-cultivated garden were envied by relatives and neighbors. And while death and poverty raged around them, the children from this family had attended school and lacked none of life's essentials.

But then, their parents began to display the dreaded signs of "Slim."[60]

---

[60]The term given to AIDS. One of the primary signs of AIDS is extreme weight loss.

The children watched silently as their parents, once strong and able to provide, gradually became gaunt and unable to move about without pain. Slowly but surely, a role reversal began to take place in the family. Instead of relying on their parents for all that a child needs, Jessica and her siblings were expected to perform all of the household chores and do whatever they could to relieve the pain that now rendered their parents helpless.

Then, all too soon, Jessica, Sempaka, Christine, Sarah, and Petero's names were added to the cold statistics of orphans and destitute children. As soon as the last shovel full of dirt had been placed upon the graves, jealous and greedy relatives and neighbors set out to plunder the family's estate. Unable to defend themselves, Jessica and her siblings watched as relatives divided their parents' possessions with not even a thought of the children's welfare. Then, as if their greed and theft had not been enough, some of the relatives moved into the children's home and transformed it into a brothel. These children were now unable to escape daily exposure to the despicable sins that saturated their community.

By the grace of God, local authorities were made aware of the appalling situation the children faced, and the relatives were forced to vacate the house. However, in revenge and spite toward the children, they carried with them every belonging they could that had once belonged to the family. Those they were not able to carry with them, they locked into a room that the children were unable to access.

No longer misused by their relatives, the children remained together, but completely alone. Although they were sponsored by a large aid organization, their funding covered school fees and nothing else. Every day, the older children would go to school, hungry and poorly clothed, frequently falling asleep several times in class due to their hunger and fatigue. At the end of the day, they would return to their empty home, scavenge in the garden for whatever leftover food they could find, cook it as best they could, and then attempt to sleep. The next morning, they would awake to face the same hopeless ritual.

In view of the immeasurable loss and pain these children had suffered, our temporary inconveniences (fleas and rats, swamp water to drink, and the same meal three times a day, for seven days) seemed infinitesimally insignificant. Indeed, what were "light and momentary afflictions" to the twenty-two of us from Kasana were the daily encounters and difficulties that made up these children's lives. And while we had the comforting knowledge that our own homes and proper food and water awaited us, these children knew that this was all they had – all they ever would have.

Physical discomforts were not the only insults that were added to the children's daily suffering. Upon our arrival in the town of Kyotera, we were warned that the girls on our team should never walk anywhere alone – either in the day or the night. A gang of men known as the "Mobile Gang," whose members were all infected with the AIDS virus, circulated throughout the village raping any unprotected girl or woman they could find. Their belief, one we heard reiterated countless times by various community members, was this: "If we are going to die, we will not go alone."

While I rested in the protection that my dad, Josiah, Sennyonjo, Paul, Kimera, and all of the other men and boys in our group provided, I could not help thinking of the countless nights that Jessica and her sisters may have been in danger, or have at least been overcome with fear.

Our time with these children opened our eyes not only to the reality of their hopeless situation, but also to the plight of the community around them. Wherever we turned it was as though a spirit of death arose to flaunt its wretched victories at us.

One man we met had just attended the funeral of his ninth son. The cause of this son's death was the same as that of his first eight: AIDS. Another young man we spoke to had once been part of a football team of twenty-two; at the time we spoke with him, only three members remained. The same man was also a member of a thirty-member choir, twenty-five of whom had been claimed by the deadly virus.

Even more upsetting was the fact that the immorality and corrupt mind-set had even penetrated the church. A twisted form of Catholicism reigned in Rakai – one that bore not even a remote resemblance to true Catholicism. Here, the priests frequently infected their parishioners, especially young girls, with HIV. Many of these same men were also practicing witch doctors. With such a warped view of Christianity as their example, the people of Rakai remained proudly resistant to the gospel and to any Christian influence.

In a town where the true light had been dimmed, there seemed no hope, nowhere to turn. A veneer of carelessness and sarcasm inadequately covered the overpowering spirits of fear and death that pervaded the community. Indeed, in this town without a vision, without hope for the future, and without the knowledge of a Savior, the people had cast off restraint and were destined to perish. Rampant immorality and promiscuity were a declaration of the community's motto: "Eat, drink, and be merry, for tomorrow we die."

What are the long-term effects that are seen in a community that has lost hope? As we walked through the villages, we were amazed to see that the population consisted almost entirely of elderly people and young children. It was as though an entire generation had been destroyed. Those of the younger generation who did remain lived on in brazen debauchery and immorality. With stunningly overt hopelessness and proactive fatalism, a group of young widows whose husbands had died of HIV and who were infected themselves opened a bar and brothel. Its name: "Abazadde Bassime," or "The Parents Will Bury." Any young man tired of life and looking for some fun could, for just the price of one beer, have an infected partner for the night. After all, if we are all going to die anyway, why not?

Throughout the community it was not uncommon to find abandoned houses gradually crumbling to the ground and once fruitful gardens overgrown with weeds, their harvests neglected and decomposing. But the most painful and constant sights were the countless children left alone in their parents' homes. Many of them had been orphaned numerous times. After the death of their parents they were passed to a relative who then died, so they were passed on again and again until no one was left. With no one to care for them, no one to provide for, comfort, and raise them, they feebly hung onto life, defeated by the despair and emptiness that surrounded them.

Emptiness: a haunting union of purposelessness, insecurity, and fear. All the children ever knew was gone. "All that remains," they were told, "will also soon be gone. We are all going to die, anyway." The countless funerals blur and become one hopeless memory in the children's minds, proving the community's despondent conviction that death is not only inevitable, but it is also imminent. The dull, despairing ache inside never goes away.

Everywhere we turned we saw children suffering in countless ways. Physically, many were barely surviving and were frequently in danger; emotionally many of them were all but dead. Many young girls gave themselves to men known to be HIV positive so they could become infected and more quickly end their agony here on earth. One young girl who had been left to nurse her dying mother would drink from her mother's cup and lick the plate after her mother had eaten. Her hope was that by doing so she too would contract AIDS and die with her mother. Anything, even a slow, painful death, seemed better to her than living alone in a hopeless world.

After a week of hard work and interaction with village children in Kyotera, the younger members of the team returned to Kasana both moved and inspired to give their lives for the lost, but also disheartened by the overwhelming need. In the face of such insurmountable evil, we thought, what *could* these young children do but succumb to the pressure? Indeed, what could we, a handful of young Christians, do to bring about a change? What we had seen was an endless, hopeless, and overpowering cycle. But through their experience and trust in the Lord, my dad and Uncle Jonnes helped us to begin to see the reality of the situation. The glorious truth was, we couldn't do anything, but *with* Him, everything is possible! Apart from Christ, they helped us understand, there is no hope, but in Him, is all hope.

The world with all of its studies, proposals, and plans has failed to make a difference. Many aid organizations have done their best to give children free education and food with the hopes that this will enable the children to rise above their situation and live with purpose and success. But these honorable intentions have failed to touch children's souls and bring them lasting healing. Victims of dissolved families, these children become victims of failed government and aid agency plans; and in the end, the community's fight to draw the children into their own deathtrap triumphs.

But in Christ, there is lasting hope to offer! In His name are forgiveness, acceptance, healing, and freedom. The call, then, is for those of us who name the name of Christ to reach out *practically* to these children and the community with the hope of the gospel – the only "plan" that can ever bring lasting results. We must *be* the hands that reach out to them, the shoulders they can cry on, the arms that hold them tight and the mouths that whisper in their ears, "You are loved, you are precious, and Jesus is with you." How long will it be until someone *tells* them that there is hope in Christ and that there is so much more to life than death? How long must they live in pain and fear before they hear that Christ's forgiveness and power bring freedom from the bondage of immorality, sin, and hopelessness? They do not need another handout, more school fees, or new programs. They need to belong, to be accepted, secure, and loved. They need family. Until the Lord's people step out and become *practical* and tangible in their love for children, His love for them will always remain distant and irrelevant. But through His body here on earth, broken hearts can be made new.

In the face of such overwhelming despair, we must remember that the Lord calls Himself the Father of the fatherless – the Father of the Sempakas and Jessicas, the father of the little girls who give themselves to HIV-positive men so that they can die quickly. If He calls Himself their Father, then He will also give all that is needed to reach them. Praise the Lord for His promise: "I have seen his ways, but I will heal him; I will guide him and restore comfort to him, creating praise on the lips of the mourners."[61]

---

[61]Isaiah 57:18-19

*The Spirit of the Sovereign LORD is on me, because the LORD has anointed me to preach good news to the poor. He has sent me to bind up the brokenhearted, to proclaim freedom for the captives and release from darkness for the prisoners, to proclaim the year of the LORD'S favor and the day of vengeance of our God, to comfort all who mourn, and provide for those who grieve... to bestow on them a crown of beauty instead of ashes, the oil of gladness instead of mourning, and a garment of praise instead of despair.*

(Isaiah 61:1-3)

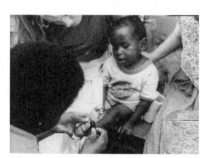

Removing jiggers from a little one's foot.

Ksana team member cutting one of the children's hair.

Kasana children and staff ready to leave on the first outreach to Rakai orphans.

246

# Chapter 20
## *PLE and Other Such Problems*

It was 7:30 in the morning one day in November 1994, but it felt like we had already been awake for hours and hours. As we all gathered outside one of the children's houses, there was a strange combination of apprehension and excitement in the air. It was the first morning of the government-set Primary Leaving Exams (PLE), and it was the first time any of our children were to "sit" the exams. If the students performed well on the exams, they would be welcomed into good schools for further academic or vocational training, thereby securing good jobs and social status in the community. If they did poorly, there would be no hope for a "bright future" in the academic and economic arenas.

Inside the boys' living room, all twelve P7 members[62] were receiving their last instructions and encouragement from Auntie Anna. The rest of us waited outside to hug them and pray for them as they boarded the van that would take them to Kiwoko for the first day of testing. We all felt as nervous as if we were the ones about to take the test.

It had been a rough year for the P7 class. With a terrible shortage of teachers in the primary school, the older students' studies had been irregular, and they had been forced to do much of their work on their own. However, all of Kasana did their best to pitch in and do their part to ensure the success of these twelve.

As Paul Kusubira, a member of our original P7 class remembers, "Every staff who knew something was called upon to give what he knew! Uncle Jay

---

[62]Primary seven is the last class of primary school – approximately sixth grade according to the American education system.

and Uncle Jonnes got involved teaching social studies whenever they had time. Auntie Laurena did a very good job teaching us science." And Auntie Edith would tutor anyone who needed help. Through it all, Anna Nyadoi stood with the class teaching English, Math, or whatever else needed to be taught at the time.

Discouraged by the irregularity of the teachers' availability, our students had other reasons to doubt their ability to succeed on the difficult exams. Unsatisfied with the academic fruit of most schools in the country (where students "crammed" for the exams without good comprehension, reasoning skills, a solid foundation, or the ability to apply what they had learned), we used many of the methods of the Master's School and the King's Schools in North America and the UK. We insisted on teaching subjects from a biblical perspective and desired that the students really *learn* what they were memorizing to be able to reason with it and apply it whenever possible. My dad also insisted that the students be fluent in the basics of addition, subtraction, multiplication, and division before they moved on to more advanced math. This stance flew in the face of the Ugandan system that taught fractions and algebra to students who could not remember how to add or subtract. True, we never covered quite as much of the syllabus as the schools around us, but at least our students *knew* what they had been taught. We also committed several other faux pas: instead of forcing our students to study for twelve hours each day except for Sunday, as most Kampala schools required, our students still had to participate in vocational training and agriculture, not to mention Bible study and family devotions. In other words, we did not teach to the test.

Many of the students were not impressed with how we taught things. Being much older than most P7 students because of their late start in school, they did not enjoy the daily multiplication facts recitations and even the occasional phonogram reviews to improve their reading skills. They also knew how the other students in the country were being prepared for this test, and how different their own preparation was.

"We wondered if we'd ever pass the exams," Betty Nalukwago, one of the first P7's, recalled. The fact that they were the *first* Essuubi Eppya students to reach the end of primary school meant there was no guarantee the teachers knew what they were doing either.

"We said to each other, 'People are getting experience from us!'" Betty continued. "I remember Uncle Jay coming into class with newspapers for us to read about current events. We would say to each other, 'What does this muzungu know about Ugandan exams? He is bringing in his muzungu ideas and ways. Will we ever pass?'"

In addition to our counter-cultural teaching methods, we also struggled to negate the social stigma that came from being a village school. According to every Ugandan stereotype, we were destined to do poorly on the exams. The community around us took part in regularly reminding our students and us that we had no hope of performing well on the exams. Only city schools – and wealthy ones at that – had students achieving first grades.[63] We were just a school for orphans out in the bush; we had no hope for good grades. Time and again we were told that we would be lucky to receive one second grade. Besides, as Paul remembers hearing time and again, "What good can come from Kasana?"

Kimera Stephen also attested to the difficulties they faced. "People in the community around Kasana looked at us children like we were no good," he said. "We were the 'bamulekwa,' the 'neglected ones,' being used to work and do whatever the bazungu wished. That's how the community viewed the whole thing. They thought that we weren't studying because we would fetch water, dig, and sing and drum and make lots of noise. The students from surrounding schools would also verbally abuse us, but we persisted and bore the shame."

With the community's continual verbal harassment and our own inexperience with government exams and the usual preparation that goes into them, it was an uphill battle for the staff to keep the attitudes of the students

---

[63]First grade is the best category of grades; grade two is second and so on. A grade four is a fail.

positive and convince them to exert even a minimal amount of effort. The taunts of the villagers continued to dig deep into the students' hearts and taint their view of the situation.

After a particularly difficult week with the P7 students, I remember my parents and Laurena Hensel sitting in our living room discussing the situation. It was a Sunday night, and the depressing prospect of facing the discouraged and indifferent P7 class the next day had instigated the conversation.

"We're losing their hearts," my dad said. "They have given up; their attitudes are terrible, and even if they do perform well on PLE, we will have succeeded in nothing if we haven't touched their hearts and made a difference in their lives.

"So, what do we do?" he asked. That was all we needed. Though Josiah, Jamie, and I had not been an official part of the conversation up to this point, the floor was now open, and one by one we began to gain interest. The discussion went back and forth for a while, but nothing seemed to present a solution. Then Dad said, "I know; let's cancel school for a week and have them come spend the week with us!" At that point, my siblings and I were immediately even more interested than before. Although we knew they hadn't been angels recently, the P7s were some of our best friends, and the idea of their school being canceled (which would guarantee the cancellation of our home schooling by Laurena as well!) and having our friends over for a week was marvelous!

What ensued over the next hour or so is a typical scene in the Dangers' household when Dad comes up with one of his big ideas. All talking at once, the rest of us added to his plan, changed it, then shot it down, built it back up again, made some slight adjustments, and by the end had come up with a "perfect" plan. But just because *we* thought it was perfect did not mean we could run ahead with it. First, Uncle Robert Tumuhairwe (our project manager at the time) and Uncle Jonnes had to be convinced that it was necessary and good. So, despite its being 9:00 on a weekend night, up we went to Uncle Robert's house and then Uncle Jonnes' house so my dad could explain the idea. And of course, we children had to jump in whenever he forgot a particularly good or convincing aspect of the plan. Fortunately, they agreed, and we all proceeded to the kids' houses to inform the students that there would be no school the next day; instead they were to report to our house by 9:00 in the morning.

It was then back to our house for a few crazy hours of planning, rearranging the living room and dining room, sharpening pencils, running to different staff houses to see who would be willing to speak on this topic, or organize that game or event. By six o'clock the next morning, after just a few hours of silence, our house was again astir with all of us making last-minute preparations.

"We could have baking lessons," my mom suggested. "Laurena, Jennie, Jamie, and I can give the girls baking lessons, and Jay and Josiah, you can give the boys a mechanics lesson."

Laurena planned games and relays, we children chose science videos to show, practiced songs to teach the kids, and planned meals that would be relatively easy to prepare and everyone would enjoy. While we bustled around the rest of the house, my dad remained in his room, praying and seeking the Lord to know what he should share with the students.

Nine o'clock came, and soon the first few students arrived. But while we Dangers kids were thrilled, the Ugandan children came in with a look of skepticism and frustration. The message was clearly written across their faces: "Now what? This is going to be some kind of pep talk, the same thing we've heard for months; nothing will change or improve, and we now have one week less to study."

I was crushed. I thought they would be excited; I thought they would appreciate the gesture and the time to get away from the "cramming." I failed to notice that there *were* a few smiles on the faces of Sennyonjo, Paul, and Senjala, and focused only on the disdain that was evident on the faces of the others. Thankfully, my parents' maturity did not allow them to give up as quickly as I did. And, following their examples, I did my best to hide my discouragement and be upbeat and welcoming.

But something broke that week. The hardness, the coldness, and frustration seemed to melt away more and more each day. We spent time talking about their pasts, praying with them, sharing testimonies, laughing, and crying. Different staff members took time to share what it means to be a godly man or woman, how to deal with bitterness and unforgiveness, how the Bible applies to different aspects of our lives. We sang and sang; we did relays, played games, learned to line dance, baked bread and cookies, and "fixed" cars. And the Lord worked in a way we had not even hoped.

On the last night, as we shared testimonies, had the students sign the "guest book," ate hamburgers (and *tried*, with much laughter and utter failure, to teach the students to say "hamburgers" with an American accent), I began to realize the work the Lord had done in such a short time. I knew that my family had always loved these students, but now our love for them was so strong it almost hurt. I knew this week had joined the students themselves together as a class and had given them a security in the love of my parents, Uncle Jonnes, Laurena, and other staff members that they had not had before. These twelve were not just part of the big New Hope family; I knew they were part of *my* family – the Dangers' family. There was a renewed sense of purpose, camaraderie, and a desire to do their best for the Lord's honor and glory. And we all knew that "P7 Week" tradition had been established at Kasana.

---

As we waved good-bye to thirteen of the "firstborns," we thought of all of the taunting and jeering they had experienced. We thought of the months of struggles, prayers, and investment. We thought of our memorable "P7 Week" and the love that had deepened between all of us.

"Father, go before Your children. Let them not be ashamed," we prayed.

---

The usual Kasana noises of drumming, shouts from children playing football, peanuts being pounded in the mortars, and chickens and cows making their presence known was suddenly interrupted by a blaring car horn. As children and staff came running out of their houses to see what the commotion was all about, there was Uncle Jonnes, waving a piece of paper out of the van window as he honked the horn and circled the roundabout again and again. The PLE results were back.

It had been three months of nervous waiting for the thirteen Primary 7 "leavers." Christmas had come and gone, and still there was no word on how they had performed on their life-or-death exams. Now the news was here. But Uncle Jonnes (once he had stopped honking the horn and brought the car to a stop) would not say a word until all twelve were there. Memories of the predictions came flooding into everyone's minds. "Can anything good come from New Hope?" "You will be lucky if you get one second grade."

Everyone stood breathless, waiting to hear Uncle Jonnes read. "Paul, first grade." Shouts rang out, and the dancing began. "Kimera, first grade." Tears began to stream down faces. "Betty, first grade." Was he just teasing, or could it really be true? The list continued. Six first grades and the rest second grades. It was unheard of. The scene was surreal. As the P7 students were embraced by everyone near them, the little children (not understanding the situation, but enjoying the chance to celebrate) jumped up and down and danced. After the rejoicing, silence came quickly as heads bowed in thanksgiving to the One who had made it all possible.

"We knew it was a way that God was exalting Himself," Paul remembered. "He proved to us that He is our Provider and Sustainer, and He stood with us. He made us do exploits because we trusted in Him."

"It was amazing," Kimera recalled. "The shame that had covered us was washed off." Of the several hundred students that had taken the exam at the Kiwoko center, ours were the only ones to receive first grades. Only one or two others from the center even received second grades. "I don't say that we were very bright," said Paul, "but God was exalting Himself."

❧❧

As the years have progressed, we have seen the Lord do amazing things through and in each of these students. And although their stories have just begun, the Lord is already using many of them in mighty ways to bring the Father-heart of God to the fatherless, to improve the nation of Uganda, and to further the Lord's kingdom.

Kimera is now the head of the Childcare Department at New Hope; he is also the "father" of David Family at Kasana. Sebwaami serves as a childcare staff member at Kasana. James, now married, serves in Administration at Esuubi Eppya, and Namubiru Margaret and Achom serve as teachers there as well. Paul has started a farm and a church twelve kilometers from Kasana where he and his wife, Susan, are caring for his orphaned nephew and serving as missionaries in the community in which they live. Betty is a nurse, and Susan, after serving as a nurse for a time, has returned to school to upgrade her nursing status. Charity and Enoch are continuing their studies at Makerere University. Sennyonjo served for a time as the administrator for the New Hope Institute for Childcare and Family. He married Gertrude, one of our Kasana daughters, and together they are adopting an abandoned little boy, Sammy. Mbonigaba is a lecturer at the University of Rwanda.

Indeed the Lord "raises the poor from the dust and lifts the needy from the ash heap; he seats them with princes, with the princes of their people."[64] He is "mindful of the humble state of his servant[s]....the Mighty One has done great things for [us]."[65]

*Author's note: Kasana's dear daughter and member of the first P7 class, Naluwooza Justine, went to be with the Lord at 3:30 a.m. on September 13, 2000, after a long and painful struggle with cancer. Her life, however, especially her last days, brought joy to those around her and glory to her heavenly Father. Though we mourn her passing for our sake and the sake of her siblings, we are certain that she is now being carried by the Father of the fatherless, and in this we rejoice.*

---

[64]Psalm 113:7-8, NIV
[65]Luke 1:48-49, NIV

Some of the first P7 students.

Some of the first P7 boys at their new secondary boarding school.

Our dear Justine Naluwooza, just months before
she went to be with the Lord.

# Chapter 21
## *Heartbreaks*

*I can't breathe; it's agony*
*Wondering where you are*
*Picture me on my knees*
*Have you run too far?*
*Can you hear*
*Can you hear the sound of my heart break*
*With each step you take*
*Can you feel*
*Can you feel me when I say:*
*Please come back to me*
*I miss you, will you come to your senses*
*Please come back to me*
*I await the day when I prepare the feast*
*And I embrace you running to me.*
*All I am*
*All I have*
*Is yours to find*
*You hide and seek*
*You think you're free*
*But you're wasting time.*
*I can hear*
*I can hear the sound of footsteps pounding*
*Regrets resounding*

*I believe*
*I believe the hour is near.*
*What would you give for a ransomed heart?*
*Would it cost too much?*
*I'm telling you now, if you run to Me*
*You will be free.*

– Michelle Tumes and Robert Arthur
(c 1998 BMG Music Pty.
Ltd./ASCAP/EMI Blackwood Music/BMI)

Her name was Namuli[66] – a bright, energetic girl with a contagious laugh and a beautiful smile. Blessed with an engaging personality and natural abilities, Namuli had great potential. But there was one major obstacle that drowned all hope for a bright future for Namuli. She was an orphan. To the community of which she was a part, she was a burden and unwanted. No one took the time to realize her potential; no one cared enough to comfort her hurts and pains. She was a drain on an already needy society. Aware of her position and hopeless plight, she knew that her life would one day become the property of some man. She would bear him children, cook for him, and obey his every command, until he found a more attractive wife. Then she would be passed to another.

But then she heard about Esuubi Eppya. It was a school for people just like her. Maybe this was her opportunity; maybe there was hope after all.

One early morning in October 1988, forty children, barefooted and with threadbare clothes, arrived for their first day of school at Esuubi Eppya. Despite the mocking and discouragement of many villagers, these children and their relatives had chosen to give the new organization a chance. Who was to say? Maybe something positive would come of it. The children were willing to take a risk – anything was better than the situations they were in,

[66]Name changed for privacy.

and the relatives saw it as at least a temporary means of relieving themselves of the burdens they so resented. And if the rumors *were* true about the white people taking the children to distant countries as slaves, or eating them, or forcing them to eat strange and dangerous foods, then it was only the "bamulekwa"[67] that were in danger. It would be no great loss to society if it all went wrong and something terrible happened to these children.

One of these children was Namuli. First timid and uncertain of the new environment, she soon began to come out of her shell, and, over the years, her involvement in school and extracurricular activities increased. Her strong and beautiful voice was always a pleasant addition to any choir, and she often led in times of singing at school and evening devotions. Taking the lead female role in an elaborate play about the story of Esther, Namuli impressed the audience with her excellent use of the English language and her theatrical talents.

When twenty-two students and staff went from Kasana to take part in the weeklong outreach to orphans in the district of Rakai, Namuli was among those chosen to go. Her smile never faded during the long days of arduous work, difficult living conditions, and possible danger.

Because she was too old to join the lower primary grades with the younger children, Namuli and several of the older boys and girls were put into a class where they would be trained in skills of self-sufficiency, basic English, and mathematics. She quickly caught on to the concepts of tailoring, knitting, and crocheting, not to mention the skills required in making many Ugandan crafts. In every way, Namuli demonstrated great potential. But unfortunately, the staff members at Kasana, who had her best interest in mind, were not the only ones to notice this.

After years of ignoring her, Namuli's relatives and neighbors, who had before seen her only as an encumbrance, a hindrance to their own progress, began to realize all that had been drawn out of and invested in her. With selfish greed they began to entice Namuli to leave New Hope.

---

[67]Orphans; literally, one's who have been left.

"We really love you," they would tell her. "Please come back to us. What are you doing at New Hope anyway? You should be married by now. Look, your cousin is only thirteen and she has her first baby. But look at you; you're much older than her, and you're still in a school for little children and orphans."

At first, Namuli withstood the temptations and pressures that were laid on her. She knew that it was only a short time until she finished her training and would graduate as a tailor. A big celebration would be held in honor of those graduating, and she would receive a brand-new sewing machine to begin her new life. No, it was not worth giving in yet.

But the pressure built. Her relatives knew that they would obtain a significant bride price if they could find the right man to marry her now. But it was not only the financial profit that motivated their enticements. Their pride had also been hurt. The girl they had all rejected as worthless now displayed confidence, spoke English, and could provide for herself. She had shamed them all by proving them wrong and even surpassing them in her abilities and training. And so they continued. "You're wasting time, Namuli. What benefit are you going to receive by staying? Come; we'll find you a good husband."

Maybe it was the constant pressure, or maybe she had been deceived into thinking that those who had once rejected her now really loved her – something she had always longed for. Whatever it was, it broke her. Just two weeks before her graduation, Namuli disappeared. The next thing we heard was that she had been given to a local man and was pregnant with her first child. The man they had found for her was not a Christian and had only been chosen because he was willing to pay the bride price. There had been no wedding ceremony, nothing that would guarantee Namuli's security in the relationship. She was his until he felt he should have another.

Caring for children, though one of the most fulfilling and rewarding opportunities, carries with it a combination of overwhelming joys and crushing heartbreaks. Placing your heart in an extremely vulnerable place, you must become real to the child, approachable, and sincere. There is no place for professionalism or superficial care. Children you once never knew existed soon become the most important people in your life. They also become your pride and joy, your constant concern, all that you live for. As you begin to open up to them and to demonstrate Christ's love to them, their broken hearts, sense of rejection, emotional and physical pains, and the abuse and abandonment they once experienced become your own. As your hearts are joined, you are able to cry with the child, rejoice with him, and feel whatever it is he is experiencing. You no longer are ashamed to cry with him, laugh with him, rebuke him, and encourage him. He has indeed become your own.

Words cannot express the joy that comes when an orphaned child, one who has never trusted anyone before, begins to open his heart to you and to share his pains and joys. You begin to see the child's pains and emotional trauma lessen with prayer and counsel. You realize that your hours of prayer and input were not in vain. No longer seeing himself as an orphan, your son or daughter begins to plan for the future. You see the choices and decisions he makes begin to take shape with purpose and vision. He becomes involved in ministry and seeks to care for younger children who are in the situation he was once in.

Then, one day it is all over. As if a light switch was turned off. The laughter and confiding turns to distant coldness. You see silent or open rebellion that refuses to be checked. Then he's gone, to where you may or may not know. But what is painfully evident is that he no longer has any desire to be near you, to look you in the eyes, or even talk to you. You are devastated and hurt; angry tears well up in your eyes. "What did I do wrong?" you ask yourself. "How did I not see this coming? What shall I do? O Lord, bring him home."

———————————————— ❧ ————————————————

It was a beautiful sunny day, the morning service had been uplifting and challenging, and we were all walking slowly back to our houses for Sunday lunch when Sennyonjo hurried up to us with a worried look on his face.

"They say Nannyonga died last night," he said, "It seems her husband beat her to death." Suddenly the beautiful day had lost all of its brilliance.

"No...no! It can't be true!" we cried. "Oh, please say there's been some mistake."

Nannyonga came to Kasana as one of our first girls in 1988. Her early childhood had been shaped by not only rejection and abandonment, but also constant exposure to witchcraft and immorality. Aware of the crippling emotional baggage with which she came, Uncle Jonnes, Auntie Sarah, and many other staff members poured themselves into her through counsel, love, discipline, and training.

Though she was four years older than me, we soon became inseparable. I helped her with English, and she taught me how to make baskets and speak Luganda. Her beginning was rough, but as time progressed, it seemed that she had truly grasped the truth of the gospel and that her life was gradually being renewed. Like Namuli, she had joined the trade-training program and had been one of those who had graduated in the class Namuli had left. Over the years, Nannyonga and I talked extensively about her future and all that God had in store for her. It was amazing to know the kind of life she had come from and to see how far she had come.

But then, in 1995, Nannyonga ran off with a man from the area. Not surprisingly, that relationship did not last more than a few months, but by then Nannyonga was pregnant, and, despite the urgings and counsel of Uncle Jonnes, my father, and many other staff members, she refused to repent and return to Kasana.

A few months later, we received a message that Nannyonga was in labor and had no one to care for her at the hospital. Her former boyfriend was nowhere to be found, and her relatives were unwilling to lift a finger to aid her. She had no supplies and had arrived at the hospital with only the clothes she was wearing. Anna Nyadoi, one of our single staff ladies, and I, laden with supplies and baby clothes that had been given by New Hope staff for Nannyonga and the baby, went quickly to help her through the delivery. We all hoped that she would respond to the love we had shown her and be restored to the Lord and the New Hope family. But her attitude remained cold and distant.

After a few days, we again received a message that Nannyonga needed help. But this time, it was not to celebrate life. Her little boy, just three days old, had died, and the funeral was to be held that afternoon. Still unwavering from her rebellious resolve, not long after the funeral it became clear that Nannyonga had chosen to follow the path that her own mother had walked, the same path that had brought her so much grief and rejection.

Her next "husband" kept her long enough to have one child, but as soon as she became inconvenient, he dismissed her. Nannyonga found another man and gave her little girl to her mother to raise. The third man in her life became the father of her next two children. However, this man was known throughout the village as being very violent. When the severity of his blows caused Nannyonga to miscarry, she returned to Kasana for advice.

"Nannyonga, don't you see the danger you are in?" one staff member questioned. "Not only you, but your children also. Please leave him. We will help you in whatever way we can." She mumbled that she would consider their advice and left. That was the last time the Kasana family saw her – alive.

As we gathered around her coffin and wept, our only hope was that at the last minute she had cried out to the Lord and claimed the grace that she knew so much about but had, up to that point, chosen to reject. The words of Isaiah best described the state of our hearts.

*Turn away from me; let me weep bitterly. Do not try to console me over the destruction of my people.*

(Isaiah 22:4)

Looking around us at the crowd that had come to the burial, we saw many of our former girls who had allowed themselves to be enticed into Nannyonga's lifestyle and that of the village around them, and our hearts broke again. Why does it have to be so? Why do they choose to remain part of this hopeless and endless cycle of pain, neglect, and abuse?

Nannyonga,

*I can't breathe*
*It's agony*
*Wondering where you are*
*Could you hear*
*Could you hear the sound of our hearts breaking*
*With each step you took...*

Girls,

*You hide and seek*
*You think you're free*
*But you're wasting time –*
*Please come back to us*
*We miss you, will you come to your senses*
*We await the day when we prepare the feast*
*And we embrace you running to us*

❦

John[68] was always laughing. His smile seemed to spread from ear to ear and was entirely contagious. He had come to us with his little brother, Ronald, in 1988, and had instantly become known for his sense of humor, his willingness to help, and his excellent athletic abilities. Most likely due to his unusual background, in addition to all of this, John had the ability to "sniff out" danger and gather information that no one else could.

Both his father and mother had served in Museveni's army during the war. And, with nothing to do himself, he had joined them around the age of eight. Armed with a machine gun, he had marched and fought with hardened soldiers. Now that he was allowed to be a child again, John flourished

---

[68]Name changed for privacy.

in the Kasana family. But some of the skills learned as a soldier did come in handy on several occasions. Several times he was sent to investigate a theft we had had, or to gain some information on unrest in the area. Every time he came back successful. Fearless, John once chased a man carrying a gun who was stealing a bicycle. Dodging the bullets, John chased him on his own bike, and soon overtook him and restored the bike to its rightful owner!

John's long legs always came in handy when he participated in a race. He was always one of the first in the Independence Day bike races we held; his long legs were perfect for the Chinese "Phoenix" bikes everyone rode. It was John who was chosen to stand at a post half a mile up the road as a lookout for Mrs. Museveni when she first came to visit us. As soon as he saw her first car escort, John was to sound an alarm and run through the bush to where we were and alert us. Of course, he arrived well before the cars reached the gate!

But, as was the case with so many, John's heart began to grow distant and hard. We do not know what caused his change, but its evidence was real. Perhaps it was wounds from his past that had not been dealt with; perhaps it was an unwillingness to submit to authority. Perhaps it was an independence brought about by an orphan spirit that hindered him from trusting others. Whatever the cause, he began intentionally avoiding anyone in authority, spreading complaints and rumors about the staff to all the children, and wearing a permanent scowl on his face. Not long after, he was gone.

After a few months passed, we met him in Kiwoko town – self-confident and self-supporting. All we could hope was that he would be wise in his choices and continue to walk with the Lord. With the prevalence of the AIDS epidemic, one mistake could cost him his life.

The next thing we heard was that he was living with one of our girls who had also run away, and she had given birth to their first child. We prayed that they would respond to God's love and would one day be married and raise a good and wholesome family.

Several years passed, then one day, a young and very attractive girl came to our home looking for a job. She spoke English clearly and well, and appeared to be well dressed and cared for. When we asked her about herself, she said she was John's wife. The news shocked us. John's wife? We thought Mary[69] was his wife.

Apparently, as we found out later, Mary and her three children had been dismissed, and the girl who was now seeking work was his new "wife." As my mom talked with her, we found, to our dismay, that John was a drunk who could not hold a job and who was doing nothing to care for his new children and wife, or his children from his first "marriage." Not long after, we heard that yet another woman was carrying his child, and John was still a drunk relying on obliging relatives for his own survival. With no thanks from John, his younger brother, Ronald, still in school at New Hope, does all he can to raise money to provide for John's numerous children.

Why do we lose them? What is it that pulls them back into the hopeless chasm that first seems appealing but in the end leads to immeasurable heartache and confusion? Why do they run from the love and commitment they are freely offered – the family security they now have, the physical and emotional and educational support they receive? We have been asking ourselves this for years now.

In a letter my father composed on February 17, 1994, he explains:

> ...several of our children have left Kasana for 'greener pastures,' this in spite of the fact that we are known to have the best school in the area, we have more special events, more personal attention and tender loving care, better medical attention, meals provided and most of the children pay nothing for any of this because they have nothing to pay with. It really is hard, on paper, to accurately describe what all is going on here, but we are under attack and <u>we need your prayer.</u>

---

[69]Name changed for privacy.

After much prayer, my dad and Uncle Jonnes felt they had some insight into the cause of these heartbreaking cases.

"The majority of our children are staying with some relative. These relatives often have little interest in their well-being, so there is very little encouragement from home for the children to stay in school. Some of these relatives brought the children to us when they were young and a burden. When they grow up and are able to do some real work, the relatives find plenty of things to use them for and begin to work against us and our desire to keep the children in school.

"Some children just leave thinking that the grass is greener somewhere else. But the main reason that children leave here, I believe, is because Satan is out to destroy us and the children that God has brought to us. It is very much like the situation in the Book of Nehemiah, where, when Nehemiah came to build the walls of Jerusalem, men rose up to resist him. Before Nehemiah came to 'promote the welfare of the Jews,' these men were satisfied to let the Jews be there.

"Satan was happy with the way things were here in Uganda and didn't need to spend much time and energy on these children. But now that people are here to bring them the gospel of Jesus Christ and to train them in things like family, Satan's territory is threatened, and he is trying to destroy us. Actually, we consider this to be a great compliment! But mostly we are thankful that 'He who is in us is greater than he who is in the world.'

"So, please don't misunderstand me. We are not defeated. We are convinced that God is on our side and that we are winning! This is a tough time, but the victory belongs to <u>our GOD!</u> And from Him to us! But we need your prayers. Second Corinthians 4:7–9 expresses how I feel about these troubles,

*But we have this treasure in jars of clay to show that this all-surpassing power is from God and not from us. We are hard pressed on every side, but not crushed; perplexed, but not in despair... struck down, but not destroyed.*

Second Corinthians 1:10–11 says what I want to say to you,

*On him we have set our hope that he will continue to deliver us, as you help us by your prayers. Then many will give thanks on our behalf for the gracious favor granted us in answer to the prayers of many.*

*Then the peoples around them set out to discourage the people of Judah and make them afraid to go on building. They hired counselors to work against them and frustrate their plans.*

(Ezra 4:4–5)

From the very first day of our involvement with children we have realized that because our task is dear to the heart of God, it is strongly opposed and hated by the enemy. As it was during the time of Ezra and Nehemiah, whenever God's people rise up to declare His Word and to rebuild all that the enemy has destroyed, they are met with conflict, discouragement, and various other trials. As the New Hope family has labored to bring the Father heart of God to the fatherless, we have faced oppositions and heartaches that, had the Lord not been on our side, would have caused us to perish.

The stories of Namuli, Nannyonga, and John are merely three of the countless others who have come and gone. As the years have progressed, and the staff has been granted more and more wisdom from the Lord, the numbers of children leaving have decreased considerably. However, the inability to trust, the desperate desire to be accepted by their relatives, and the resentment of discipline and guidelines continue to tear children away into Satan's trap. But we know that seeds were planted in their hearts. Each of them knows there *is* a place they can run to if they need help. Each of them knows that their heavenly Father loves them and will forgive them of their sins. And, with bated breath, like the father of the prodigal son, we watch and wait for their return and will run to greet them when we see them in the distance!

*When the LORD brought back the captives to Zion, we were like men who dreamed. Our mouths were filled with laughter, our tongues with songs of joy. Then it was said among the nations, 'The LORD has done great things for them.' The LORD has done great things for us, and we are filled with joy....Those who sow in tears will reap with songs of joy. He who goes out weeping, carrying seed to sow, will return with songs of joy, carrying sheaves with him.*

(Psalm 126)

*Return to us, O God Almighty! Look down from heaven and see! Watch over this vine, the root your right hand has planted, the son you have raised up for yourself.*

(Psalm 80:14–15)

# Chapter 22
## *Kasana Has Lost a Mother!*

❧❦

*Newsletter from Dad, June 10, 1995*

"'Kasana has lost a mother!' Jonnes said as his voice cracked with emotion and tears flowed down the cheeks of many. Yes, people, we have lost a mother in Kasana! And such a mother she was. Her name was Evelyn Ruyondo, wife to Joseph Ruyondo and mother to Emmanuel, Esther, Joel, and Dan, as well as many, many children orphaned by war and AIDS. In a very real sense she was also a mother to many staff members at Kasana and villagers from the surrounding community.

"She was our nurse and involved in countless other activities with the children. How many of our children are alive today because of her? Only God knows, but surely through the measles epidemics where she nursed desperately sick children at all hours of the day or night, some pulled through just because of her. And Bizimungu, who, at the age of about eleven was disowned by his father because he was too sickly and had massive ulcers all over his legs and arms, wouldn't be here if she had given up on him as so many before had done. And what about the many who would have given up on school and life in general just to fall into the sinful and hopeless ways of the community around, but for her loving care and motherly wisdom? Day and night, she was on call if not on duty, and she was called on at all hours. Yes, Kasana has lost a mother – a dearly loved mother. A nurse can be replaced, but how do you replace a mother?

"On May 23, at 11:00 p.m., after having suffered some fairly severe 'morning sickness,' she was rushed to Kiwoko Hospital after having collapsed by her bed. The next day, she was much better, and each day after that she continued to improve. After about four days, we all expected that she would be released from the hospital because she was doing so well. The doctors, however, decided that she should be at the hospital because she needed the rest. They knew her well and judged rightly that with all of the needs of her own family and the Kasana family, she would not be able to resist the temptation to sacrifice her own well-being for that of others. But their precautions were suddenly of no use, and with no sign of warning, she died."

*Evelyn indeed was one of the pillars of Kasana's early days. Her love and care, her advice, hard work, and patience will never be forgotten. In memory of a dear mother, friend, and co-worker, I have asked several people she touched to share their memories of her. May the Lord be glorified for the lives His faithful servant touched and changed!*

---

"I was there attending to Auntie Evelyn when she died," Betty Nalukwago began. "She was so good to us. She guided and counseled us, and talked to us about how girls should grow. Growing up as a girl is a difficult thing if you do not have parents to guide you, so Auntie Evelyn became our mother. She even talked to us about things many parents even fear talking to their children about. She also spent time with us and taught us how to cook. When we would go see her in the clinic, she would talk to us about anything. We wouldn't just go there for treatment when we were sick, but we'd go there for everything we needed for life.

"When I was little," Betty continued, "I used to walk from my home in the village here to school barefooted. Whenever she would look at me she would feel bad. So one day, she called me and gave me shoes – she had bought them herself! I felt so loved! Another time, I pierced my toe with a thorn. I still have the scar!" Betty smiled. "I limped to and from school for several days, and I didn't know she was observing me. She called me and took care of it, and in just two days I was fine.

"When she was sick," Betty's face became contemplative, "I was asked to go with her to the hospital to take care of her. She didn't look sick, but she was there mainly to rest. While I stayed with her, I remember her lying in the hospital bed and talking to me. She kept saying, 'My daughter, please always keep my words.' Just before she died, she was talking about her children. I remembered the Bible was in her hands; she had just finished reading.

"It was then that she asked me for water to bathe. As she stood up, she suddenly collapsed. I ran to get the nurses, and they did all they could, but she died. It was the saddest moment. I don't think I'll ever forget it. I was there when she died. The nurses told me to go tell people in Kasana, but I couldn't even walk. I don't know who took the news, but it seemed to get there so fast. It was so sad. We missed her, we really missed her. We didn't think that anybody would replace her."

"She was a good mother to New Hope," Sebuchu Nathan began. "She worked so hard to help me become healthy. I had skin rashes all over and a kind of syphilis. I remember going to Kiwoko Hospital and they failed to find the cure for what I had. But Auntie Evelyn didn't give up. She went and explained the situation to Uncle Jay, and they tried to find me medicine that could help me. All the while, she tried to encourage me, but I was so discouraged and most times I could cry.

"Then, one Sunday after the service, she called me to come to her. She said, 'Sebuchu, I know God still loves you! Uncle Jay got the medicine!' Although she was so excited," Sebuchu continued, "I didn't believe her because I thought there was no way I could get better. For a whole month, she would inject me twice a day – I had sixty injections. And after that month, my skin became normal! I remember she invited my mother, and we had a party to celebrate!"

❧

"She was the nurse and a mother," Kaleera Augustine reminisced. "She really did a great job and was so committed. I remember the kids who came in from the villages each day suffering from jiggers and malnutrition, and she would care for them. She would also come day and night and check on those of us who lived in the dormitories. She would check to make sure our meals were nutritious and would come into our rooms to check the hygiene. She was so committed and loving. I remember we would often go to her house, and she would care for us so well. Sometimes we would enjoy being sick because she took such good care of us!"

❧

Bizimungu Charles shared, "It was Auntie Evelyn who organized for me to come and live at Kasana. I was covered in wounds, and she would dress them so carefully. I was afraid of other people working on me, but Auntie Evelyn would do everything so gently and lovingly, and even with many tears.

"I was staying at Uncle Jay's house when she got sick and died. I wished that I could have died instead of her, because she was the best person in my life," Bizimungu's eyes filled with tears as he continued. "She died! But before she died, I thought I could get better. But when she died, I completely lost hope. When she died, I felt bad, and said, 'I'm the next one,' because I knew she was not there to care for me anymore."[70]

❧

I will never forget the evening that Auntie Evelyn passed away. The sunset that night was spectacular, almost as if we had caught a glimpse of heaven where Evelyn now resided. However, the wailing could be heard all across the site. Children and staff, not to mention her own dear family, ached with the knowledge that one so dear was now gone forever. But I will also never forget my father's words to all of us as we gathered for prayer at the Ruyondo household that night.

---

[70] See the rest of Bizimungu's and Auntie Evelyn's story in Chapter 23, "Our Brother Bizi."

"Let us not weep as those who have no hope." Hope: the knowledge that the Lord holds our tomorrow, that there is more to life than death, that the King of kings and Lord of lords holds Auntie Evelyn and we would one day see her again. The confidence that, although one who had meant so much to each of the children was gone, the Lord would send others in her place to love and care for them. Though the pain remained, a sense of fragile peace began to permeate those gathered near her coffin. Our Father is still on the throne. He is still the Father of the fatherless, and will bring about His perfect will in each of our lives.

*O people of Zion, who live in Jerusalem, you will weep no more. How gracious he will be when you cry for help! As soon as he hears, he will answer you.*

(Isaiah 30:19)

*Though [the Lord] brings grief, he will show compassion, so great is his unfailing love. For he does not willingly bring affliction or grief to the children of men.*

(Lamentations 3:32–33)

"Like all tragedies that come into the lives of those who love God," my dad's newsletter continued, "He brings good out of them. We have already seen one person brought to a saving knowledge of the Lord Jesus Christ and many other lives have been powerfully affected by all of the events surrounding Evelyn's death and burial. I'm very glad to be able to say that Joseph and his children have been greatly supported through this time, and it shows. They are on firm ground. They still need your prayers, but they are strong. They receive many visitors, and many have pitched in to take care of the house, the cooking, and the children. It is a pleasure and a privilege to serve those who have served so faithfully."

*Precious in the sight of the LORD is the death of his saints.*

(Psalm 116:15)

Today, Joseph Ruyondo, the late Evelyn's husband, has now been on staff for fourteen years. His commitment to the ministry and to the children at Kasana also must not be overlooked. In April 1997, we rejoiced with him as he was wedded to Ruth, a dear sister in the Lord. Now, in addition to Joseph's first four children, they have little Faith, Jesse, and Joshua. We are so grateful that though this dear family has passed through many difficulties and much grief, the Lord has been faithful to them, and we are thankful that they remain a part of the Kasana family to this day.

Evelyn, Mom, and Sarah

Ruyondo family, 1992

# Chapter 23
## Our Brother Bizi

❧

*Do not reject me or forsake me, O God my Savior. Though my father and mother forsake me, the LORD will receive me....I am still confident of this: I will see the goodness of the LORD in the land of the living. Wait for the LORD; be strong and take heart and wait for the LORD.*

(Psalm 27:9-10, 13-14)

Bizimungu - in his mother tongue his name means "the Lord knows." His quick smile, sense of humor, mischievous personality, and servantlike spirit are merely a few of the things my family and I love about our "brother" Bizi. But the road has not always been easy for our brother. Indeed, there have been countless times when he questioned the meaning of his own name - "the Lord knows." Does He? Does He know the pain of the rejected child, the disowned son, the wounded, hopeless invalid? Does He see and look with love, or merely acknowledge with a distant coldness?

Though it seemed dark at times, Bizi's life story is one of the persistent and forgiving love of the Father of the fatherless - the love of a God who *does* see and *does* hear, a God who weeps when His children weep and feels their every pain, rejection, and distress. Yes, our God does see! May Bizimungu's story be an encouragement to all those who may ever doubt that truth.

❧

"So do you think he could come to school at New Hope?" Karen Morgan, a dear family friend and lab technician at Kiwoko Hospital, said to my parents. "He will still live at Kiwoko to receive medical attention, but something must be done for him. He sits alone all day at the hospital doing nothing. He can't go home either - his father has disowned him."

When we first saw Bizimungu, his legs, arms, and stomach were covered with gauze and bandages so that all that could be seen of him were his feet, hands, and face. From a young age he had suffered from what was thought to be a rare disease that caused his skin to eat away at itself. After months of cleaning and bandaging, his skin would heal, but its paper-thin structure did nothing to protect him from the daily "wear and tear" that normal skin can handle. Often the smallest bump to his skin would reopen an old wound, and sometimes develop into a wound far worse than the one before it.

Though they continued to test and research Bizimungu's condition, as far as the doctors knew, there was nothing that could be done for him except frequent cleaning and bandaging of the wounds.

"I came to Kiwoko in 1987," Bizimungu began to reminisce over the years. "I was sick and had wounds all over my body. My parents would bring me to the clinic when I was very bad, I would get better, we'd return home, and I would get worse again. Finally, my father got tired and said, 'This is not my child. I can't have a child who is sick like this.'

"My mother, however, never wanted to give up on me, and she soon brought me back to the hospital, because she had seen that I improved there. But eventually, because my father refused to support her, my mom ran out of money and couldn't bring me back to the hospital. Somehow, Karen Morgan heard about me and asked what was wrong. When she found out what the situation was, she offered to let me stay at Kiwoko and to do tests on me for free. But even though I was staying at Kiwoko, my wounds continued to get worse. The doctors never knew what the problem really was.

"When it was time for Karen Morgan to return to the States, she came and asked if I could come to school at Kasana."

In 1993, Bizimungu joined the Kasana family as a day student. Each day he would arrive at school in the Kiwoko pickup, which carried the hospital staff children to school. He would spend the day at New Hope, doing what he could despite his condition, and then return to the hospital's nutrition ward, which he now called home.

"When Karen left," Bizi continued, "I began to get very sick again as I was not getting the medical care that I had when she was there."

Very concerned at Bizimungu's deteriorating state Auntie Evelyn arranged for Bizi to come and stay at New Hope so that she could oversee his care.

"But instead of improving once I came to New Hope, I only worsened. Everyone at Kasana tried to encourage me," Bizi continued, "but I had lost most of my hope. My father had told me that I was useless."

Despite the encouragement of the Kasana kids and staff, Bizimungu remained in despair and hopelessness. "Whenever people would come to see me, I would not see it as an encouragement. I thought they were coming to mock me, and I never wanted anyone to come near me."

Nothing seemed to help Bizi. "My wounds got so bad that I could no longer walk. No medicine could help," he said.

The pain was so intense that he could no longer straighten his legs lest his paper-thin skin would tear. Eventually, he developed contractures, making it physically impossible for him to straighten his legs. But Auntie Evelyn did not give up.

"She would clean me with a lot of tears," he remembered. Her mother's heart overflowed with love for Bizi, and she spent countless hours caring for both his emotional and his physical wounds.

"While other nurses had been so rough with me, Auntie Evelyn was so gentle," Bizi said. "She would dress my wounds so carefully, three times each day, soaking them first before she removed the bandages."

In addition to Auntie Evelyn's tireless love, many members of the Kasana family reached out to Bizi. Each night, Wamala Fred, one of our boys, and Laurena Hensel would go down to the clinic to care for Bizi and spend the evening with him. Later on, because he couldn't walk, between five and ten boys would come each morning to my family's house where Bizi was staying, lift him onto a comfortable armchair, and carry him in it to school. This chair served not only as a glorified stretcher, but also as a work area while he attended class. Though the Kasana family did whatever they could to encourage Bizi and to lift his spirits, he continued to be depressed and hopeless.

"During those days many people would come and pray for me," Bizi continued, "but I never took it seriously. I never wanted anyone to come and visit me because I thought they were just wasting their time. And yet, during the days when I was too sick to go to school, I would just sit there feeling lonely, hearing the sound of the kids coming and going.

"Then, one day, Uncle Jay and Auntie Vicki were on a walk and passed by to come and check on me. While they were there, they asked if I would come to their house for the weekend, because Auntie Evelyn would be away. But I didn't want to go to their house. I thought I would be a burden to them. I also knew that my wounds smelled very badly, and I didn't want to share that with anyone. I told Auntie Evelyn that I didn't want to go. But she said, 'You know what, Bizi? It's only a weekend, and then I'll be back.'"

"When Auntie Vicki and Uncle Jay came to visit me the next time," Bizi continued, "they said again that they wanted me to spend the weekend with the family. With my mouth I said it was fine, but in my heart I was saying, 'I don't care what happens to me now. I'm going to die soon anyway.'

"The Dangers took very good care of me while I was there that weekend. I shared a room with Josiah, and he would always sit and talk to me. I felt somehow loved, but still in my heart, I was hopeless. I had seen many people in wheelchairs, and they couldn't do anything good with their lives. I felt that if I was going to always be lame, even if my skin healed, I wanted to die. Before I was so sick and couldn't walk, I had always wanted to do something very great. But now that I could no longer walk, I saw that my dreams were completely dying. Throughout the day, I would sit and wish that I could die."

Bizi had begun to feel more at home at my family's house, so after Auntie Evelyn returned it was decided that it was best for him to stay with us. Auntie Evelyn continued to come daily to care for Bizi's wounds, and with much prayer and time, Bizi began to smile again.

But, as if Bizi's life had not been scarred with enough pain, the Lord chose to take away the person that had become dearest to his heart – Auntie Evelyn.

Bizi's voice began to quaver as he shared the painful memories of Evelyn's death. "I wished that I would have died instead of her. She was the best person in my life," he said, now openly crying from the agony of this painful memory. "But she died. Before she had died, I had hoped I could get better. But when she died, I completely lost hope and I said to myself, 'I'm the next one,' because I knew no one could care for me like she had. In my heart, I knew that I was going to be the next one."

The tiny flicker of hope's flame that we had started to see in Bizimungu's life seemed to have been snuffed out. *God must not care,* he thought. *God must not know Bizimungu.* Once again his name meant nothing to him.

But, God *did* know, and He *did* see. The Father of the abandoned one, the One who cares more than we could ever imagine, had not left Bizimungu alone.

*"You, O God, do see trouble and grief...You hear, O* LORD, *the desire of the afflicted...you listen to their cry."*[71]

During the darkness of the days following Evelyn's death, many more people began to reach out to Bizi. Mary Silk, our new nurse, began to take a personal interest in Bizi's welfare, doing her best to fill the void that Evelyn's death had left in Bizi's life. Dr. Ben Kingi, a doctor at Kiwoko Hospital, also spent hours researching Bizi's physical condition, listening to Bizi's heartaches, praying with him and encouraging him.

Still not sure of the cause or proper treatment of Bizi's skin disease, Dr. Ben suggested a surgical procedure that would, Lord willing, restore mobility in his knee joints and eventually enable him to learn to walk again.

---

[71]Psalm 10:14, 17

"They would put me to sleep every other day – Monday, Wednesday, and Friday," Bizimungu recalled. "Once I was asleep, they would straighten my legs. I didn't know what was happening, until the morning when I would feel a lot of pain. But Uncle Jay, who came with me to the surgeries, would tell me what had happened. They would straighten my legs, and my knee would just crack. It was as if they had broken me. The next morning I would just feel pain, but I would see no difference. This went on for several weeks. I never wanted to disappoint them and stop them from doing it because I thought I would keep burdening people who weren't my real parents. I thought, *These people are trying to help you, but you just want to refuse what they are doing for you.* So I kept quiet because I knew I would die soon anyway. I gave up saying anything about my body apart from doing what they told me. It reached a point when I would say, 'I am like an animal on which they are doing all sorts of tests.'"

<hr />

It was almost dark, and our living room was filled with people – staff members, a team from Oxford, England, and Bizimungu, who was asleep on the couch. Nothing we had tried had worked – prayer, medical research and tests, surgeries, and more.

Although a medical doctor herself, missionary Jan White felt strongly that this was not merely a medical condition, and that we needed to spend time in focused and fervent prayer for Bizimungu. Could we have an evening of prayer while they were all here? So we had called those who loved and knew Bizi well. Each one came with an expectant heart and the faith that nothing is impossible with the Lord.

We began to pray individually and corporately, begging the Lord for mercy on Bizimungu's life.

"Bizimungu," Uncle Jonnes was kneeling by the couch by Bizi's head. Bizi woke up, confused as to where he was and looked around to see all of us gathered around him, praying.

"I was asleep when everyone arrived," Bizi smiled as he remembered. "I never knew when they carried me from my room to the couch. I only remember waking up when they were praying for me and anointing me with oil."

"Bizimungu, I want to talk to you about your relationship with your father," Uncle Jonnes looked at Bizi with love in his eyes. His father? What did this time have to do with his father? We were here to pray for his legs and his skin, not the fact that his father had abandoned him.

But Uncle Jonnes, prompted by the Holy Spirit, knew exactly what to say. "I feel you are harboring bitterness and anger toward your father, and the Lord wants you to forgive him." Bizi began to cry as he and Uncle Jonnes, ignoring the crowded room, walked through Bizi's past and prayed that the Lord would give Bizimungu the grace to forgive his father.

"Now," Uncle Jonnes continued, "I want you to look at me and pretend I'm your father. What would you like to say to me?"

What transpired next, I will never forget. As Bizi, with tears in his eyes, looked at Uncle Jonnes and spoke forgiveness and love to his father, his legs began to straighten before our eyes. Legs, usually pulled tightly toward him, legs that even a doctor could not properly straighten through surgical methods began to relax and slide down on the couch. His eyes remained fixed on Uncle Jonnes, and we watched in amazement as the Lord answered our prayers. Yet Bizimungu was oblivious to his physical change!

When their time of sharing and prayer was over, Uncle Jonnes smiled, "Bizi – look! Look at your legs! Look what the Lord has done!" The time of intense prayer and beseeching the Lord for mercy instantly erupted into a time of praise and thanksgiving to the Lord for faithfully answering our prayers. *Bizimungu* – Your heavenly Father *does* know; He heard your cries and He answered!

───────────────── ❧ ─────────────────

Over the next few days, Bizimungu's improvement was remarkable. While his legs were not entirely straight after the night of prayer and had lost most of their muscle tone due to months of inaction, by the next day he was able to sit on the seat of a child-sized bicycle and use his feet to push against the ground. He was mobile again, and we began to see something we had nearly lost hope of seeing again – Bizimungu's contagious smile!

Not long after his first discovery of mobility, he was able to begin slowly peddling on the bike. With the exercise causing strength to return to his legs, it was not long at all until Bizi was walking, then running. Bizimungu's wounds also began to heal rapidly. His skin began to grow back, and with each passing day the bandaging process became easier and easier. I will never forget the exciting announcement Bizi made to the family one day: "Guess what? I do not have a single sore on my whole body!" Oh, God is good!

At each stage of Bizi's recovery, we gave thanks to Him who made it all possible. Bizimungu's life was drastically changed. He was able to play with other children and attend school – even walk there himself!—instead of spending hours each day cleaning his wounds. His joy, his laughter, and his mischievous pranks and jokes that kept my family in stitches had returned.

What a contrast! He had been transformed from a boy who saw himself as rotten – inside and out – who had been disowned by his own father then lost the woman who had been such a tangible expression of Christ's love, to a boy filled with inexpressible joy who laughed again. His heart was free from bitterness, and his body was well on its way to recovery!

Bizimungu's words say it best: "I wish people could open up my heart and look inside! It is laughing in there!"

The Lord also continued to work miracles in Bizi's relationship with his father. Uncle Jonnes, not long after the time of prayer, took Bizi to meet his father. Their time was a blessed one – with his father welcoming him as a son and showing obvious signs of the pleasure of being reunited with Bizimungu. Not two years later, when his father died, he once again expressed his love to his son by making Bizimungu the heir to all he owned – an honor Bizimungu never dreamt of receiving. Not only had his physical body received healing, but the Lord had also healed his relationship with his father.

The years since Bizimungu's healing have not been perfect or void of pain and times of trouble. Despite all the Lord had done for him, Bizi has struggled to believe that *all* things work together for good. When his father's inheritance became a burden for Bizimungu to defend from greedy relatives, when a small new wound opened on his leg, or malaria kept him in bed for days, Bizi would often allow himself to slide back into the depression he had been slave to for so long.

But our God is so merciful and faithful, even when we are faithless! Each time, when Bizi realizes the truth of his situation and chooses to see the Lord's hand at work, the Lord raises him up again, and he is able to go on again in confidence. Those who love Bizi have also remained faithful to him – my parents, Dr. Ben, Uncle Jonnes, Uncle Kimera, and so many more. Our persistently merciful Father is not through with Bizimungu! His ups and downs do not scare the Lord! Faithfully, the Lord continues to grow Bizimungu into the man He would have him be.

Today, Bizimungu's faith continues to grow. His life choices are reflecting a maturity and wisdom previously not seen, and he has sacrificially cared for his mother and siblings. Now an independent man, Bizimungu knows there are always people at Kasana to whom he can run when he needs advice, encouragement, or help. More and more, he is coming to know the love of his heavenly Father, who works all things out for Bizi's good and who will never leave him or forsake him. He is beginning to see and accept how the Lord used the difficulties in his life to work out His perfect plan for him. Had he been a healthy child, he would have been raised by his parents, but he would have remained illiterate, would easily have been pulled into the immoral lifestyles that have brought early deaths to others of his siblings and relatives, and, most importantly, he may never have come to know his heavenly Father – who does know and does care!

*Why do you say, O Jacob, and complain, O Israel, 'My way is hidden from the LORD; my cause is disregarded by my God'? Do you not know? Have* you not heard? The LORD is the everlasting God, the Creator of the ends of the earth....He gives strength to the weary and increases the power of the weak....Those who hope in the LORD will renew their strength. They will soar on wings like eagles; they will run and not grow weary, they will walk and not be faint.

(Isaiah 40:27–31)

Bizi on a boat.

Bizi on a bike.

Bizi being carried.

# Chapter 24
# *Not an Orphanage*

*"Please don't call me an orphan. I am not an orphan because I have a Father, and I have a family! My Father is God. My family is here all around me – the Kasana family."*

– Matthew Namanya, a Kasana son,
sharing his testimony at a staff envisioning week

*"Have you noticed something, Jennie?" Kimera asked me. "No matter how children leave – be it in a good way or a bad way, they all look at Kasana as home! They do! They'll always come home. And we will be here to welcome them!"*

"Jay, I really like the vision of New Hope that you and Jonnes and the others speak of, but it's too vague. I can't get my mind around it. I need you to put it down on paper." Robert Tumuhairwe was our new manager at Kasana. He had joined the team while my family was on furlough in 1992 and had brought with him a fresh excitement and an ability to organize things.

Up to this point, most of the ideas and principles upon which the children's center had been founded were in my dad's and Uncle Jonnes's minds. They would pass on their ideas to the new staff, who would each add their own personal touch, and so the vision was carried out. But now with a new manager who had not been there since the ministry's inception, there was a need for a simple and clear way of passing on the vision.

My dad accepted Robert's request and sat down to compose a summary of what was on his heart. Satisfied that he had condensed and explained things sufficiently, he presented a one-page document to Uncle Robert. "This is great, Jay," was his response, "but I still can't really grasp it. Can you condense it some more?" And so, once again, Dad sat down to whittle away the unnecessary words, leaving only the focus, the heart of the vision.

"I worked on it again," my dad reminisced, "and was able to get it down to a paragraph this time. Robert appreciated my work, but said, 'Can't you give me just one sentence?'"

One sentence! How could one sentence encompass all he wanted Kasana to be and to do? And then it came – simple, yet fully encompassing the heart of New Hope – its purpose was simply the message of Psalm 68:5–6: to bring the Fatherhood of God to the fatherless.

"Yes," Uncle Robert had said. "*This* is something I can work with!"

---
❧
---

*"I remember having Christmas holiday with the Dangers family one year with several other children. We had a great time eating hamburgers for the first time, sitting round the camp fire, and just having fun being with everyone. During that holiday, Uncle Jay also began to explain to us older children the vision for family villages. All the children were still living in the general houses up the hill at that time, so this was all new to us. He began to share what the circular villages were to look like, and what their purpose was, and began to envision us, hoping that one day one of us would help in bringing this dream to reality."*

*– Kimera Steven*

"Jay, we now have a clear and concise purpose for Kasana," Uncle Robert began, "'bringing the Fatherhood of God to the fatherless.' And from the beginning, you've talked of family and family villages. But what we have now are dormitories, not families."

My dad had been aware for a long time that this part of the vision was yet to become a reality, but he felt stuck. We were very low on finances, we didn't have near the number of staff we needed, and we were struggling with the behavior of some of the children. How could we break free from what we were doing and bring about such a drastic change?

The discussion went on as to when we might be able to afford to build the first village, and the date discussed seemed very far off. It was true. It had always been about family – our theme verses stated it clearly—"God sets the lonely in families."[72] Yet somehow we had been unable to fully make this verse a reality at Kasana up to this point.

"Wait a minute," Uncle Robert said. "Let's think about this. We do not need permanent structures for the families! We started with a mud building, and it worked just fine! Why not go back to that same structure! We can't wait until everything has come together. Let's just do it!"

*"While I was in YWAM, I said, 'God, I need to hear You; I need to know what Your plan for my life is.' He had been stirring my heart with verses about caring for orphans and spending my life for others, but I didn't know specifically how this would look. So, I prayed and prayed that God would direct me, and then He gave me a dream. I didn't know what it meant at the time, but later, I saw its meaning unfolding. In my dream Uncle Jonnes and I and others were walking, and we went behind a big house and into the bush. The whole time we were moving in a circle. There were a lot of activities going on around us, and then we began working and setting up huts in round circles. When I woke up, I had no idea what it meant, but I continued to pray and ask the Lord to show me. Again, He gave me another dream. I was with Uncle Jonnes again, and he was driving a long thing like a train, then he turned to me and said, 'Now it's your turn to operate it.' So I began operating the machine with him."*

– Kimera Steven

"Kimera, we would like to offer you a job in childcare!" Uncle Jonnes, Uncle Robert, and my dad smiled as they offered the first Kasana son a position as staff member. It was June 1995, and Kimera had just completed training in YWAM and had applied for a job working with children. The only

---

[72]Psalm 68:5-6

clarity the Lord had given him was that he should return to work at Kasana. The rest was still unclear – at least for the time being!

Not long after his work began, Uncle Robert approached Kimera with an idea. "Kimera, we need to begin to carry out the vision practically. We need to begin to place children in families. We say we are not an orphanage, and yet, our children are living in dormitories like in an orphanage. Will you be the first father of our first family at Kasana? I will help you, but I want you to be the main father."

Although the blueprints showed round villages at the end of each of the seven "spokes" (roads), the blueprints were still just blueprints. The reality was that there was still thick bush in each of the places where family villages were to be built. The "Kasana Sheraton"[73] would have to suffice for the first family home.

In late 1995, all of the children in group two packed their bags and moved back to where it had all started. The change was almost instant. Group two became David Family, and the children began to take pride in their new home, their new "siblings," and the fact that they had a place they now belonged. That next year, David Family began clearing the land that would become their permanent home. Still, there was not enough money for permanent round houses, so four round huts were built.

"It was then that I began to realize what my dream had been about!" Kimera smiled. As in his dream, behind a big house (the "Sheraton") he and Uncle Jonnes and others, the children the Lord had brought him, began clearing and building round homes in a circle.[74] Ten years after we had arrived in Uganda, the first children's village was built and established. It hadn't been in our timing, but God had taught us so many valuable lessons in the meantime, and now it was His timing.

---

[73]The original mud building, which housed the first children and staff, was eventually turned into our guest-house. When a visiting team came from California they painted a large sign to be displayed outside the guesthouse. It read "Kasana Sheraton," and the name stuck ever since!

[74]Kimera's dream regarding Uncle Jonnes and him working together and then Uncle Jonnes handing him the controls was clarified when he bagan to work as Uncle Jonnes' assistant in the childcare department and was later handed Uncle Jonnes' position as head of the childcare department as Uncle Jonnes continued to mentor him and guide him in his new position.

It wasn't long after David Family was established that it became so clear how desperately important it was for the other children to also be divided into families. And this fact was not just clear to the staff. The children themselves began to see the benefit of living in a family as opposed to a dormitory.

"I'll never forget the day that several of the students came up to me and asked me a question that changed my life," recalled Uncle Willy, Worcester Family's first father and a member of staff for over eleven years. "It was Bosco, Lydia, Dan, Rukundo, and Justine. I was young and a new staff member at Kasana working mainly in construction, but also helping this group of children in their gardens, so we'd become good friends. But I was not prepared for the question they asked me. 'Uncle,' they said, 'we want you to be our father. We want our group to move out of the dormitories like David Family has, and we want you to be our father.' I was shocked," Uncle Willy recalled with tears in his eyes. "I mean, I was so young, and I had never even been fathered myself. I knew I didn't know how to *be* a father. But I also knew I could not say no to them."

Not long after the children's request, City Church Worcester in England raised funds, and the first permanent family village was built. And the same year David Family moved into their village, Worcester Family, with Willy as their father, was established.

And so the blueprints finally began to come alive! Pacific Family came next, named after the Lutheran church in Pacific Palisades, California, that funded the building of their family village. Calvary Family was funded by Calvary Chapel Costa Mesa. The children and staff of "group 1" had been praying that the Lord would give them land and a place to have as their own.

"We prayed and prayed that the Lord would let us become a real family like the others had experienced," remembered Simon Katabaazi, one of the leaders of group one. "So when we were told there was a piece of land for us and that the building process would begin soon, we began to think of a name for our new family."

After much prayer, group one's children and staff decided on the name "Samuel Family." "Because, like Hannah in the Bible had prayed for a son and the Lord heard her and gave her Samuel, we had prayed for a family and the Lord had heard our prayers," Simon reminisced. And so, Samuel Family was born.

Later, the members of family five were given a piece of land and a home of their own. Being good friends with those in David Family, the children's vote for their family name was Jonathan Family.

And last but not least, in 1999, a final family, made up of twenty-six children nearly all brand-new to Kasana, began. They named themselves Ebenezer Family, meaning—"Thus far the Lord has brought us." In 2001, Ebenezer Family, who had been living in the former "General Paddock," moved down into the last of the seven villages. The circle was finally complete, and the buildings of the "General Paddock" graduated to staff housing.

"I really see that New Hope has changed so much from the early days," Matthew Namanya, a New Hope son and member of Jonathan Family recollected. "When I arrived at Kasana, it was struggling financially. We found the era of good food on the weekends was over. We lived in the 'General Paddock,' as we called it, but that was not bringing the identity of family. All the children lived together. We had dorm inspections, and many would easily dodge their responsibilities because there were so many children. The older children, too, would often mistreat the younger ones, but because there were so many of us, the staff was not aware of all that went on. At that time, there was talk of family, but we didn't really see it. It wasn't clear then that our goal was to create families. But as soon as we were disbanded and put into our family villages, there was a huge change. Children have now found their identity in their families."

A perfect example of how putting the children into families gave them identity and a sense of belonging was with Jonathan Family. Several years ago, there was a time when the children in Jonathan were as divided as they could possibly be. The family lacked consistent, solid fatherhood, adding to the children's frustration and lack of cooperation. Consequently, New Hope leadership decided the only option was to disband the family and allocate different children from Jonathan to the other six families. Besides, the children acted as if there was nothing they would prefer more than to be far away from each other – their only way of relating to each other was through fighting and arguing. Well, when news of this reached the children, there was nearly a riot.

"We are a *family!*" they protested. "You *cannot* separate us!" And there was instant unity where before there had been strife! Needless to say, this was not the response that had been expected!

"Even though we had not been unified before," Matthew recalled, "we knew we had become a family, and family had become so important to us. We could not be separated."

It is these seven families that daily portray the vision of Kasana. It is here that children are raised, prayed for, corrected, and find security and identity. It is here that "aunties" and "uncles" become "moms" and "dads," and the orphan finds a home.

Yes, there have been struggles. Not all families blend instantly and beautifully. There are tribal differences, language and cultural differences, painful backgrounds that must be dealt with, children who are too wounded to want to be loved, personality conflicts, and more. And the Kasana staff is certainly continuing to learn. As the years have progressed, the Lord has given wisdom and guidance in new and confusing situations. And the seven families remain strong. Those who have grown up and gone out on their own come home and are warmly welcomed by their younger siblings and parents – just like a real family.

Indeed, the New Hope Uganda Kasana Children's Centre is not an orphanage. It is a home for orphans who are one by one giving up their orphan status by accepting the love of their heavenly Father and becoming sons and daughters of the King of kings and choosing to belong.

                                    ço

For the remainder of this chapter, I would like you to "meet" a few of the wonderful family parents and staff who have sacrificed their lives, time, and love for the Kasana children. I would like you to hear from them what they've learned and experienced, and to glean from their wisdom as they answer questions I asked them in interviews.

What have you learned as you've served the fatherless children in your family groups?

- *"Don't expect a quick thank you. At times you may never get it. I have learned patience – plant the seed and do not demand for a quick yield but wait for God's time – keep watering and in time, it will yield fruit. I have received big thank you hugs after a while."*

  Francis Mugwanya, Worcester Family Father

- *"They are not different from other children. They are insecure and have lost trust – they need us (me) around even if they don't show that they need it, so we need to be available and give them love and assurance that we care."*

  Joseph Ruyondo, responsible for the children who are part of the Kasana family but live out in the villages

- *"That it's more blessed to give than to receive. That it's more important to serve even if you feel like you're getting nowhere. We don't always know when the fruit will be seen!"*

  Alison Casebow, a mother figure to many

- *"God has shown me how selfish I am and how much I presume to know when I really don't know much. I've also learned that what to me might seem little is actually significant."*

  Nancy Kirsch, David Family Mother

● *"I've learned patience, pressing on, and that God can use these children to be wonderful people in the future. I've learned that I need to depend on God to change the attitudes of the children, not our own efforts."*

Kairanga Everest, Calvary Family Father

● *"I have learned that it is impossible to meet all their needs in my own strength. Until Christ touches them, they are never satisfied and always show that there is something missing or lacking inside them."*

Simon Katabazi, Samuel Family Father

● *"Whatever kindness or goodness I show them I should do it as unto the Lord, not to them, because people forget easily. I shouldn't expect to be appreciated or remembered. But God remembers!"*

Grace Nassaka, Samuel Family Mother

● *"I have learned that I have to remind myself of the Father's heart in order to reach them. I have learned that they are children who have lost security, identity and love as they lost their parents."*

Lydia Sseddinda, Ebenezer Family Mother

● *"The best part of being a family father is the fact that there's a lot to learn from the kids. First of all, you have to learn self-control. If a child does something that really makes your mood become angry, and you say, 'I could finish this one off!' Can you control yourself or not? Self-control is so important in your life. If you don't have it, you could spank a child like you're spanking a cow. That hurts them, and they will never forget it. Self-control is number one, listening is number two. Don't act immediately after you've listened. You can easily do harm to someone because you haven't listened. But, if you listen, it gives you the base to stand on and help you. I now know how to handle a child, because you are dealing with a human being; you've got to give this human being your attention and your whole heart. I have learned to be open, and that's what I say to them. It has blessed my heart so much, in that sometimes kids have told me their stories and I've burst into tears with them. Sometimes the kids will tease me, but they see it and they really know that I easily cry and they don't see that in me I don't pretend. I'm not perfect, I'm still learning, I'm still in 'school.' I'm still learning a lot. Disciplining a child is helping a child become something tomorrow – you're shaping him – helping him be what he couldn't otherwise be."*

Rukundo William, Pacific Family Father

What challenges did you face being a Family Parent?

- *"Treating all the children in the family equally because some were outgoing and others were hard."*

Kairanga Everest

- *"Facing rejection from the children."*

Grace Nassaka

- *"To continually love and accept the unlovable and those children who can't trust and accept me."*

Lydia Sseddinda

What are some hurtful statements you've received from the children you are raising and love?

- "You're not my *real* father."
- "Even if you *say* you love me, you can't love me like my real father."
- Never saying thank you
- "You're just doing this for the money."
- "How *can* I trust you?"
- "Were there no jobs left in America? Is that why you are here?"

What are some things that make you get choked up or make it all worthwhile?

- *"I get all choked up when the children say to me, 'Aunt, are you coming home tonight?' I love it when kids call their family group home and not 'the family group.'"*

  Nancy Kirsch

- *"Even when the children didn't appreciate me for anything, I knew I was doing it all to the One called 'God.' Whatever He has used me to do has been for His glory, not my own fame or glory, so I continue."*
  Francis Mugwanya

- *"In the last eight years, I have received four very special thank you letters from kids which I read any time I want to go back home to the States. I've also had many students who have left the school come and say thank you for teaching me."*

  Nancy Kirsch

- *"Knowing whose business we are involved in and seeing some fruits of our labor."*

  Joseph Ruyondo

What has kept you here at Kasana?

- *"Understanding the vision, visualizing my role in the ministry, waiting upon God and getting encouragement from God during hard times or when tempted to quit."*

  Joseph Ruyondo

- *"I lost my father when I was young, and my mother suffered as she cared for all of us children as a widow. I enjoy serving in Kasana because to me it is one of the ways I can say, 'Thank You, God, for making me what I am.'"*

Kairanga Everest

- *"The spirit of family that is evident in and around Kasana has kept me here."*

Simon Katabazi

- *"Knowing that God loves me and lifts me up even when I fall down; knowing that this is where He wants me to be at this time; seeking counsel through praying and sharing with godly friends in times when I definitely would have quit."*

Grace Nassaka

Childcare staff members and David, Samuel, Jonathan, Ebenezer, Worcester, Calvary, and Pacific family parents from years past and today, you have been a blessing! The seeds you have planted in the hearts of your children, the hours of your time you have sacrificed, the tears you have cried and prayers you have prayed have not been in vain! And though you may not see the fruit of your labor yet, it is with confidence that we remember, *"Those who sow in tears will reap with songs of joy. He who goes out weeping, carrying seed to sow, will return with songs of joy, carrying sheaves with him"*![75] And indeed, as the author of Hebrews writes, *"God is not unjust; he will not forget your work and the love you have shown him as you have helped his people and continue to help them."*[76]

---

[75] Psalm 126:5-6
[76] Hebrews 6:10

Worcester Family village, 2004

Calvary Family

Ebenezer Family, 2004

Worcester Family, 2004

# Chapter 25
## *Family Matters*
〜

*"I liked the spiritual parenting that was offered here at Kasana, and I knew that if I left, no one else would give me that. I also knew that no one outside of Kasana would counsel and handle me in the way they do here. Instead, they would just counsel me to do what was wrong. When others encouraged me to leave Kasana in the early days, I decided to stay because of the parenting I was given."*

— Scovia (Nakacwa) Oundo, a New Hope daughter
and current staff member

## A FAMILY AFFAIR

He first came to spend one night with our family. His brother, Ziwa, had died the day before, and we knew we couldn't send him home to an empty house. Their parents had already been separated for years when their father was brutally murdered during the war, just feet from where the boys stood. After witnessing their father's death and then experiencing abuse and rejection in the home of their new stepfather, the boys decided it would be better to fend for themselves than to continue suffering daily abuse.

At the ages of seven and nine, Ziwa and Sennyonjo moved out on their own, built themselves a house made of grass, and began working in people's gardens for food and the money they needed to pay school fees. Carrying a load far bigger than should ever be required of a small child, Ziwa became not just a big brother, but also a father figure to Sennyonjo. And then, after a two-day bout of malaria, Ziwa was gone.

Sennyonjo's one night at our house became two nights, a week, and then months. My family loved having Sennyonjo in our home. He had been Josiah's, Jamie's and my good friend even before he and Ziwa had joined the Kasana family. Then, once they had become day students, we spent even more time each day with Sennyonjo. Now we were thrilled to have him in our home! However, my parents soon began to be concerned that our having Sennyonjo live with us was showing favoritism. We feared that the other children would feel second-rate if they had to live in the "General Paddock" while Sennyonjo got to be part of a real family. And so, after three months, it was decided that Sennyonjo should move in with the other children. I'll never forget the tears that flowed as my parents talked to Sennyonjo, my siblings, and me. It was hard for Sennyonjo to move out, but soon he grew used to life with the other children and began to flourish as a real leader among them.

Then, two years later, after we had returned from a sixteen-month furlough in Canada and the U.S., things changed once again.

"We have realized," my dad explained, "that while Jesus loved the multitudes, He also had those He was closest to. He had the seventy, the twelve, the three, and even the one." My parents had begun to realize how impossible it was to give the depth of discipleship they desired to *each* of the children. There were just too many. As they prayed about it, they realized that it was better to invest much in some than little in many. Quality was definitely better than quantity. If they could choose a few that they could pour into, those few would, in turn, reach out to others. It was what the Lord did – within the limitations of His humanity, He chose to pour Himself into a few. But it was those few who changed the world.

"So! Can he move back in with us?" we children nearly shouted when our parents shared their thoughts with us. "Can we go tell him *now?*" And so, Sennyonjo moved back in with us and became an official part of the Dangers family. Along with him, my parents also brought in Esther Birabwa, a friend of mine, who had shown real leadership potential, but who was also struggling with negative influences from friends and with difficulties at home.[77] And so it was time to play "musical bedrooms," make a new chore chart, and celebrate that there were two exciting new additions to the family!

Bringing Sennyonjo and Esther into our home was a turning point in our family – the beginning of "enlarging the place of our tent, and stretching our tent curtains wide."[78] My parents knew that often the results would take a while – that those invested in might not instantly flourish and be ready to change the world. But they also knew that no spiritual investment is in vain. The Lord's Word never returns to Him void, but it accomplishes the purpose for which it was sent. Our job is just to plant the seed. It is His to make it grow and bear fruit.

We were sitting in the classroom working, when suddenly Sennyonjo and Kimera came running up shouting. "Auntie Laurena! We need your help quickly – Paul has broken his arm!"

"Are you sure it's broken?" Laurena said as she quickly followed the boys back to their classroom. The question seemed almost silly as soon as she saw it. His arm had been completely fractured, and half of his forearm was at least an inch above the other half. "It's broken all right," Laurena said, as her first aid skills quickly came in handy.

It was Paul's right arm, and he was right-handed. The doctors said it would take at least six weeks to heal. This would not have been as serious had he been living with a family who could help him, but Paul lived with his younger siblings in the village, and he depended on his ability to work in his garden to feed them. It was soon decided that his older brother would look after his other siblings, and Paul would move in with us until his arm healed. As it did with the others, Paul's time with us joined our hearts to his in a

---

[77]Esther's father had died, but her mother, Mary, worked for my mom and was struggling to raise her five children on her own. After discussions with Mary, it was decided that the best way to help Esther was to have her move in with us for a time, but to still remain in frequent contact with her mom. Esther eventually moved back in with her mom, but will always be an important part of our family.

[78]Paraphrase of Isaiah 54:2

real and lasting way. Though he moved back to live with his own siblings, Paul has a permanent place in the Dangers family. His wife became our first sister-in-law, and his children some of Mom and Dad's first grandchildren.

Bizimungu joined our family when his health was at its lowest point. He too joined us for the weekend and then became a permanent part of the family.

Richard, who had joined our family for several Christmas vacations, was struggling. His background had been filled with abuse and neglect. And when the amount of individual attention in the "General Paddock" was not sufficient to meet Richard's needs, it was decided that he should live with a family that could give him the parental involvement and care he needed. Now, the ratio of boys to girls in our home was 1-1! Four girls and four boys. Richard also joined our family in the United States for five months during one of our furloughs so that he could continue to live in a family.

Wasswa, also a regular Christmas-vacation-Dangers-family member, joined our family officially when it was discovered he had a severe case of diabetes. My parents knew that it would be very difficult to maintain a good diet and keep an eye on his blood sugar levels unless he was in a home. By this time, Esther had moved back in with her mom and Paul had returned home. Another mattress was added to the boys' ever-filling room, and with Esther gone, the ratio wasn't looking good for the girls!

One of the greatest blessings of growing up in Uganda was how the entire work at Kasana was a family ministry – in its focus, in its set-up, and practically in how our own family was run. To this day, my parents believe very strongly that in order to truly build and solidify the faith of a child, that child must be involved in age-appropriate "battles" that will give him his *own* stories of how the Lord answered prayer or worked on his behalf.

Too often, second- and third-generation Christians merely hear their parents' testimonies of the Lord's work in their lives, but because they have few testimonies of their own, they receive a "second-hand" faith whose flame quickly dies down. Too often missionary kids ("MKs") are not given the opportunity to join in with their parents' work, and they see the ministry as "Mom's and Dad's thing."

However, because of my parents' convictions, our immediate and extended Dangers family – Sennyonjo, Paul, myself, Esther, Bizimungu, Josiah, Jamie, Wasswa, Richard, Joyanne, Jeremiah, and Julia – have always been included in as many aspects of the ministry as was possible. It was always a family ministry – never just Dad's. We knew we were a team, and each member had a vital part to play.

When we were too young to hold official staff positions, we often filled in where there was a need – in the school, clinic, farm, or carpentry workshop. Later, we were able to fill specific roles. Sennyonjo, Paul, and I were a Sunday school teaching trio when I was ten and they were twelve. Many years later, Sennyonjo worked with teams and helped with the running of the Institute of Childcare and Family, and Paul, my cousin Jon, and I helped organize youth outreaches to other parts of the country. Esther, Richard, Josiah, Jamie, Joyanne, and I were often on the worship team. Joyanne participated in community outreaches, and Wasswa helped teach in the primary school and taught English as a second language to some of our staff.

Often, our "roles" were less obvious. Take our Jeremiah and Julia, for example! Though they are still too young to carry a real position (at this writing in 2006 they are nine and six), their warm and welcoming spirits do wonders in breaking down barriers between my parents and children who are hurting and would otherwise have been afraid to come to them for counsel and love. When dealing with children whose main interaction with adults prior to Kasana was abusive and filled with fear, shame, or neglect, the staff often struggled to draw the children to themselves. Frequently, we children filled the role of "go-betweens" or mediators between the kids and staff – turning the hearts of the fathers to their new children and the hearts of the children to their new fathers.

The "family business" has also spread throughout our extended family in the States, Uncle Jonnes' family, and that of many other staff members.[79] The Bakimi children, younger than most of us Dangers' kids, are becoming increasingly involved in leadership and ministry at Kasana as well. The Bakimi household makes our "full house" seem empty, as they gladly welcome anyone needing a place to live, comfort, or a family.

Uncle Jonnes' brother, Godfrey, is also a long-standing member of the Kasana family. For a time, we had three sisters all on staff, Anne, Rose, and Gertrude. Currently, Charles Francis and his cousin, Christopher, are both teachers at the secondary school. Both my mom's and dad's parents have spent much time at Kasana and have made significant contributions to what New Hope Uganda is today. My dad's sister, Jacquie, travels to Uganda frequently to assist in any way she can. Her husband, Ron, serves on the board of New Hope Uganda Ministries, Incorporated.

Stateside, my mom's mother, her cousin DeAnn, and her aunt and uncle, Fran and Duane, have worked tirelessly on financial and logistical issues for New Hope and our family. My cousin Jonathan Dangers also worked with us in Kasana for a year.

The list goes on and on of family members who have prayed, given, visited, and made things possible here in Kasana. This ministry is truly a ministry of family and of many families!

## THE FATHERHOOD OF GOD

As many organizations that work with children do, my father had originally intended to structure the children's center with children placed in homes and widows or childless couples placed as the care takers in each home. After all, women are known for being nurturing and the ones to care for children. World over, the role of raising children is seen as a woman's job. However, it was not long after we had started that my dad and Uncle

---

[79] It is impossible to mention all the family members who have joined in the work at Kasana: the relatives of the Clays, Shoracks, Casebows, Robin Hancock, the Woods, and so many more. We are grateful for the part every single family member has played and could not have done it without them!

Jonnes began realizing the importance of fatherhood. Indeed, of all the titles He could have chosen, the Lord calls Himself a Father. As they began to study the Scriptures, to look around them, and study history, it became clear to them that the vast majority of the world's problems come as a direct result of poor fatherhood. If men were truly taking their roles as father seriously, think of how empty prisons would be, think of how marriages would be reformed and restored, think of how the number of girls selling themselves to gain a man's affection would be reduced! Every child, every adult needs the affirmation, guidance, and acceptance of a *father*.

Not long after the first children were brought to Kasana, the New Hope Uganda leadership was faced with a sobering question: the next generation was in their hands, history would be formed at Kasana, so *how* were they going to make this generation different from the one that came before it? Crying out to the Lord for guidance, they asked for wisdom to end the cycle of sin that had ravished Uganda for generations. They knew that unless the Lord gave them real wisdom, this generation, orphaned from wars caused by men who had not been raised by godly fathers, by AIDS brought about by mothers desperate for a man's affection, or fathers who were never trained in godly behavior, would grow up with the same emptiness and lack of direction and would continue the fatal cycle. They too would become men with no boundaries, direction, or affirmation, trying to "prove" their manhood through immorality and violence. The girls would grow up with the need for affirmation and would look for it in all the wrong places; they would not be valued and would either have to fight for their "rights" or succumb to abuse and a "doormat" status.

In order to stop this vicious cycle, the Kasana leadership knew that a step back must first be taken to restore the broken foundations of fatherhood. Men must first be trained and discipled to be servant leaders, godly husbands, and faithful fathers. Men must take their rightful place in society and in the home. Then, as women see godly men taking their roles in the home seriously, sacrificially raising children who are not their own and taking their proper role of leadership, they too will be encouraged to carry out their God-given roles in the home and in reaching out to those who have no home.

And so, a new theme in Kasana's history began – a theme that stands strong until this day – the theme of fatherhood.

⁊⊷⥀

On the surface, it all sounds good and exciting: offering godly fatherhood and motherhood to the next generation, raising them up to be better parents than their fathers and mothers were, and training them to raise their children to be better mothers and fathers than themselves. What a wonderful cycle to begin! But what is one to do when even the staff members come from broken families and have never *experienced* fatherhood and family? One cannot give what one has never received.

Often those the Lord brings to staff Kasana, both foreign and Ugandan, have never received the true love of a father or mother or witnessed true "family life." In fact, at one point we had a Ugandan staff of over twenty, and only one had grown up in a two-parent, loving, still intact family. The message of family is intended for more than just the children the Lord brings to Kasana. Taking a step back in order to move forward, the focus at Kasana had to be turned somewhat toward those the Lord had brought to *be* fathers and mothers – *they* first must be loved, parented, and trained to father and mother the next generation. Now, years after this turning point, there are countless stories of adults who have been touched by family – many of whom had no family yet are now "mothers" and "fathers."

"Having been brought up by a single mother, being in Kasana has given me a sense of both physical fatherhood and spiritual fatherhood," shared Simon Katabazi, Samuel Family's former father during his single days and now headmaster of our primary school. Simon is husband to Noelina and the father of two little boys, along with several other children he and Noelina care for. "I've learned how a godly father should conduct himself in a family, and I have also received fathering from people like Uncle Jonnes. When many people from my tribe see me caring for my children and helping my wife with things like changing nappies or washing dishes, they think she has bewitched me and is manipulating me into helping her. But I get to share with them why I do this, and our family is able to be a living testimony of God's love." The fruit in Simon's life is seen in the way he is raising his two little boys and how he and Noelina have opened their home to several other fatherless children and loved them as their own.

"My view of parenting and fatherhood in particular has been deeply and positively affected," adds Francis Mugwanya, a single Worcester Family father. "I used to believe the myth that having a 'tough' face as a father would win respect from my children. Other myths like men are not to cry have also been undone in my mind. I believe that through the teaching of family at Kasana, my future wife and children will have a better husband and father than they otherwise would have had!"

Everest Kairanga, raised by a godly yet widowed mother, states, "Uncle Jay and Uncle Jonnes are models to me of what a father can be. It is my prayer always to embrace their teaching on family, which is to always have Christ at the center."

Anna Okello has been a staff member at Kasana for over eleven years. "When I first arrived in Kasana," she shared, "I lived with Uncle Jonnes and his family. I loved the time I stayed with them. Although I was an adult, my time with the Bakimis was my first experience with real fatherhood and motherhood. The Bakimis introduced me to family. I was loved in a way I'd never been loved before, and my eyes started opening to the true meaning of family."

While extremely uncommon in most places in Uganda, it is not at all uncommon to see a man at Kasana holding a child, playing with a group of children, sitting and talking or even crying with children. It is as if they've been freed to be what the Lord created them to be - examples of their heavenly Father to the children the Lord brings them. Consequently, many women have found new freedom and joy as they serve as family mothers or mothers to their own biological children. They no longer carry the full burden of raising children on their own, nor do they have to fight to prove their worth and value. They are being cared for and loved and are also able to flourish in the supportive and nurturing roles the Lord has given them in the home.

Deborah, in the Book of Judges, sang, "When the princes in Israel take the lead, when the people willingly offer themselves – praise the LORD!"[80] Indeed, it is when the princes take the lead, when men step into their godly servant-leadership roles as fathers and husbands, that the family can truly become whole. Women can flourish in their roles, cherished and protected by their husbands; biological children and orphans can find security, affirmation, and identity, and the pain-filled cycle can end. The next generation *can* be different!

## BEHIND EVERY GREAT MAN

"Trouble started as soon as I began telling our friends and family that Gertrude and I were going to move out to the village!" Uncle Jonnes began. "People instantly began saying, 'How dare you do such a thing!'

"When a British friend of ours came to visit us in our home in Kampala one day, we told her we were moving to Luweero. She knew what Luweero was really like and knew that there was nothing there that could compare to the house we had in town.

"She looked at us and said, 'You must be crazy! How can you leave such a house! Everyone is searching for good housing now that the war is over. How dare you talk of leaving such a house to go to live in the jungle?'

"I said, 'Well, God has called us to better things than a house! We are just responding to God.'

"Her response was simple; 'I don't understand you,' was all she said!

"Then there was a friend of ours, a doctor, who came and said, 'Jonnes,

---

[80]Judges 5:2, NIV

I've heard what you're trying to do, and I need to talk to you. Do you realize that you are being unfair to your wife?'

"When I asked him how I was being unfair, he said, 'Don't you know that you are destroying her career?'

"I didn't want to hear any more. I cut him short and said, 'Well, we didn't marry to build a career; we married to build a family.'

"Our friend smiled and said, 'I thought you could have both.'

"'Possibly,' I said, 'but our first priority is a family, and that's why we're going to Luweero to build it together.'"

"I had grown up in an empty home," Uncle Jonnes shared with tears in his eyes, "because my parents had divorced and there was no mother in the home. I had such pain in my heart – a pain that I do not want my children to ever have to experience! I want my children to come home and find their mother there, ready to welcome them, talk to them, and just *be* with them. Before I'd met Gertrude, when I imagined who I would marry, I really didn't care how educated she would be, or what her qualifications were – I just wanted her to be *there* with me and my children. What a blessing it is that this dream has come true!"

They say that behind every great man is a great woman. The Kasana story would not be complete if it did not include the stories of the roles that Auntie Gertrude, my mom, and many other great women play daily here at Kasana. They serve their husbands, raise their children, and provide a living example to those who've never experienced "family" or what a godly family can be. Each day my mom and Auntie Gertrude follow their pioneering husbands and bring order to what otherwise could be chaos. They have gifts of welcoming people, caring for the hurting, and making their homes havens of peace and respite for their families and those the Lord has added to them. Through the lens of the world, they and others like them have suffered huge injustices – being brought into the bush to support their husbands. The living conditions were often rough and the daily routine exhausting. Thousands of people have flowed in and out of their homes. What consideration has been given to their own careers and desires? Yet when you speak to them, this is not at all their perspective. In fact, it is quite the opposite!

"I feel so fulfilled!" Auntie Gertrude shared with a smile. "I really do not see my decision as a sacrifice at all! I am so grateful that the Lord brought me to Kasana and has allowed me to serve my husband and family here. I do not miss my former life in Kampala at all!"

As our Lord says, "Whoever loses his life for my sake will find it,"[81] and, "Everyone who has left houses...and fields for my sake will receive a hundred times as much and will inherit eternal life."[82] Although in the world's eyes, Auntie Gertrude has "lost her life," at Kasana her life has been multiplied. The number of children and adults who look to her as a mother cannot be numbered. The impact she has made for the kingdom can never be measured.

My mother too rejoices in her decision to follow her husband into the unknown.

"From the time I was a little girl, I knew I was supposed to be a missionary, and most likely to Africa," my mom recalled. "But I had no idea what I would be doing. I toyed with different possibilities, but nothing seemed to fit my gifting and interests. But when I met Jay and heard his vision for Africa, all I could think of was, 'I can go and help him!' There have been times when people have asked me what my position here at New Hope is. When I've told them that I'm a wife and a mom, I home school my children, and I take care of many visitors, many look at me as if to say, 'You poor thing.' But I have *loved* that aspect of my life. To me that is a very satisfying role, and I love it. When I imagined myself helping Jay, this is exactly what I imagined myself doing."

My parents work well as a team. While my dad is a visionary, my mom takes care of the details, the communication, and the relationships. She

---

[81]Matthew 10:39, NIV
[82]Matthew 19:29, NIV

helps my dad to "sense" the needs of people on staff that Dad otherwise would never notice. Dad is also the pioneer, and Mom follows him, making the frontier into a homestead. When people come in to see and take part in Dad's vision, Mom makes them comfortable and well fed.

A perfect example of this happened just recently. My parents received an e-mail from a man serving in the U.S. military in Iraq. He said he had been in our home in 1987 when Uganda was still in its recovery stage. He had never forgotten the way my parents had welcomed him and the hamburgers and chocolate cake my mom had served him. While he was in Iraq, something happened that reminded him of my mom's hospitality, and he felt the Lord wanted him to track us down and send my parents a financial gift. This message came at a time of real financial strain. Who would have thought eighteen years ago that a warm welcome, a hamburger, and piece of chocolate cake would make such an impact on someone and result in such a blessing to the ministry!

Would my mom and Auntie Gertrude trade their lives for anything? "Sometimes I've thought it would be nice to have a more 'normal' life," my mom admits. "Being married to a pioneer is not always easy! God certainly gave me a 'Caleb'—one with a different spirit who serves the Lord whole-heartedly.[83] Jay usually does things against the grain – to the best of his ability – as God would have him do it, but it is almost never the easy way! Each time, though, when I get tired of the hard work of taking the brunt of being pioneers, I think, *I wouldn't trade this life for anything.* If I ever imagine what life would have been like had we taken the 'easy route,' I think of how many lives wouldn't have been touched here, and I'm so thankful for where the Lord has led us regardless of the difficulties."

"I am a person who really doesn't like taking risks," Auntie Gertrude laughed, "so it is not always easy being the wife of someone who is always stepping out in faith! But I have made a commitment that if it is God's will, I would follow wherever He may lead us. I want God to help me to not be a

---

[83]Numbers 14:24

stumbling block in the way of what He is doing. When I am worried about what new step of faith Jonnes is taking, I can rest knowing that God is the One leading us, and I am able to follow and support my husband with confidence."

In addition to my mom and Auntie Gertrude, there are so many other great women who have served their husbands and families and consequently provided a beautiful and living picture of godly families for our children to witness. Alison Casebow, Anne Imusatlaba, Milly Mwase, Jodene Kessel, Raych Clay, and Susan Kusuubira are just some of the *many* great women who have been a blessing to their own families and the Kasana family. And those who are not "stay-at-home-moms," such as Sarah Muwanguzi, Anna Okello, Grace Mwanje, Cate Okoth, Lydia Ssedinda, and many, many others, still hold their homes as their number one priority.

"Because of being at Kasana, I now *value* my family," Grace Nassaka shared, a single mother of two. "I could never abandon them for the sake of ministry. I am working on winning *their* hearts so they can serve the Lord with me! We want to serve God as a family, not me alone. This wouldn't be the case if I hadn't come to New Hope."

Not only are each of these godly women blessings to their own husbands and families, but they also provide a daily example to the Kasana children of what a godly family can look like. Children who know nothing of a loving and close-knit family can observe daily what it means to be a family and can aspire to having their own one day.

Indeed, as the older Kasana children have moved on, it has been so exciting to see these whose own families were torn apart for one reason or another begin to create wholesome and faithful families and become fathers who are dedicated to their children and wives, and wives who joyfully support their husbands and love and care for their children. Kabogoza, Levi, and Matthias are just some of the many Kasana sons who are making a difference in their communities by simply being loving fathers and dedicated husbands. Kizza is a faithful and dedicated mother, Paul and Susan and Julius and Scovia are beautiful examples of godly couples, and the list goes on and on. Even those who are not yet married or do not yet have children of their own show signs of the "family values" they've learned.

It is not uncommon to see a teenage boy or girl pick up a little child and hold her, talk to her, and play with her. Indeed, we at Kasana believe that through one family at a time, even one former orphan at a time, Uganda's heritage of broken marriages, absent parents, and hurting homes is being exchanged for the miracle of beautiful, Christ-centered families!

## GOD SETS THE LONELY IN FAMILIES

What about those of us who are single or widowed and cannot offer the completeness of a whole family? Our role in the family here is equally vital.

Nancy Kirsch is one of the mainstays in the Kasana family. "As a single woman here at New Hope I am not a single woman; I am 'Auntie Nancy.' I have my job as a teacher, yes, but I have kids – a whole family of them – sons and daughters! Although I can't do for them *all* that a real mother might, what I *can* do on their birthday, when they are sick, when they are discouraged, when they are away from home, makes a difference and gives them a picture of what a real mom does."

Lydia Sseddinda, a widowed mother of four, is the mother of twenty-six in the Ebenezer Family. She testifies to how the emphasis on family has helped her biological family and her Ebenezer Family.

"It has continually reminded me of my relationship with God as a Father – my Father and my children's Father. It has also helped me in the parenting of my children. My own children and my Ebenezer Family children now receive fatherhood from the 'uncles' here. I know that this will help them and the other Kasana children to have better families in the future."

And what about the single men? Only at Kasana can a twenty-five-year-old man talk of his twenty or thirty children without people being shocked and quite concerned! Actually, we have had more single family fathers than married ones! They have soaked up the teaching on family and fatherhood, and they have chosen to pour themselves into the lives of the orphaned children the Lord brings to them!

Kimera Steven, Willy Mwase, Francis Mugwanya, Rukundo William, Kokas Otim, Charles Francis Ikwarit, Chris Sperling, Francis Opio, Kaleera Augustine, Simon Katabaazi, Shadrach Okiror, Everest Kairanga, Dan Kizito, and Ebenezer Nahabwe are many of the single-family fathers who have served and loved our children.

Indeed, the Lord does place the lonely in families – those who are orphaned, widowed, single, or have simply never experienced what a Christ-centered family can be. And what a joy it is for each of us – no matter what our background, past family experiences, or current marital status – to experience the richness of family, the joys of parenting, and the blessing of belonging.

> Sing...you who never bore a child; burst into song, shout for joy...enlarge the place of your tent, stretch your tent curtains wide, do not hold back...for you will spread out to the right and to the left; your descendants will dispossess nations.
>
> (Isaiah 54:1–3, NIV)

> Sons are a heritage from the LORD, children a reward from him. Like arrows in the hands of a warrior are sons born in one's youth. Blessed is the man whose quiver is full of them.
>
> (Psalm 127:3–5, NIV)

Bizimungu, Josiah, Richard, and Sennyonjo

Siblings in height order, Christmas 1999.

The Dangers' extended family, December 2001.

Josiah, Esther, Jennie, Jamie, Sennyonjo, and Joyanne, 1994

# Chapter 26
## *The Lord Gives and the Lord Takes Away*

❧❧

BLESSED BE THE NAME OF THE LORD, (JOB 1:21)

*Over the years, the Lord has seen it right to take members of the Kasana family to be with Him. Each of the stories in this chapter is an important memory and lesson to us. Each of the lives that are no longer with us will always remain as memories in our hearts. Each situation turned our eyes all the more to the Lord and proved again His faithfulness and closeness in times of heartache.*

*Some of the following stories are excerpts from newsletters that my father wrote to our supporters, friends, and family; others are my own attempts to do justice to their stories.*

**Ziwa William,** From a newsletter written in May 1990:
"Doctor Ian Clarke handed me the medical record. It read:
  'Patient's name: Ziwa William
  Address: Kasana.
  The patient arrived at 4:00 a.m. Dead on arrival. Had been treated here yesterday.'
"The diagnosis was cerebral malaria.
"As I walked out of the clinic, I saw Sennyonjo, Ziwa's thirteen-year-old brother and the only surviving child of their mother and deceased father. I

pulled him to me and held him tight as we cried. He knew without me having to say a word.

"Ziwa's illness had been very brief. He had spent Tuesday night at one of the children's homes in order to help the resident students make beehives. Wednesday morning I found him in their garden working alongside them before school. He was like that, very industrious and helpful. At about noon he developed a fever, which persisted to the next day, so he was sent to the clinic for a blood test. Malaria parasites were discovered, though not a severe case. He was given the standard treatment, and we took him back. After we had prayed with him, he wanted to sleep. It was 5:00 p.m.

"At 3:20 a.m. Thursday morning, I was awakened by Emmanuel. 'Ziwa is very sick. Can we take him to the clinic?' I dressed and jumped on my bicycle to ride the one mile to Kabubbu, where my parents were still living, in order to get our van. By about 3:45 we were racing down the rough, two-mile road to the clinic. Ziwa had been unconscious when we had carried him to the van, and I decided that speed was probably more important than comfort at this time. But I still was not sure how serious his condition really was. I had heard of other people becoming unconscious with malaria, but then being fine after treatment. Besides, he hadn't actually been all that feverish.

"'He's still breathing,' was the reply from the back seat as we approached the clinic. From the crying, I knew Sennyonjo was afraid. He was unusually close to his fifteen-year-old brother.

"Margaret Kacence, the nurse on duty and a close friend of the Kasana family, took Ziwa's temperature as I explained the situation. Ziwa seemed to be resting quietly under a blanket. It was about 3:58. We carried him inside and laid him uncovered on a bed. 'He's not breathing!' Margaret exclaimed, and she began checking for pulse. None. A minute later Dr. Ian was there to confirm her findings. It was 4:00 a.m. Ziwa was gone.

"Naturally we've been dealing with the question *Why?* Ziwa was a model student, a quiet but effective leader, and an example of integrity to the other children, especially for Sennyonjo. The two of them had been living on their

Later, when Kimera gave his life to the Lord, the man he was living with was furious. "This man had let me stay with him although I was not related to him because he liked the fact that I contributed to the family income through my hunting. But their home was filled with witchcraft," Kimera explained. "They were always carrying out their rituals and honoring evil spirits."

"Either you choose to quit this business of Christianity," the man threatened, "or you will no longer be welcome here, and you will be on your own."

"I shared my situation with Uncle Peter and Auntie Sarah and the others, and they welcomed me to join them. In those days," Kimera smiled, "everyone stayed in one house – the 'Sheraton.'[106] One room was for Uncle Emmanuel and Uncle Peter, one was for Auntie Sarah and little Wasswa Michael, another room was for the girls, and another room was for the boys. Several boys also slept in the sitting room, as there were so many of us. This was where I stayed."

৵৽

# 1995

A crowd had gathered to listen to the singing and to watch the skits this group of visitors was presenting. It had all been decently entertaining and interesting, but not riveting. That is, until a man they hadn't seen before stood up. His strange accent, brown skin, and short, stocky build made it obvious that he was a 'foreigner.' "Hello, everyone," the man began. "My name is Kimera Stephen, and I am from Luweero."

"Luweero!" the name passed through the crowd like wildfire. Instantly those who were only half-listening gave him their utmost attention. What could possibly bring a person from Luweero all the way to Gulu?

"I have come to share with you the love of Christ," Kimera continued. "But before I share that, I must tell you of my sincere love for you and of my

---

[106]The original mud building which housed the first children and staff was eventually turned into our guesthouse. When a visiting team came from California, they painted a large sign to be displayed outside of the guesthouse. It read "Kasana Sheraton," and the name has stuck ever since!

complete forgiveness of all that was done by your people to my people." And Kimera proceeded to share the gospel with his captive audience.

Gulu and Luweero: two areas in Uganda that had nothing in common but hate and mistrust. It was men from Gulu and other northern areas that had massacred thousands of innocent civilians in the Luweero Triangle – including Kimera's own father. So what *was* it that brought such a man here – and in peace?

"But sir," people from the crowd continued to ask, "have you *really* forgiven us? Is such a thing really possible?"

Kimera smiled at them. "Yes. By God's grace in my life, I have completely forgiven you, and I love you. Why would I ever come here if I didn't come to preach to you the gospel? And in order to carry the gospel, I must have forgiveness and love in my heart. Without forgiving you, this could never be."

The Lord has continued to do amazing work in Kimera's life during the sixteen years he has been at Kasana. He came to us a timid yet self-made young man, filled with fear and bitterness; he now walks in freedom and security. Kimera's role at Kasana has also grown immensely. From the beginning of his time here, he rose to positions of leadership. Then, upon completion of his studies and after his training in YWAM, Kimera came back to serve in the childcare department at New Hope Uganda.

"During my time in YWAM, I prayed very seriously about how I could serve the Lord and if I should go back to Kasana or not. My theme verses at the time were Isaiah 58:6–14, which talk about spending yourself on behalf of the poor. Also, the Kasana theme verses, Psalm 68:5, 6 and James 1:27 continually were in my mind. So I asked the Lord and said, 'God, I need to hear You.' And He spoke to me several times in dreams. In each of my dreams, I was with Uncle Jonnes, working, traveling, and doing all sorts of things. I was still not completely sure what the dreams meant, but I knew the Lord would show me in His time."

Declining a job to work for YWAM after completing the Discipleship Training School, Kimera chose to come home and apply for a job working with children. His addition to the Childcare Department was immediately significant. Kimera was able to understand the children and where they were coming from in a way that the other staff could not. He had been one. He had suffered what they had suffered and had even been a Kasana kid just like them.

With wisdom beyond his years, Kimera became an invaluable assistant to Uncle Jonnes, and the two have worked hand in hand even to this day. Kimera's dreams came true, and the desires of his heart to fulfill the verses God gave him during his time at YWAM have been granted. Daily he cares for orphans and widows in their distress,[107] spends himself on behalf of the hungry, loosens the chains of injustice, provides the wanderer with shelter, satisfies the needs of the oppressed,[108] and brings the fatherhood of God to the fatherless.[109] And consequently the Lord has blessed him and continues to make him a blessing to many.

# RUKUNDO WILLIAM

He sat alone in a corner of the house, dejected and hopeless. *You've been rejected,* Rukundo's thoughts told him. *You are nothing.* And, based on every circumstance in his life up to that point, he could only agree with the lies that crowded his mind. In addition to the painful state of his heart, the wound on his leg had continued to worsen. It had already been there for two years, and the cousin in whose house he lived seemed to think nothing of it. After all, he was just an orphan.

When Reverend Livingstone, the local Anglican reverend, saw the situation Rukundo was in, he had insisted that his cousin take him to the new clinic in Kiwoko. Not wanting to offend the reverend, his cousin agreed to

---

[107]James 1:27
[108]Isaiah 58:6-14
[109]Psalm 68:5-6

ride him on the back of his bicycle each day to see a doctor. There, Rukundo's festering wound would be treated and he would be given pills to combat the infection. But as soon as they would return from the clinic each day, Rukundo's cousin would tell him to go into the bush and collect firewood or do other jobs that would aggravate the wound and cause it to worsen.

"Rukundo," Doctor Ian Clarke's eyes looked concerned, "I'm afraid your wound is only getting worse. It looks like the only solution might have to be amputation."

"NO!" Rukundo's heart had screamed. "Not my leg." His life had already been nothing but suffering, but to take away his leg would cause it to be unbearable.

That night, as he lay quietly on his mat, Rukundo cried out to God. "God, it is You who gave me two legs. Please do not let me lose one of them."

The next day at the clinic, the nurses seemed pleasantly surprised. "Rukundo, it looks like we don't need to dress your wound today! We'll just put some iodine on it as it's looking so much better!"

Not even knowing the Lord, Rukundo had cried out in desperation, and the Lord had heard – and answered!

---

"His name is Rukundo William," Karen Morgan explained to Uncle Jonnes. "I got to know him when he had to come each day for a wound to be dressed. His wound is now better, Gudruna[110] and I have been paying his school fees at City of Faith in Kiwoko. But his home situation is not good. His grandparents, who had been raising him, have died, and he's living with a cousin that really doesn't care about him. Do you think he could come and live at Kasana?"

And so Rukundo joined the Kasana family in 1994. At first he was quiet and insecure, but as he began to get used to the people around him, his true

---

[110]One of Kiwoko's first nurses.

personality began to break through. Soon, his formerly dormant, yet excellent, sense of humor and constant string of witty comments became his trademark, and he became instantly popular throughout Kasana.

The Lord also began to draw Rukundo's heart more and more to His. It had been Karen Morgan who had first led him to the Lord, and since then the Lord's work in his life has been evident and real.

"Once I got used to things at Kasana, I loved it here," Rukundo reminisced. "Uncle Jonnes and Uncle Jay would often sit us down as a big group of boys and talk to us and just spend time with us. I was still new to English, so I missed a lot at first, but I soon caught on! Uncle Jonnes used to say things like, 'One day, you'll be a pastor, a father, or anything! You can do all things through Christ!' I loved hearing his encouraging words. Soon, I also began to be given different leadership positions among the other children, and my faith in the Lord grew through these times. I always remembered the counsel we'd received from the uncles, and I would do my best to put their words into practice."

Over the years, Rukundo continued to grow in his faith and in his love for life. In 1997, he completed Primary Seven and was then accepted into Nile Vocational Institute where he studied plumbing.

"It was the first time since I'd come to Kasana that I was away from my Worcester Family, and it was so hard for me to be away from them and the rest of the Kasana family," Rukundo continued. "I'll never forget the time Uncle Richard Casebow and Uncle Rob and Auntie Kitty came to visit me at school. They had just been passing through the area and decided to come and say hello. As soon as I saw Uncle Richard, tears came from nowhere, and I was overwhelmed with how loved I was! He held me in his arms and let me just cry and cry! I felt so loved!"

As the months progressed, Rukundo began to get used to being away at school, and year after year rose to positions of leadership, especially within the Christian groups at school.

"It really caused my faith to grow," he shared. "I saw that God was using me to be a leader, and when I remembered all the things Uncle Jonnes had told me, I realized that God's hand was on me. I really didn't know much, but what I did know, I tried to put into practice, and the Lord blessed it. I remember getting letters from Uncle Jonnes saying, 'You are my son, and I miss you!' and I would be strengthened and encouraged to keep going because I knew I was loved."

In 2001, Rukundo graduated from NVI and was soon encouraged to join Youth With A Mission's Discipleship Training School (DTS). It was then that the Lord began to give Rukundo a vision for his future.

"I saw what had been given to me," Rukundo recalled, "the love that I got, the correction, the care, and I knew that a way I could give back would be to serve with children. I was offered a job several times with YWAM and also had an offer with National Water, but in my heart, I knew I wanted to serve the Lord by working with children.

"Before I graduated from DTS, I told Uncle Jonnes and Uncle Kimera and Uncle Jay the vision I had on my heart to work with children. They seemed pleased to hear what I had to say and offered me a job working in the childcare department. I assumed I'd start with basic administrative work in the department and eventually get to move into something directly working with children. But what they offered me when I arrived for my first day of work was a complete astonishment!"

"Rukundo, welcome!" Uncle Kimera called him over to his desk. "We've been discussing which position we need you to fill. We'd like to give you a family. We need you to be a family father."

"What?" Rukundo was stunned. He had left Kasana as a boy just years ago, and now to return and be given the responsibility of raising other children was more than daunting. "Can I manage such a job?"

"Can anyone manage such a job?" was Kimera's reply.

And so, with fear and trembling and God's wonderful grace, in 2002 Rukundo was given the Pacific Family to father. Its former father, Chris Sperling, had recently been married, and he and his wife, Jane, would be moving to another part of Uganda to work, and Pacific Family was in desperate need of a father figure.

"I found big boys in the family, some who threatened and tested me," Rukundo recalled. I certainly learned from them! God gave me courage and the strength to stand, because I didn't take my own power or wisdom and knowledge in to the family; I went in His grace. I told the children I didn't come there to teach but to learn from them. I would share the little I knew, but I wanted to learn. Since that time, I've really seen the hand of God upon my family. I've just asked Him to lead me as I lead the young ones. Now, I am seeing those same older boys finishing A-levels or nursing school, and our relationship is so good!"

─────────────────────── ⤳⤶ ───────────────────────

# 2002

"If you find out where she is," Matthew Shorack had said, "I'll take you to see her - wherever she is."

As the car rounded the bend in the narrow path, Rukundo's heart began to beat faster. "Yes, here it is," his uncle's wife pointed. "This is the place where your mother is staying right now."

It had been nineteen years since Rukundo had last seen his mother. Was it possible his uncle's wife was correct and she was still alive? And if she was, would she want to see him?

Just a year earlier, while he was attending the Discipleship Training School, Rukundo had attended a session on forgiveness. "Is there anyone you've held in your heart in bitterness that you need to release?" the speaker challenged the class. Rukundo's mind instantly drifted into the past. He was a four-year-old boy again and could see his mother and father standing there in front of him. There had been a lot of disagreements and shouting during the previous few days, but now there was silence.

His mom reached down and handed him a gift - a new pair of green shorts and a green shirt. Normally he would have been excited about the gift, but today he knew there was something wrong. His parents then each said good-bye and left. He was too young to understand that his parents were now divorced and each had chosen to go his own way, leaving him with his grandparents. But regardless of Rukundo's limited understanding, that last memory would forever be burned in his mind.

Now, he was 22, and that had been the last time he had seen his mother and father. Not long after his parents' divorce, the Luweero war reached its climax, and Rukundo's grandparents took him into hiding in the bush. They later heard that his father had been killed, but nothing was ever discovered about his mother's whereabouts.

Rukundo's mind jolted back into the present. The message about forgiveness was continuing. *If my mom is still alive,* Rukundo thought, *why can't she look for me? She rejected me, and I'm sure she no longer loves me.* His own bitter thoughts surprised him. As the man continued speaking, Rukundo knew he had to release his mother.

"I don't know what caused me to be able to forgive my mom," Rukundo shared years later. "It had to have been the Lord. But during that session, I wrote my mom's name on a piece of paper; I prayed for her, forgave her, and then burned the paper, symbolizing that I no longer held her in bitterness in my heart and that I'd forgiven her for rejecting me. I felt so relieved that day, and a love toward my mom began to slowly grow in my heart. I remember saying, 'God, if she is still alive, please save her; help her to know You! It would be my joy to find her when she has come to know You!' I didn't even know if she was still alive, but from that day on, I began praying for her, and you know what? Our God listens to our prayers!"

A year later, while serving as the Pacific Family father, Rukundo had enrolled in the New Hope Institute of Childcare and Family for more training in working with children. "Again, here at the Institute, the topic of forgiveness came up," he shared. "Though I'd forgiven my mom, there was still pain in my heart. Once again, I prayed and forgave my mom. This time, I knew the forgiveness was complete, and I immediately began missing her and longing to see her. 'Lord,' I prayed, 'may I see her one day?'

"Not long after this, a wife of my late uncle came to visit me. 'Your mom is still alive!' she told me. 'I saw her earlier this year.'"

"You're joking," Rukundo had told her. "It must have been someone else."

But the woman had insisted. "I even spent the night in her home." But Rukundo still had his doubts. It was too good to be true.

And now, here they were, in Uncle Matthew's vehicle about to arrive at the home his aunt insisted was his mom's.

Rukundo's heart beat faster. There were several women sitting out on the verandah. How was he to know which was his mother? It had been nineteen years, she must have changed, and even his formerly vivid memories seemed to have faded away.

"Phoebe," Rukundo's aunt began, "Phoebe, this is Rukundo, your son."

What took place during the next few minutes cannot be adequately described. Rukundo scanned the group of women sitting before him. Then, one stood up slowly. She was wearing the full traditional Rwandese dress, but there was nothing else about her that immediately convinced him it was her.

"Is that my son?" She walked toward him. "Is that my boy?" Tears sprang to his eyes.

"Yes, Mamma, it's me, Rukundo William."

"My son!" tears began to flow. "It's my son!" As they embraced for the first time since he was four years old, no words were adequate.

"Mamma, I forgive you," Rukundo finally was able to say weeping as she held him. "I had held you in bitterness in my heart and thought you didn't love me any more."

"Oh, my son, I love you!" her tears now came in a torrent. "I love you, and you are *my* son. I am your mom, you are Rukundo, and I am your mother!"

"Oh, that day was the one I will never forget," Rukundo told me years later. "There was just too much joy, and it turned into tears! My mother had always wondered where I was, but after the war there'd been no way of finding me. Then, when she remarried, her new husband refused to let her leave, so there was no way to search for me. But the thing that blessed me the most was that not long before we met, she had given her life to the Lord! Oh, that caused my faith to grow! The Lord had heard my prayers!"

*Since that joyful reunion, Rukundo's mother has come to visit him at Kasana several times, and their relationship has continued to grow. On one of her visits, Rukundo's mother prepared a feast for all of the men and women who had raised her son for her. She then gave her testimony of the Lord's work in her life and her son's life, and thanked each person who had invested in Rukundo and made him who he is today!*

---

And the list of first fruits continues. There is Namayanja Susan, who is serving faithfully as an excellent nurse in the community; Chandia John, who is serving his country in the military; Mbonigaba Edward, who has gone beyond Uganda's borders and is working in Rwanda; and Matthias Segirinya, who is making a difference in his own community by being a hard-working builder and a good father and husband, and so many more.

Rukundo's, Kimera's, and Scovia's lives continue to witness of the Lord's goodness and faithfulness. Currently, Scovia is the main preschool teacher at New Hope and a supportive wife to Julius, the Mabaale church's pastor. Kimera serves as the David Family father, the head of the childcare department and a member of the Management Committee. The input he has had on Kasana Children's Center cannot be measured. Rukundo also continues as the Pacific Family father, a family known for its unity and joy. He also works in the childcare department with administrative responsibilities and serves as the church's worship leader.

What joy it is for me to get to work alongside my brothers and sisters in ministry! But an even greater joy is felt by their Kasana parents who see that all they invested was not in vain. The seeds they planted have grown and borne fruit, and now they not only call them dear sons and daughters, but co-workers in the kingdom and fellow ministers to the children the Lord brings our way.

These and many others like them are indeed Kasana's first fruits. And with excitement and anticipation, they and their parents till the soil of the next generation of children, preparing the way for the Lord to raise up hundreds more godly sons and daughters of the King!

Rukundo welcoming new children on their dedication and "welcome to the family" day.

David Family (Kimera, second from the left in the front), as family father.

Julius and Scovia with their wedding party and relatives.

# Chapter 30
## *His Kids*

⟿

Muyango, Kimuli, Namaganda, Eva, Fatuma...the list goes on. When I was just sixteen, I was given an opportunity for which I will be eternally grateful. From June 1995 to May 1996, after my eleventh grade in high school,[111] I was able to take a year off of school to teach full time at Kasana. Little did I know that year would be perhaps the most influential year of my life in molding my vision for the future.

Beginning with a class of forty-two first-graders[112] and then moving up with them into second grade, the Lord put a love in my heart for teaching and working with children that has grown stronger over the years. Through the years, the Lord has allowed me to remain close to this class and work with them during the summers between my years in university, and even now while I am once again in Uganda full time. It always seemed like there was a need for a teacher in whatever class they were in each time I returned – P5 and P6 social studies and English, S1 Bible studies, S2 and S3 English. While distance has often been the biggest issue to deal with, letters have continued to be sent to and from Uganda, maintaining the relationships to the best of our abilities.

Now, eleven years after our first year together, several of my boys, once tiny six- and seven-year-olds and now nearly a foot taller than me, often look down at me and laughingly say things like, "Auntie Jennie, do you remember the time I lied to you and you had to spank me?" How could I forget!

[111]Equivalent to S5 in Uganda

[112]The Ugandan education system is similar to the british system Primary 1 (P1) is equivalent to American kindergarten: P2, first grade, and so on up to P7, sixth grade.

There were times of such laughter and joy, and times when I felt I had come to my wit's end as I daily did my best to teach and love them.

I'll never forget the time Auntie Margaret Musinguzi and I were team-teaching. That day, the class's continuous disobedience, rowdiness, and sulky attitudes were too much to handle. When Auntie Margaret left the classroom crying, I was left with forty-two frustrated and out-of-control children. While I had more experience in the classroom than most sixteen-year-olds, I was clueless as to how to best handle such a large group of second-graders under such circumstances. My only resort had been to "bite the bullet" until recess, quickly run home, explain the situation to my dad, and return with him. I will never forget him and Uncle Tonny (the headmaster at the time) lining up the entire class and, through much discussion and investigation, determining the "guilty" from the "not guilty" and then spanking each offender. I stood at the end of the line to hug and hold each crying child after they had been spanked and hugged by either my dad or Uncle Tonny. But these times of frustration and misunderstandings are all part of child rearing, and the joys and laughter far outweighed the struggles!

Teaching at New Hope is unlike most teaching positions. Not only do you become a class teacher, passing on information about math, science, and grammar, but you also become a parent figure. Has the child you are teaching eaten this morning, or did the village relative they live with decide they didn't deserve it today? When was the last time they had a hug? What verbal or physical abuse had this little one gone through the night before? Had they slept in fear or in peace and safety? Then there were the health and hygiene issues to attend. Of course, the children who lived on site were usually clean and well-cared for, but the majority of my students lived in the villages and walked to school each morning.

My students were required to line up outside the classroom door each morning, and when the bell rang, they would quietly come through the door, one by one. However, they weren't allowed through without first receiving a hug from me and whoever I was team-teaching with at the time.[113] Next came the hygiene check.

"Good morning, class!"

"Good morning, Auntie Jennie!"

"Let's see how many of you remembered to do all we talked about yesterday." They would quickly stand by their desks (long tables with benches so crowded the children nearly sat on top of each other), and one at a time we'd look at their fingernails and toenails. Had they been cleaned and cut recently? How about jiggers – any of those to remove? "Did you brush your teeth this morning? How about combing your hair?"

Depending on the results of the class inspection, we may go on to lessons right away or we may not. If there were jiggers to remove or fingernails to be clipped, lessons would be postponed until proper hygiene was attained. Break time was often spent continuing to deal with jiggers or giving haircuts.

Of course, there were other unexpected health and hygiene interruptions as well. There were the numerous times when I would turn around to see one of the little ones crouched over the table, shivering – their sudden malaria-induced fever so high they could hardly stand up. The lesson would quickly come to a halt while one of us teachers would pick up the little one and carry him up the hill to the nurse, who would take over from there. During break we ran quickly back up the hill to see how our little guy was doing.

Once Nalute, who used to walk more than three miles to school each day, arrived very late and so sick it was a miracle she had made it at all. Her case of malaria was so bad she became incapable of moving, and we decided it was best for her to come home and stay with Alisha and me until the medicine had successfully combated the parasites in her little body. Four days later, she was strong enough to walk home again. Then there was the time Tonny "accidentally" poked the boil on his finger with his pencil lead, and

---

[113]I first began teaching for Auntie Sarah Muwanguzi during her maternity leave along with Alisha Beck, a friend from Canada who had also taken time out of high school to work in Uganda. Not long before Alisha left, Simon Katabazi came to join us. When I moved up to second grade, I team-taught with Auntie Margaret Musinguzi.

all the pus squirted several feet across the table and onto several other children. Needless to say, the twin girls next to him were thoroughly disgusted, but all the little boys thought it was amazing, and couldn't figure out *how* Tonny had managed something so spectacular! As Alisha whisked Tonny out of his seat and to the clinic, he grinned sheepishly and was quite proud of his "accomplishment." The task at hand was to figure out how to sterilize the desk *and* the kids!

How can one adequately record all the memories – each child, each story, each tear and shy smile? There was the time Ndawula got his first 100 percent on a spelling test. The entire class erupted in applause, and my eyes filled with tears of joy. Or the time that Emmanuel, who was convinced he *couldn't* write neatly but who I'd been working with for months, won the prize for the neatest notebook! There were the hot afternoons when I'd see one head after another begin to nod. Up we'd all stand and march outside for a few minutes of races, stretches, and other various "waking up" activities, and then head back to class, our blood pumping and smiles on everyone's faces.

The list of memories goes on and on, and all I can say is "Thank You, Lord for each and every one."

His older brother had come to see him. But I knew something was wrong. He wasn't just there for a visit – he was finding out where Muyango's things were, what belonged to him, and what belonged to New Hope, and how long he could be gone for. My heart skipped a beat. I knew he wasn't there just to see him or take him for a short holiday. He was taking him away. The war in Rwanda had just ended, and countless Rwandese were leaving Uganda and returning to their home country. But for some reason, I had not even thought they would take away *my* little Rwandan boy. I ran as quickly as I could to my dad and Uncle Jonnes. They looked into the situation and were assured by Muyango's brother that he would bring him back in a week.

Legally, we have no claim over these children, but that fact cannot negate the unbreakable heart ties that had been created between us. I knew his parents were no longer alive, and I knew his relatives were not Christians. Would they care for him? Would they make sure this amazingly bright boy would receive the education he needed? But most importantly, would he be raised in the ways of the Lord if he were taken from New Hope? I hugged Muyango and prayed silently that the Lord would bring him back. Then I ran home and wept.

The week passed, and there was no sign of Muyango. I knew there would be none. I knew I might never see him again, and my heart broke. *Who will care for him? Who will make sure he goes to school, and who will teach him about the Lord?* Because of past experiences with children being taken from us, I pictured him growing up with no training and guidance, his talents squandered. I pictured him on the streets of Kigali – still a war-torn and dangerous city – and sought the Lord for several days, begging Him to bring Muyango back. He was only eight, and so small.

"Protect my little boy," I cried each night to the Lord. Then one night, I felt a sense so strong that it could only have been the Lord. "He's not yours; he's Mine," I heard a voice say. "I do not *need* you to take care of him. I chose to use you and New Hope for this time; but Muyango is *Mine*, and I can and will care for him so much better than you can."

I felt a weight fall off of my shoulders. He *was* the Lord's, not mine. I had been given the amazing privilege of loving him for this short time, but now God had other plans. And though we often can't understand His plans, though they are sometimes hard and painful, they are always good, always the best.

My prayers did not decrease, but the frustration and despair gave way to a poignant, fragile peace as each day I made the decision to trust the Lord that He was watching over Muyango.

A year passed, and we still had not heard from Muyango. It was time for our furlough, and my good-byes were even more difficult than usual. I was to complete my last year of high school in Canada while we were away, and then I would stay somewhere in the States for university while my family returned to Uganda. I had no idea when I would be home again. I wept as I hugged each of the children, now P3s, and prayed again that Muyango might be restored to them. Seven months after our good-byes, my parents returned to Uganda to see how the work was progressing and to be an encouragement to the children and staff. I will never forget receiving a fax from them halfway through their trip. It read: "Jennie, sit down while you read this. We have some good news for you. Muyango is home." I couldn't read another word. My eyes filled with tears, and I ran to tell my brother and sisters the good news.

Muyango is home! He is safe; God was faithful! He cared for him and brought him back!

Muyango's relatives *had* taken him with them to Rwanda, and yes, he had been in the city of Kigali, not going to school. Life had been difficult, and his family had decided they could no longer care for him. Their only solution was to return him to New Hope. I could hardly sleep that night, as my heart overflowed with thankfulness. "I think he's back to stay," the words of my dad's fax echoed through my mind.

The next time I returned to Uganda, I rejoiced to see that Muyango was doing well in school and had completely caught up with his classmates, despite missing a full year of school. His command of the English language had returned (he had been surrounded only by Kinyarwanda and French for more than a year), and he was doing well in general. But while I was there that summer, Muyango fell out of a tree and was stabbed in the eye by a branch as he fell. Thankfully, his eye was still intact, but he lost sight in it and could not open it. The doctors hoped that he would be able to see again, but they could give no certainty of that. Again, I questioned the Lord, and begged that He would return Muyango's sight to him.

When it was time for me to return to university again, I did not realize that it would be the last time I would see Muyango for many years. Once again, his relatives came and took him away. To this day, we do not know where he is, though we assume he is in Rwanda. Is he going to school? Is he safe? Is he walking with the Lord? I cannot answer these questions. I do not know if his sight returned to his eye. But I do know that His heavenly Father knows and cares.

*O Lord, protect him; comfort him, provide for him.* I'm sure he's so tall and grown up. He is eighteen now, almost a man. Not a day goes by that I do not think of him and pray that the Lord will be with him. Many times I have imagined the day when I will see him again. I'm sure he'll be so tall – those in his tribe always are. But even if I do not see him in this life, I pray that the Lord will cause the seeds that were planted in his heart when he was a young boy to take root, and that he will grow to be a man of God. If His eye is on the sparrows, I know His eye is on my little boy!

It was just getting dark. The crickets and cicada bugs were already beginning to make their presence known. As darkness settled over Kasana, there certainly was not silence in my house! Fifteen Senior 2[114] grade students were crammed into my little living room and dining room. The girls were in the kitchen washing the dishes; it had been the boys' turn to cook that night. As I looked around the room my heart swelled with gratitude to my heavenly Father. Here were fifteen of the most important people in my life, sitting in my living room laughing, singing, and talking nonstop. Of course, the guitar was out, and several students were singing along with Emmanuel, the class guitar player. And at the same time, there were Serwadda and Kimuli with the CD player, dancing to their own choice of music. The girls in the kitchen were also singing their own songs and laughing. Yes, it was chaos, but such joyful chaos. I treasured these times with my kids, who were no longer children but young adults. The Lord had blessed us over the years, and it was so refreshing to see the depth of their relationships with each other.

---

[114]Equivalent to eighth grade.

Once the dishes were done, we all crowded into the living room. The guitar was put away, the CD player turned off, and all became quiet. It was time for our tradition. I pulled out my Bible, and we began to read off the names of those who had been in our class but were no longer there – Nalute, Loyce, Musoke, Kabugo... The list went on and on.

Many had left in good ways – moved on to learn a trade and then work full time. Others had either moved ahead a grade or had been held back a grade. The departure of others had left painful, gaping holes in the class. Poor choices had sucked them into lifestyles they would one day regret. Several of the former classmates were pregnant, living with an abusive man, or struggling to care for their new child on their own. We knew where some were; others had disappeared. But we still considered them part of us.

As we came to the end of the list of names the floor was open for prayer. "Lord, protect each one no longer with us," Mugabi prayed. "Father, bless each one of them, and let them know that they are loved by us and by You," Fatuma continued. "Lord, You know where each of our former classmates are. Please care for them and show them Your love for them," Ntambala agreed.

Having children who've left has been the hardest part of working with this class. During the years of living in the States I was almost afraid to open any letter I received from Kasana. "Lord, don't tell me someone else has left," I would pray each time I opened the envelope. Sometimes the letter would fill me with joy. "Kimuli is doing so well, you'd be proud of him!" Or, "Eva has begun working at the Baby House, and she loves it! She's turning out to be a great 'mom.'" But all too often it was heart-wrenching news I received.

"Christine[115] just ran away, and we have no idea where she is. She had just found out she was pregnant before she disappeared. We'll let you know what we find out."

---

[115]Names changed for privacy.

"Margaret's[116] relatives took her out of school, and she is working for her aunt who is a witch doctor. Her relatives have turned her against us and against Christianity, and when we offered to bring her back, she refused to come with us."

But, each time, after weeping when I heard of one more who had left for unhealthy reasons, I had to remember that they are *His*, not mine. He loves each one of them far more than I could ever imagine. Seeds were planted in their hearts and minds – each one knows the truth of their Father's love for them and the sacrifice of our Savior on their behalf. And one day, I pray that they will remember these truths and return to the One who can forgive all sins and heal all pain.

"You need to be the one to tell them," Peggy said as she choked back a sob. The sun had just set as Peggy and her husband, Jim, short-term missionaries with us, returned from Kampala with Joyce.[117] "Joyce says she just can't do it."

*Why me?* I thought. *Why do I have to carry this burden?* And yet, I knew someone had to do it. So I called for Betty and Samuel.[118] Betty had been one of my kids for eight years. She and Samuel were Joyce's little siblings. Peggy and Jim brought Joyce into my living room; her face was expressionless, and she said nothing. My eyes filled with tears. *I can't do this*, I thought. *Lord, give me Your strength.*

"Betty and Samuel," my voice shook, "Joyce has asked me to share something with you that is very difficult. Joyce has cancer in the bone in her leg. It is very serious..."

I'll never forget that night, the four of us standing in a circle, holding each other and weeping, praying for the Lord's mercy on Joyce. My fear was

---

[116]Name changed for privacy.
[117]Name changed for privacy.
[118]Names changed for privacy.

also for Betty and Samuel. While they had never had huge behavior problems, they had, for years, been distant and closed to love and affection. I knew that, like all of our kids, their pasts had been filled with rejection and the deaths of those closest to them. For eight years I had tried everything I could to reach out to Betty and convince her that she was loved and accepted. Yet for eight years she remained polite, but ever so closed. Given this news, my fear was that her heart would become more and more closed and hardened toward us and, more importantly, toward the Lord.

My prayers for her intensified. "Lord, do not let this time cause hardness toward You in her heart. May You become so real to her during this time, and may You give us wisdom to show her and Samuel and Joyce Your unconditional love."

I'll never forget the letter I received from Betty not long after I had told her the terrible news. Not wanting to invade her privacy by continuously asking her to talk to me, I had written a letter to her to express that I loved her and was praying so much for her. Her response made me weep.

> Dear Jennie Dangers. Thank you so much for the letter. It was so encouraging. I really felt that you cared for me....For sure I did not know that you really loved me. I have just seen it and I know that you mean it from the bottom of your heart....It has taken me a long time to know that you really care, but pray for me so that I will learn how to be free....I love you so much (I mean it)....From Betty

For eight years, I had tried to reach out to her, yet to no avail. Now this difficult situation had finally broken through to her, and the Lord had opened her orphaned spirit to see that there were those who loved her. Since that fateful night two years ago, much has happened. The Lord saw fit to take our sister and daughter, Joyce, home to be with Him, and once again, Betty and Samuel were forced to deal with the grief of a lost loved one. But while there have continued to be struggles in their lives, there is no doubt in my mind that they both know they are loved. This knowledge has not developed to the extent it needs to be, but they have found a place where they are accepted. Their Kasana family and family parents have demonstrated unconditional love to them through the hard times, and the Lord continues to use even difficult situations to open their eyes more and more to His love for them through people in new ways.

---

"OK, does everyone have their new pairs of socks? How about pens and pencils? Jerry cans and basins? Money for drinking water?" It would be a miracle if we had not forgotten something immensely important. It was a hot afternoon during the dry season, and the Early Adulthood staff, Constance and Sebwami and I, were in Masaka with six of the students from my class. They had completed all the education New Hope had to offer, and they were now moving on to "A-levels"[119] at a boarding school far away from home.

Upon the completion of their studies at New Hope, others in their class had decided to move on to other courses and forms of training – nursing school, cosmetology school, and more. My kids would no longer all be in the same place. Our days of being together were now over. They had each entered a new stage in their lives. No longer children, they were leaving home to follow what the Lord had called each to pursue.

How my heart burst with love and thanksgiving as I saw each of them standing in line to hand in their application letters to the new school. I knew the Lord had done so much in their lives and hearts over the years. They were ready to begin standing on their own without the ever-present care and oversight of their New Hope parents.

"Lord, help them to stand firm. Captivate their hearts in a new way this year." As we all prayed together before we left, my mind flashed back to ten years earlier. Then they were so little and so desperate to be loved, so cute and so ready to be guided and cared for. Now they were ready to stand on their own.

---

[119]Equivalent to eleventh and twelfth grade.

After the last round of hugs and words of encouragement, the three of us staff members drove off. *It's a new stage of life,* I thought. *This must be what it feels like to watch your child leave for his or her first day of school – excited, sad, nervous. Thank goodness they are His and not mine!*

I commended them to Him and rested in His sovereign plan. "Thank You, Lord, for my kids. Please complete the good work You started in them! I can hardly wait to see all You will do in and through them in the years to come!"

*Author's note:*

*It was Saturday, November 8, 2003, not long after I had finished writing this chapter, and I was sitting at my desk in the fifth-grade classroom where I was teaching in Colorado Springs. I had finished grading and doing my lesson plans and decided to check my e-mail. Suddenly, my heart began to race as I read the address and title of one e-mail that caught my eye. "I guess you know Me!!" read the subject line. The message was short and simple—"Hello. It is Muyango David. I will write soon." Alone in my room, I wept for the next thirty minutes. He's alive! Thank You, Jesus, for watching over my little boy!*

*Through our e-mail connection, I was able to find out that Muyango was studying in Rwanda, walking with the Lord, and living with an older brother who is the assistant pastor of a church in Kigali! Later, through the provision of a dear friend, Mary Moorman, I had the privilege of traveling to Rwanda to visit my not so little boy!*

*There are others I still have not seen for years – others who weigh heavily on my heart, and I must continually lift them up to the Lord – Nalute, Nakawooya, and many more. O Jesus, watch over them, I pray!! And from the lesson I learned through Muyango's story, I choose to place them in His hands – He who loves them more than I could ever imagine, and who will never leave them or forsake them! But, my prayers for them will not cease!*

Simon, Alisha, and I with "our kids" in P2, 1995.

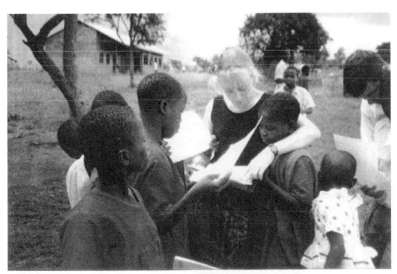

Jennie giving out P2 report cards.

Smaller math group outside, Primary 3.

Primary six, 1999.

# Chapter 31
## *Blessed to Be a Blessing*
&∽&

*I will bless you...and you will be a blessing...all peoples on earth will be blessed through you.*

(Genesis 12:2-3)

At the core of New Hope's vision is a desire to raise up a generation of young people equipped and envisioned to reach out and make a difference in their world. In Genesis, the Lord blessed Abraham and his family. However, Abraham did not receive such a gift so that he could sit on his blessings and enjoy a good life. The Lord blessed him so that he could bless the nations.

While our children in Kasana do not have all of the comforts and amenities that most children from the West enjoy, they have received so very much. Most of them came from desperate situations - abuse, neglect, abandonment, and the loss of one or both of their parents. When they are brought to New Hope they are given a sense of belonging, they become part of a family, and they receive free education, medical care, food, clothing, love, and discipleship. And, like Abraham, our desire for these children is for them to flourish in the blessings they've been given and then, in turn, reach out to others in situations similar to the ones they once were in. Through this, they will see that true blessing comes from investing in eternal priorities, "spending oneself"[120] on behalf of others. For when you spend yourself on behalf of others and satisfy the needs of the oppressed, "He will satisfy *your* needs...and

---

[120]Isaiah 58:10

will strengthen your frame. You will be like a well-watered garden, like a spring whose waters never fail....You will find your joy in the LORD, and...[will] feast on the inheritance of your father Jacob."[121]

### From a newsletter I wrote in January 2002

*Your people will rebuild the ancient ruins and will raise up the age-old foundations; you will be called Repairer of Broken Walls, Restorer of Streets with Dwellings...*

(Isaiah 58:12)

As we began to clear away the rubble that had once been the walls of a village home and prepare the foundation for a new home in its place, the words of Isaiah 58 rang in our ears. A new excitement came over us as we realized that our work was part of God's plan – it was near to His heart.

On January 23, thirty "Kasana kids" and eight staff members, all equipped with our own bedding, foam mattresses, jerry cans, tools, and food, boarded our "lorry" and began the seven-hour trip to the southern part of Uganda. Our purpose: to allow our Kasana children to experience the joy of "spending [themselves] in behalf of the hungry and satisfying the needs of the oppressed" by sharing the many blessings they have with those who have nothing. It was a trip that none of us will ever forget.

We were gone from Kasana for one week, staying in a school in the town of Kibaale in the district of Rakai and working every day with children and widows in the surrounding villages. The plight of the children of Rakai, left desolate as a result of AIDS, has been on our hearts since our first trips there ten years ago. Finally, the Lord provided another opportunity for us to take some of our own young people to reach out to children who know nothing of their heavenly Father's love for them. We wanted the Kasana children to reach out not only to the physical needs of these orphans, but also to their spiritual and emotional needs.

---

[121]Isaiah 58:11-14

What a joy and encouragement it was to see these students, who had not long ago been helpless orphans themselves, begin to share the Father's love with those around them. The joy on their own faces was so evident as they worked hard to build houses for two families (composed of several orphans and their elderly grandmothers), shared their testimonies, presented the gospel to the crowds of people hungry to hear the Word of God, and sang and danced to songs that glorified their heavenly Father.

While we worked on the buildings, several of the students took turns visiting with the village children who gathered to watch us – telling them Bible stories and teaching them songs that would remind them of the love of Christ even after we left. The students also helped remove jiggers from the village children's feet and hands. Not willing to miss an opportunity, they used the chance to share the gospel with their "captive" audience!

On two occasions, we were able to show the Luganda version of the *JESUS* film. After both presentations, our young people quickly dispersed into the crowd to share their own testimonies with the observers and to answer their questions. The Lord's blessing was there, and most of our children were able to lead at least one person to the Lord!

As a result of the young people's testimony while they worked on one of the houses, the two wives of a local witch doctor gave their lives to Christ! Not only that, but these women asked one of our staff members and several of our boys to come and share the gospel with their husband. This was, needless to say, a real step of faith for the boys, especially since they had all witnessed the power of witch doctors. However, with much prayer and trusting in their heavenly Father, they went into his home (witch doctors will almost never allow a Christian to step across their threshold, but this man invited them in!) and boldly shared the Word of God with him. Although he did not accept the Lord there, we know that seeds were planted, and we pray that one day the Holy Spirit will free this man from bondage and draw him to Himself.

The words of one of our student team members, Sebuchu Nathan, provides a picture of what the Lord is doing in the hearts of these young people. "I never realized that *I* could be a part of the solution! I never realized *I* could offer something to someone and really help them!" How exciting it is to see sons and daughters who once had nothing at all now giving and blessing those around them!

༺༻

**From a newsletter I wrote in May 2002**

*Arise, shine, for your light has come, and the glory of the* LORD *rises upon you. See, darkness covers the earth and thick darkness is over the peoples, but the* LORD *rises upon you and his glory appears over you.*

(Isaiah 60:1-2, NIV)

"The second outreach of the year has also taken much of my time over the last couple of months – preparation and planning, a one-day mud house–building outreach in a nearby village for team preparation, the actual weeklong outreach, and then the follow-up work with the students. On May 11, forty-four of us climbed onto the lorry once again and set off this time for Masaka district for an outreach similar to the one in January. It was in many ways much more difficult than last time, but the Lord really worked in and through us, and I know that it was not in vain. All of the team leaders and many of the students were sick (some completely out of commission) at some point during the week. We also had a terrible accident on the lorry with a little village boy. Despite his mother's insisting that he stay away from the truck, and many team members shouting at him to stay away as the lorry was moving, the young boy, about eleven years old, jumped onto the back of the lorry just as it passed a huge tree. While I was not there on the scene, what I saw when they came running to the house where I was, was one of the most terrible things I've ever witnessed. The boy had somehow been pinned between the truck and the tree and had had both of his calves torn off to the bone. What followed during the next few minutes was utter chaos and panic – village women running around screaming and wailing, the mother of the child hysterical and incoherent, and our team members running around to get what was needed to tend to the boy and to calm those around us. One of our team members quickly washed the screaming boy's legs and tied clean cloths around them to slow down the bleeding, and then our faithful lorry driver – now traumatized by all that had happened – raced him to the closest hospital – one and a half hours away.

"In a nation where mob justice often ends the life of the driver involved in any kind of automobile accident (regardless of whether or not he is guilty), we were extremely thankful for Godfrey's (the driver's) safety, but were very prepared to be forced to leave the village. We knew we would now be seen as bad luck, and no one would listen to our message. However, what the enemy had intended to end the work, the Lord used to open new doors for us to share His message. Rather than being angry at us, many in the village came to apologize for the little boy's behavior and to assure us that they knew we were innocent. Through the situation, we were able to get to know new members of the community and share with them and to demonstrate God's love to the boy and his family. Indeed, God works all things for our good! (The boy is also recovering remarkably well.)

"Without a doubt, the most rewarding time of the outreach for me was spending time with the students. Seeing their countenances change as they participated in serving others and hearing them share about the work the Lord is doing in their hearts made every disappointment and difficulty on the trip infinitely worth while.

"One boy, Muwanguzi, had been allowed to join the team, but not without a bit of uncertainty from many of us leaders as to the wisdom of our decision. His attitude had been far from perfect during the last term, and we had no idea whether he would be an asset or real hindrance on this trip. But God worked in amazing ways in Muwanguzi's heart during the week. Every day he would return from work or from sharing with villagers with countless questions – deep and searching questions from the Word of God. 'I was speaking to a man,' he'd say, 'and I tried to answer his questions, but I want to know a scripture that would explain the truth to him better than I could.'

"When Muwanguzi returned from the outreach, everyone at home noticed a huge change in his attitude and his openness to speak about the Lord. Then, one morning Muwanguzi was brought to the clinic in great pain – he had fallen more than twenty feet from a mango tree and had broken one of his vertebrae. He will be kept on bed rest for quite some time and will not be able to play soccer or do anything with excess movement for a year. At first, I was afraid of what his attitude might be. Would he be angry with the Lord? Would the work the Lord had begun in his heart on the outreach be to no avail? How wrong I was! When we went to visit him in the hospital a few days after the accident, I was shocked to see his face. It was more open and joyful than I had ever seen it. And next to him sat a little boy, leaning on him and talking to him. Not long after he'd arrived, Muwanguzi had found this little boy, maybe seven or eight, who had been in the hospital with a broken foot for two weeks. 'He's my friend, now!' he told us. 'We play, and he sings to me, and I take care of him.' Every time we go to see Muwanguzi, the little boy is still with him, and we hear of Muwanguzi's continued 'outreach' in the hospital.

"The man next to him had nothing to cover himself with and no one to care for him, so Muwanguzi had given his sheets to the man and had even helped to bathe him when the man's fever broke. He has also begun to share his faith with the men in the beds around him. When I thanked Muwanguzi for his care for others (after cautioning him to be careful with his own back!), his response was, 'People are taking care of me, and so I'm going to take care of others! It's like a line that starts with others, goes through me and then goes to others – I get taken care of, and then I can go and help someone else!'

"Every staff member who visits Muwanguzi returns marveling at the goodness of the Lord and His work in the life of one we'd been so worried about! He has had no self-pity or anger, but is instead using his time in the hospital to share the love of the Lord with those around him!"

*Three years after our outreach to Masaka, Paul Kusuubira returned to visit the small church that was started by the men and women who had given their lives to the Lord during our time there. What he found astounded us all. The church had not only remained, but had doubled in size. And the faith of the church members had not only affected their "spiritual" lives, but had practically changed their entire community. Convicted by the sacrifice and service of the children who had come to serve them before, their decision was, "We've received; now we must also give!"*

*Formerly impoverished people were now working hard in their gardens and consequently harvesting amazing amounts of crops and giving large portions of them away. Former homeless drunks were now contributing members of the community who gave part of what they earned to the poor. Widows were being cared for, poverty was diminishing, and lives were being changed. A member of the congregation had donated a piece of land on which to build a church, and the church had raised enough money to build a permanent structure in which to meet.*

*The change in the community was so drastic that when the local Catholic priests demanded that the political authorities stop this spread of Christianity, the local authorities' response was, "There is no way we would ever stop whatever is causing former drunks to reach out and care for the poor. If anything, we should be joining these people!" The Lord is faithful, and the seeds that these young people planted bore fruit that has, in turn, blessed others we had not even hoped to be able to reach!*

⤜⤏⤚

**The People of Jesus,** from a newsletter dated May 2001 by Richard Casebow

"This year Alison has been getting quite involved with some of the more needy people in the villages around and about Kasana. The needs out there are huge, and it is quite easy to forget them, surrounded as we are with our little community here at New Hope. She has found it very fulfilling getting involved in a number of families and more recently with an old man called Maggala, from the village of Mabale, not far away.

"Maggala really is old. We asked his age and he says he was born in 1903 and fought in the Second World War in Ethiopia. When Alison visited him he was in a really bad way, needing many hospital visits and with his feet swollen and full of jiggers....

"We have carried out several jigger picking sessions with him, one of which yielded thirty-five jiggers, and have now attempted to deal with the source, which is the dusty floor of his house. Whilst he was in hospital we sprayed the floor and walls with insecticide and got someone to re-smear the floor to get rid of the dust. Before we did this, Alison managed to bring some of the little blighters home with her, and we have had to have a few jigger picks on our own feet! Emily and a few of the older children from Kasana have also accompanied Alison on her trips to the bush and ended up really enjoying themselves. A few ladies from the Mabale church, a satellite church of our Kasana Community Church, are starting to look after him now, washing his clothes, contributing food, and picking jiggers. Maggala keeps telling his neighbors, 'Look, the people of Jesus have come to wash my feet!'"

---

The children's outreach into communities has not only happened during arranged events. The hearts of the children have been touched, and many of them continuously reach out even to their next door neighbors.

There is Mwesige Steven, for example, who is a current Senior Four student. Though he formerly lived with relatives and attended New Hope as a day student, he now lives on his own. But instead of living the "fun life" that most young guys his age would choose, Mwesige's heart is burdened for those who live around him. Each day when he returns from school, children from the surrounding neighborhood flock to his house.

"Some of them are orphans, some are not," Mwesige explained. "I just do what I can with them. Sometimes I just talk to them and spend time with them. If they are young, I teach them basic life skills about cleanliness and good behavior. If they are older, I tutor them in whatever they're struggling with in school. I also teach them how to ride a bike and fix a bike. In return, they carry water for me, and then I let them use my bike to carry water for their families. I also try to get odd jobs to make money so that I can supply them with things like soap and medicine. It's not much, but I do what I can." If only we had more "Mwesiges" in our communities!

There are two students, Sarah and George, who have seen how the Lord has blessed them and are now earning money to purchase building supplies to build a new house for their widowed and impoverished mother. Not only have they raised much of the money already, but they've done most of the laying of bricks themselves as well!

There is Calvary Family, who recently built a house for a poor villager, and Ebenezer Family, who went and cleared land and planted crops for Jjumba's mother. There is Kimuli, who, though he's still in school, works to pay for his nephews and nieces to go to school. There is Kalera, who has chosen to love his father even though his father disowned him – and not just to love him, but to care for him in his old age by purchasing land and building him a house where he can live.

There is Medie, Kimuli, Emma, James, and Mugabi, who found a senile elderly man living under a tree near the secondary site and determined to do whatever they could. They stopped to visit him and found he was sick. So, they went and purchased painkillers and anti-malarial drugs. They later bought him some new clothes with their own hard-earned money. When his sickness began to worsen, they approached Uncle Matthew, their Bible study leader, and asked for help. Together, they took the man to Kiwoko Hospital, where he was admitted. In a country where it is the relatives' responsibility to care for sick patients in the hospital, this man's fate seemed bleak. But each day these boys went to visit him, bathed him, bought him food, prayed, and shared the gospel with him. One of the boys used up his entire savings to help pay for the man's hospital bills. Eventually, his sickness worsened and claimed his life. It was the boys who dug his grave, notified the local authorities, and carried out his funeral ceremony.

There is Ibra, who, when his uncle lay dying of meningitis and AIDS in the hospital, rejected by many of his other relatives, spent his whole vacation caring for him. He spent sleepless nights watching over his uncle in the hospital, bathed him, and turned him every few hours. Even when school had started, Ibra would go to class during the day and return to the hospital for the night. His good friend and another one of our boys, Tonny, joined him, and for two months they showed unconditional love for this man who had never shown them love.

And these are just a few of the many children and family groups who have not sat on their blessings, but reached out to those around them. Many of them speak of the day when they get to adopt orphaned children, or how they can't wait to become nurses so they can better care for the sick, or how they will care for many orphans and give as much as they can to the poor when they are wealthy businessmen.

As all of the "Kasana kids" grow up and catch the vision God has for them as individuals, I know it will be astonishing to see how the Lord uses them. I also know that Satan looks ahead and trembles, for the Lord is preparing a mighty army of His children to further His kingdom in ways we have yet to see!

The "People of Jesus," (also known as the Casebow family) and some local
church members and Maggala (center).

Nsubuga, Jennie, and Fatuma tying bamboo reeds to build a mud hut.

Mudding the walls of a new house.

Kasana men and boys singing at a church we visited in Kyotera.

# Chapter 32
## Credit Where Credit Is Due

Well, many stories have been told. However, this book would not be complete without mention of a group of men and women who actually are a constant, but often overlooked part of the Kasana family. This is the team of people who serve "behind the scenes" within Uganda (though not at Kasana), in the U.S., Canada, and the U.K.

Behind the scenes here in Uganda, yet giving clear direction and wisdom, is the Board of Trustees of New Hope Uganda. From its inception, New Hope Uganda has also been blessed with a board whose wisdom and love for the Lord surpassed what we had ever hoped for. Its first chairman was Pastor Nicolas Waffula, who served faithfully for many years. Pastor Nicholas not only watched over the ministry as it began, but he also gave personal pastoral care to my own family, the Bakimis, and many others at Kasana. Past and current board members and dear friends are Pastor Titus Oundo, James Ameda, Ben Oluka, Peter Kiyimba Kisaka, Bishop Bugimbi, Joy Angulo, David Ndyagenda, David Kabiswa, Sam Sakwa, and Happy James Tumwebaze.

Those serving Stateside include the Franklins, the Woods, the New Hope Uganda Ministries, Inc. (NHUM) board, and the Becks. Lin Franklin, my father's boss when he worked in California, took up the job of forming New Hope Uganda Ministries, Inc., a sister ministry that serves New Hope Uganda. He has been the chairman of the NHUM board now for six years. His wife, Judy, has served voluntarily for years as the NHUM accountant, receipting all donations, sending thank you notes to donors, and keeping all the books for NHUM. Other past and present members of the NHUM board are Jerry White; our pastor and family friend, Brian Watts of Langley, B.C.; my uncle Ron Demolar; my mom's cousin DeAnn (Snipes) Lueken; Reverend Gary Wood; my father, Jay Dangers; Dr. Mark Emmerich of North Dakota; and Pastor Steve Holt of Colorado Springs. In addition to his role on the NHUM board, Gary Wood serves as the New Hope North American Director. Gary lives in Dickinson, North Dakota with his wife, Louise, and works tirelessly handling finances for individual foreign staff, answering countless e-mails, giving advice and counsel to the leadership at Kasana, coordinating all North American teams and staff, running the Stateside part of our sponsorship program, and much more. Gary also travels to Kasana each year to teach in the Institute of Childcare and Family.

In 1993, Rob and Kitty Beck from Langley, B.C. began our sponsorship program. At the time we had 21 staff members and 191 children. After beginning and running this program successfully for eleven years, Rob and Kitty handed over to Kasana staff memeber, Marian Kinghorn, a program that now cares for 500 children, over 50 Ugandan staff, and 330 sponsors.

Gina Charsley in the U.K. served New Hope for years by handling funds donated to the ministry Church Relief International (CRI). Also through CRI, Barney Coombs, Bruce Blow, Ron McLean, John Olhausen, and Dave and Jeanette Downer have given pastoral input and care for many years to the leadership at New Hope.

And then, where would we be without the faithful prayer warriors, the children's and staff's sponsors, and the ministry's other financial supporters who have stood with us for years? To each of you who have walked with us in prayer or financially who are reading this now, this story is your story. Each victory, each success, can be directly attributed to each of you who spent time on your knees before the Father on our behalf and on behalf of the children. To each of you who sacrificed monthly to support a child, to each of you who gave faithfully to support the work here, or spent hours of your personal time to make the work at Kasana possible – the value of the part you played in the Kasana story can never be calculated.

On behalf of New Hope Uganda, I would like to thank all of the men and women who have served and who continue to serve behind the scenes to make the work here possible. Indeed, as the writer of Hebrews assures us, "God is not unjust; he will not forget your work and the love you have shown him as you have helped his people and continue to help them."[122]

The NHUM board- Gary Wood, Jay Dangers, Lin Franklin, DeAnn (Snipes) Lueken, Jerry White, December 1997.

---

[122]Hebrews 6:10

Calvin and Dorothy Young, Jonnes Bakimi,
Gary Wood and Yolanda White in Southern California

# Chapter 33
## *Not to Us*

And the story continues. Indeed, what has transpired at Kasana *since* this story began to be written is a book in and of itself. It is a story of God's faithfulness, grace, forgiveness, and love. It is a story whose ending only He knows, but we can be certain that it is a victorious ending in which He will be glorified.

Each day a child is touched, a tear is shed, and laughter is heard. Each day decisions are made, lives are changed, and challenges are faced. There will continue to be victories and disappointments, rejoicing and weeping, conflict and resolution. But we know that He who calls Himself the Father of the fatherless and the Defender of widows will walk with us, giving us strength and wisdom. We rest in His sovereignty and the fact that His love never runs dry. His patience is never stretched further than He can bear. His mercies are new every morning. And to Him we say,

"Not to us, O LORD, not to us but to your name be the glory
because of your love and faithfulness...."[123]

Receive all the praise and honor and glory! "For the LORD has done this, and it is marvelous in our eyes!"[124]

---

[123]Psalm 115:1
[124]Psalm 118:23

Dad teaching at the New Hope Institute of Childcare and Family.

Our boys love football (soccer).

Black Bird Preschoolers.

Mom with Deborah and Nissi.

Jill welcoming Rebekah into the Kasana Family.